Harold Monro and the Poetry Bookshop

Harold Monro at the Poetry Bookshop, 38 Great Russell Street, London, in 1926

Harold Monro
and the
Poetry Bookshop

JOY GRANT

LONDON
ROUTLEDGE AND KEGAN PAUL

First published 1967
by Routledge and Kegan Paul Limited
Broadway House, 68–74 Carter Lane
London, E.C.4

Printed in Great Britain
by Western Printing Services Ltd., Bristol

© Joy Grant 1967

Contents

v

CONTENTS

Illustrations

vii

Acknowledgements

Acknowledgements are due to the many writers and others who, in response to press advertisements and personal enquiries, gave me their reminiscences of Harold Monro. Some I saw personally, and I wish to thank Mr. Joseph Bard, Professor Edmund Blunden, Mr. John Crow, Professor Bonamy Dobrée, Mr. Eric Gillett, Mr. David Garnett, Professor J. Isaacs, Mr. Galloway Kyle, Mr. Noel Monro, Sir Herbert Read and Mr. Michael Rothenstein for giving me their time in this way. Special acknowledgement must be made to Mrs. Alida Monro. In a series of interviews, she has provided me with facts and insights of the greatest value. I am deeply indebted to Dr. Arundel del Re, of the University of Wellington, New Zealand, who has written me many letters about his association with Monro before the First World War.

Mrs. Rose Sabin has kindly allowed me to quote from the unpublished autobiography of her husband, the late A. K. Sabin, and Mr. Harold Owen and the Oxford University Press from two unpublished letters of Wilfred Owen. Mrs. Alida Monro and Messrs. Gerald Duckworth have allowed me to quote from the work of Harold Monro and Charlotte Mew; Mrs. Ianthe Price from that of her father, F. S. Flint; and Mr. George Hepburn from that of his mother, Anna Wickham. Messrs. Faber and Faber and Harcourt, Brace and World, Inc. have permitted quotation from 'The Waste Land' in *Collected Poems 1909–1962* by T. S. Eliot; and Messrs Faber and Faber and New Directions, New York, have allowed me to reprint '*Δώρια*' from *Personae* by Ezra Pound. Messrs. Macmillan and Sir Osbert Sitwell allowed me to quote from *Laughter in the Next Room*; and the World Publishing Co. and Mr. Conrad Aiken from *Ushant*.

ACKNOWLEDGEMENTS

For access to unpublished Monro correspondence I am indebted to the Harvard College Library; the Henry W. and Albert A. Berg Collection of the New York Public Library; the Lockwood Library, University of Buffalo; the University of Chicago Library; the University of Michigan Library. The main repository of Monro's papers is the University of California Library, Los Angeles. For the kind assistance of the Library's staff during my stay there I am most grateful.

Finally, my sincere thanks are due to Professor Geoffrey Bullough, of King's College, London, for his advice and support in all stages of my work, and to the Central Research Fund of the University of London who gave me the grant of money which enabled me to travel to America.

Introduction

This book concerns a man who over a period of twenty years played a unique part in the life of literary London. When he died in 1932 Ezra Pound could securely write: 'I doubt if any death in, or in the vicinity of literary circles could have caused so much general regret as that of Harold Monro.'[1] Since then occasional tribute has been paid him in the autobiographies of writers who were his friends, and reminiscent anecdotes re-told, but in the main his reputation has receded into the margins of literary history. This has happened, in part, because much of his energy was spent in practical fieldwork for poetry, which ceased with, or shortly after, his death; and in part because the nature of his own poetic talent has been misunderstood—he has tended to be remembered as a poet for the wrong things. An attempt is made here to re-present the man in both aspects of his achievement.

A disinterested ambition to promote the cause of poetry was the mainspring of Monro's varied activities as poet, bookseller, publisher, editor and versespeaker. Though many years of contact with poets and poetry-lovers helped to rid him of his illusions about what he personally might hope to achieve, they did not rob him of the quasi-religious commitment to the Idea of Poetry which in 1913 had led him to write: 'I think I only know one thing about myself for quite certain, which amounts to this: that if anyone can imagine an earth without poetry he need not imagine me one of its inhabitants.'[2]

But Shelleyan idealism was counterbalanced by a good measure

[1] 'Harold Monro', *Criterion*, XI (July 1932), p. 581.
[2] 'How I Began', *T.P.'s Weekly*, XXI (4 April 1913). p. 419.

1

of commonsense, and the two together directed his activities. He was, in the words of his widow, a 'practical idealist'.[1] His friend F. S. Flint extends the paradox further, and sees him as 'a living contradiction in terms': 'He was hardworking and lazy; he was generous and mean; he was a lover of freedom and a tyrant; unconventional and conventional; a bohemian and a bourgeois.'[2] His contradictions were reconciled, Flint thinks, only in the service he gave to poetry.

Be that as it may, for twenty years his energies and his private income were expended in practical schemes to help poets and to bring poetry before the public, and it is a remarkable tribute to his conduct of this invidious task that in his obituary Ezra Pound said: 'One's strongest regret is for the passing of an honest man from a milieu where honesty, in the degree he possessed it, is by no means a matter of course.'[3]

It was the knowledge that Monro was dedicated to poetry rather than to poets that gave him his peculiar prestige. 'I hate literary gossip and anecdote', he wrote in notes for a lecture given before the First World War, and his constant fear, in running poetry-readings at the Bookshop, was lest 'curiosity about poets' rather than about poetry should draw the people in. He preserved a studious detachment from literary coteries and movements, for they produced, in his view, lamentable divisions among brothers. It was generally understood among literary people that Harold Monro was above considerations of fashion, fame, faction or financial profit.

Sir Osbert Sitwell has paid tribute to Monro's role as host:

> The Poetry Bookshop constituted, under the most considerate and, indeed, inspiring of hosts, Harold Monro, a great meeting-place; for not only was he a friend to all the poets of his own generation, but new work always attracted, though it may sometimes have irritated, him. He was indulgent to all

---

[1] In a talk given at the Harvard Summer School (19 July 1961).
[2] 'Biographical Sketch', *Collected Poems of Harold Monro* (London, 1933), p. vi.
[3] Op. cit.

poets. He liked new ideas even when they did not match his own, and in the large, comfortable panelled rooms above the shop, he would often of an evening bring together whole schools of poets of the most diverse faith, opinions and temperament. Since his death there has been no one to match him in this respect.[1]

Monro had the advantage of being a poet among poets. He was also, T. S. Eliot has written, 'One of the few poets of whom it can be said that they cared more for poetry in general than for their own work.'[2] Douglas Goldring comments on the irony of fate by which

> the harder and more successfully Harold worked to establish the reputation of his brother poets and to make the publication of new verse commercially possible, the less attention was paid to his own output. He was primarily regarded by his colleagues as a bookseller and publisher, and a source of small but welcome cheques.[3]

Yet for Monro himself, Mrs. Monro has told me, his poetry was the most serious and meaningful part of his work. It throws a curious light on his role as host and on his other extraverted, public activities—disclosing a constitutional melancholy, nagging tensions, a bleak sense of isolation. The sensitive gloom of his countenance was an index of his character. He looked like a Guards officer, John Drinkwater recorded, but 'a rather serious, one might almost say dejected Guards officer'.[4] 'He had', wrote Flint, 'one skin fewer than other people';[5] and he protected himself from painful encounters behind a reserve of manner that could hinder relationships.

[1] *Laughter in the Next Room* (London, 1949), p. 34.
[2] In a letter to Marvin Magalaner (21 Jan. 1947). Quoted by him in 'Harold Monro—Literary Midwife', *Arizona Quarterly*, V (Winter 1949), p. 155.
[3] *The Nineteen-Twenties* (London, 1945), p. 155.
[4] *Discovery* (London, 1932), p. 224.
[5] 'Verse Chronicle', *Criterion*, XI (July 1932), p. 684.

The part that Monro invented and played was an original one: it may be said with confidence that his vision was unique in his time, and that he did more to bring poetry to the public than any other man of his generation.

1

The Preparatory Years

Harold Edward Monro was born on 14 March 1879, at St. Gilles, near Brussels, and spent the first six or seven years of his life in Belgium.

His father, Edward William Monro, who was a civil engineer employed by the Neuchatel Asphalte Company, had previously spent four years in Budapest, and was for fourteen years in Belgium; he later opened works for the company in Spain and America. In 1872 he married Anabel Sophia Margary, whose father was also a civil engineer, and they had three children, of whom Harold was the youngest. The elder brother, Arthur Russell, died of a 'disease of the lungs' while still at school, and Mary Winifred, the eldest child, also predeceased Harold. In 1889, when Harold was ten, his father died, and his mother later remarried.

Though Monro was often spoken of as a Scot, his forebears had been in England since 1691, when the Reverend Alexander Monro, D.D., formerly principal of Edinburgh University, came to London, having been deprived of all his offices for refusing to take the oath of allegiance to William and Mary. His son, James, was elected Physician to Bethlem Hospital in 1728, and was the first of the family to hold this office, which passed from father to son for five generations. When Edward Thomas Monro retired in 1858 the tradition of a hundred years was broken. The doctors were authorities on the treatment of the insane, and between them produced a number of books on the subject.[1]

---

[1] See *Dictionary of National Biography*; see also Denis Leigh, *The Historical Development of British Psychiatry* (London, 1961), pp. 48–51, 104–6; and E. D. Monro, 'Five Physicians of the Fyrish Family', *Clan Monro Magazine*, iii (1951). p. 27–31.

The Royal College of Physicians owns a series of portraits of the Monros, and their family resemblance is striking. The resemblance between Thomas Monro (1759–1833) and his great-great-grandson Harold is especially noticeable: the long, lean, melancholy face, with the curious, almost oriental eyes under dark brows. There may have been a similarity in their temperaments, for Thomas Monro was well known in his day as a patron of young artists, and played a significant part in the formation of the school of English water-colourists.[1] Artists came to his house at 2 Adelphi Terrace in the evenings to paint or sketch, sometimes selling to their host the products of their labours. J. M. W. Turner, like Thomas Girtin, J. R. Cozens, Cornelius Varley and others, enjoyed the doctor's patronage, and was a favoured visitor in London, and later at Bushey. 'Girtin and I have often walked to Bushey and back, to make sketches for good Doctor Monro at half-a-crown a piece, and a supper of oysters,' said Turner. 'Good Doctor Monro' became something of an eccentric in his later years—he loved colour, and when it snowed he would have his paths swept clean and artificial roses fixed in the trees. He built up a valuable collection of paintings and drawings, and was himself an artist of some distinction.

Henry, Harold Monro's grandfather, was the sixth in the direct line of succession to become a doctor, though he was not connected with Bethlem. He had a practice in Wimpole Street, and attended Brooke House, Hackney, a private lunatic asylum which had been in the family since 1781, and from which Harold Monro derived the largest part of his income.[2] The medical tradition was re-established when Harold's son, Nigel, became a doctor.

[1] Henri Lemaitre, *Le Paysage Anglais à l'Aquarelle 1760–1851* (Paris, 1955), p. 217; see also C. E. Coode, 'Turner's First Patron', *Art Journal* (May 1901), p. 133.

[2] Brooke House was severely damaged by a high-explosive bomb in October 1940, after the patients had been evacuated. It was acquired by Hackney Borough Council in 1944, but, the cost of converting it to educational use proving too high, it was demolished in 1954–5. (See *Survey of London, Vol. XXVIII: Parish of Hackney*, Part I, 'Brooke House' (London, 1960).)

The Monros were a solid upper-middle-class family with a tradition of service to medicine and the Church, and with considerable family pride, still alive among their descendants to-day. Monro's education followed the pattern usual for boys of this class. From a preparatory school in Wells, Somerset, he went to Radley, the public school founded on High Church principles, to which his father, two of his uncles, and his elder brother had preceded him. A contemporary at Radley recalls him as 'rather a lonely boy with no particular friend', and *The Radleian* for 1892–6 has little to say about him. He left school not long after his sixteenth birthday, in circumstances explained in a letter from the Venerable Adam Fox, D.D., who was Warden of Radley in later years:

> I always understood that he had to leave the school rather suddenly, I believe for introducing a bottle or bottles of wine into his study, which would then be a great crime, and may be still for all I know. At any rate it created amusement when he came to recite or read his poems at the school, and I said inadvertently when I was introducing him, that 'it isn't often that a public school turns out a poet!'

How much the anger of the clan was roused by this disgrace can only be guessed. Monro's father being dead, authority had passed in part to his widow. All his life Monro was haunted by considerations of 'what his mother would think', which suggests that her moral influence was powerful. Some authority was vested, too, in his father's eldest brother, Russell, who had been to Radley himself and shone as Senior Prefect, winner of the History Essay Prize, and member of the school VIII. He had followed up these triumphs by success at boxing at Oxford, by marrying the daughter of a baronet, and by gaining a considerable fortune, partly through his interests in brewing. He lived in style at Somerby Hall, Rutland. His disapproval of his nephew was at least sufficient to drive the lad to some show of spirit: Harold determined that he would become Prime Minister, and to this end he started learning shorthand. 'I think my chief impulse in the matter was to prove to my uncle, who had suggested I had no grit, that, in fact, I had some.' But, Monro confessed, 'I was too slow and dreamy, and I could stick at nothing.'[1]

But there was, in fact, one newly discovered interest at which he did 'stick', for the two years between Radley and Cambridge were filled with turbid adolescent yearnings which found some outlet in a passion for poetry.

His experience of poetry, up to the age of sixteen, had been strictly limited:

> ... save for 'Elijah' and other poems by B.M.,[2] or verses by Proctor and Hemans which my mother read to me on Sunday evenings, the Longfellow and Scott I learned in the schoolroom, and the Keble's *Christian Year* and Macaulay which I learnt later in English schools, I remained in total ignorance of the existence of poetry . . .[3]

His expulsion from school he regarded as a happy release into a new world of poetry:

> By a stroke of good fortune I left school young, and then I suddenly became conscious of myself as a solitary and wayward person, and in the seclusion of my bedroom I wrote a dozen poems and the same number of stories, all about an individual too obviously myself . . . Safe away from school, I began to read Virgil with a cousin who took some pains with me, and to think it the most delightful adventure book and to wonder why I had not been more interested in it at school.[4]

He went to Cannes with his mother, had congestion of the lungs, and discovered, while he was ill, *Childe Harold* and *Endymion*. His enthusiasm grew apace:

> I immediately wrote a long poem in rhymed couplets called 'The Madonna'. I became morose and developed the surly atti-

---

[1] 'How I Began'.
[2] Barbara Macandrew, the author of two volumes of pious verse: *Ezekiel and other Poems* (1871), and *Elijah and other Poems* (1880).
[3] Ibid.
[4] Ibid.

tude I have kept ever since towards people who interrupt me at 'work'. Then at a tutor's in England I extended my discoveries to Milton's minor poems and Tennyson, and by this time I had become fully conscious of the existence of poetry and had filled a dozen copy-books as fast as I could buy them with my own verses, all ghastly immature. I wrote a Christmas play in verse, and acted it with friends in a Suffolk village —and I wrote dozens of love poems.[1]

In this state of mind, he went up to Caius College, Cambridge, in 1898, and read for the Modern and Medieval Languages tripos. He took a third, and proceeded B.A. in 1901. Looking back over his Cambridge career, he was glad that he

. . . had to study about a hundred thousand lines of French and German. I took six months off in Germany, and worked hard for the first time in my life, read the whole of Goethe, Schiller and Molière, and much else, and began the habit of long walks, which I have kept.

The *furor poeticus* did not abate:

By the time I went to Cambridge poetry had become an obsession, but I kept this a close secret and not till my third year did I form a little group with three other undergraduates to discuss and criticise each other's verses.[2]

The other three were Leonard Pass, G. N. Pocock and Maurice Browne.[3] It is clear that F. S. Flint was misinformed when he declared that Monro was, as an undergraduate, 'not interested in books, still less in English literature, least of all in poetry. What interested him was horse-racing . . .'[4] The correspondence between Monro and Maurice Browne supports Monro's account (quoted

---

[1] 'How I Began'.
[2] Ibid.
[3] Maurice Browne (1881–1955) became an actor-manager, and was best known for his production of R. C. Sherriff's *Journey's End* (1929).
[4] 'Biographical Sketch', *Collected Poems of Harold Monro*, p. vii.

above) and reveals them, in the words of Browne's autobiography, as 'two fledgling poets soaring rapturously from peak to peak'.[1]

However, a letter from Browne in 1903, recalling their college-days, shows that Flint was not entirely wrong. Evidently both horses and literature appealed to Monro as an undergraduate:

> Your room at Cambridge savoured chiefly of roulette, horses and prize poems, with myself reading some absurd and inordinately long thing aloud . . .[2]

An evocation of a happy evening spent in Browne's rooms follows:

> You come in and sit down on the sofa, and you tell me to read you something. Afterwards there is silence; then very softly you recite something; another silence; I make tea and put on fresh coals, and we talk of poetry; probably I read you what I am writing, then there is another long silence, after which you insist on going to bed, but stay to hear something out of 'Epipsychidion' that I have just discovered. Then—then you do not go to bed yet; but we stay up a little longer and talk of sacred things, the innermost secrets of poesy, and love . . .

Browne was two years younger than Monro, and their friendship set a pattern that was to be repeated in Monro's life—that of teacher and eager disciple. 'The elder's encouragement of his friend had no bounds', Browne wrote years later. 'A tall dark youth with large brown eyes, those [sic] eyes blazed when Maurice wrote a poem which pleased him.'[3]

Monro and Browne arranged to go on a walking-tour together in the Harz mountains of North Germany during April 1902. Dorothy, Browne's pretty younger sister, joined them. Predictably,

---

[1] *Too Late to Lament* (London, 1955), p. 65.

[2] The letters from Monro, Browne, Dorothy Monro and A. K. Sabin which are quoted in this chapter are in the Maurice Browne Collection in the University of Michigan Library. None of this correspondence has been published.

[3] *Too Late to Lament.* p. 65.

Dorothy and Harold fell in love. In the letter from India, quoted above, Browne recalls the idyllic mood of the holiday:

> . . . the room with the musical machines playing and a waiter passing through it, the restaurant with the dais at Goslau, empty, and the great bell there, and the chapel . . . a bit of the pine-forest just outside Harzburg, with many paths and a sign-board, and three dim figures, ourselves . . . a tea-room, with a beautiful child, very vague; and witch-like shadows on a rock at night in the Bodenthal . . . the dining-room at Treseburg; we three are sitting at the corner-table, and laughing at the innkeeper who has dozens of plates and lasses round him; his wife is a formless shadow somewhere near the fire-place; Gretchen—no, she is on the hill outside with Dorothy, and you are telling me, and I am sitting on a rock screaming with laughter while you look at me so ludicrously reproachful. Our room upstairs at Treseburg; Dorothy comes in, looking radiant —she says nothing, but kisses me, and goes out again.

So much radiance, laughter and reproach can only mean that they had all three admitted the presence of Eros among the party; and from this time on there was an understanding that Harold and Dorothy would be married.

From Cambridge, Monro had gone to London to read for the Bar, but he wrote, his heart was not in the law:

> I had to pretend I was working, but I usually had *Paradise Lost* or Keats open on my knees or in my Justinian. I developed the habit of writing my verses at night, and I walked by various roundabout ways back home every evening, preparing myself for the night's work and repeating my verses over and over to myself with the object of improving them.[1]

In an undated letter to Hall, a Cambridge friend, Browne gives a very different picture, lamenting the wasted life of Monro, 'now practising at the Bar and in Society', attending in the space of a month 'seven balls and five private theatricals, and eleven at homes, and fourteen dinner-parties'.

[1] 'How I Began'.

11

Whatever the truth of the matter, the state of affairs did not last for, having passed a couple of Bar examinations, Monro threw up the law and went to live in Ireland, becoming a land-agent and very small farmer, his address c/o A. F. Maude, Esq., Drumna-dravey, Irvinestown, Co. Fermanagh. In a verse epistle to Browne, undated, he rejoices that he has 'fled the dingy haunts of frowning law' and says he is intent

> On staying here to try and understand
> The wiles of rent-collecting, tilling land.
> And I shall keep a cow, some pigs, some hens,
> Some noisy geese (I'll use their quills for pens).

The dilemma of a poet fallen among farmers is treated with humorous resignation in a letter to Browne:

> It is wrong that the waving corn should have become merely good 'crops', the autumn-tinted woods 'fine coverts for phea-sant' . . . There is no sweet in life without some sour. I've got a lovely little mare and usually get two days' hunting a week.

Meanwhile he was waiting for Dorothy, who, it seems, showed some reluctance to face the rigours of rural Ireland and to join him as his wife. There was another snag: Dorothy Browne was a first-class hockey-player, and his letters to her brother suggest that Monro resented the place which 'that hockey' held in her heart, though he had to admit that 'it's a great thing playing for England'. But Monro was enjoying 'improving' her: 'Dorothy's mind is open-ing to Beauty and Truth like a flower's to the sun', he wrote.

On 2 December 1903 they were married, and their honeymoon was spent in their beloved Harz Mountains. Thence to Ireland, where a pastoral life did not entirely suit them. Monro wrote to his brother-in-law, 'One wants a town sometimes, with theatres and par-ticularly pictures and sculpture, and then there is this eternal rain.'

In December 1904 a son was born, and christened Nigel Harold Maurice Russell. Dorothy gave a fond account of the child in a letter to her brother which suggests, besides, a good deal about their situation:

12

His intelligence is startling ... He has a slightly olive skin, large dark blue eyes, beautiful long dark eyelashes, very well marked eyebrows for a baby, a perfect mouth and a nose that varies day by day ... He was christened at Christ Church, by the Bishop of Ossery of whom we saw a good deal in Dublin. He is awfully nice for a clergyman, which means he is quite nice for a man ... I spend most of my time making baby clothes, and being read to by Harold (chiefly St. Paul's Epistles and *Paradise Lost*) ... funds extremely low.

The child was healthy but the mother's strength much depleted, and she returned to England to escape the Irish climate. Harold soon followed, and after an unsettled year, they moved into a cottage near Haslemere in 1906. 'At last! *At last!*' Monro wrote to Browne in September, 'I have a charming little study with all my gods round me again including the picture of the world: Watts' *Galahad* ... To-day I enter upon the 10 year [*sic*] of literary production of my life ...'

From its commencement in 1902, the correspondence between the two young men was urgently preoccupied with the poetry-writing which each of them regarded as his most important and exciting activity. It mirrors very well the attitudes and aspirations of youths of poetic taste, nourished on Romanticism and its late-Victorian aftermath. They shared a quasi-religious attitude to poetry; the poet was an inspired being separated from society, and in many respects opposed to its ideals.

Browne, with a volatile, readily excitable emotional nature, was swept further off the ground than his friend. It is amusing to see Monro adopting a restraining, avuncular attitude towards the younger man. Browne wrote, hot with his poetic vocation after watching the sun go down over the Backs:

Has it struck you—do you know—that we are sacrosanct, dedicated to God, whoever, whatever, he may be, the god of truth and beauty, as much as any ordained minister of his ...

13

the feeling has come to us . . . Every day, every hour, every
minute, we do not devote to it, is useless, and not only useless,
but wasted, criminally wasted. Harold, am I going mad? or am
I different from other men? dowered by God himself? with
feelings other than the multitude's? . . . I must stop; my brain
is reeling, and feels as if it would burst. I have not felt like this
before . . . it either means insanity, or some greater thing,
something that is poesy. What is to happen? Ought I to go
down at the end of this term, despite of everything? What, o
what must I do? For God's sake write to me.—Maurice.

This letter is undated, but Monro replied on 27 May 1902 in a
manner reminiscent of Keats:

I can imagine how lovely the Backs must have been. . . . God
even doesn't know where we shall end. . . . nothing will be
accomplished by mad long rushes, but all by gradual steady
striving. We are mortals and men like everyone else (that
annoys you!). Poetical feelings have been common to the king
and the crossing-sweeper and Shakespeare. The distinction is
that a poet can be everyman but everyman cannot be a poet.
The crossing-sweeper and Shakespeare thought together but
Shakespeare interpreted the common thoughts which the
crossing-sweeper could not have done. . . . Therefore let us
wait—if we fail to please the world we shall be crossing-
sweepers, if we succeed we shall be Shakespeares.

One fears that the moderate, sensible and realistic tone of this
letter inflamed Browne even more.

The correspondence also reveals the state of Monro's taste. In
commenting on work by Browne, he is concerned with perfection
of diction and metre based on standards derived from his reading
of the Romantics and Victorians, and with the pursuit of an obsoles-
cent 'Beauty'. In an undated criticism of some manuscript Browne
sent him, Monro writes:

I think the following lines are most original and beautiful:

When the rippling stream
With a silver gleam
Goes singing down the glade. . . .

Later, in criticising Browne's 'Job', he disapproves when he thinks the verse unscannable, the grammar tortured, when the meaning is obscured by the syntax, when there is empty rhodomontade. No more searching discontent is expressed with this inflated piece of verbiage, mixing influences from Milton, Swinburne and Shelley—a dramatic poem with Buddha, the Shadow of Christ, Elihu, Bildad the Sunhite, the Morning Stars and the Voice of God among the *dramatis personae*—unless it is subtly conveyed in the remark that 'it does not altogether grip me'. A friend's partiality and considerateness may be partly responsible for this moderation.

Monro was aware that they were at the end of an outworn tradition. In May 1903 he wrote:

To follow on Tennyson, Browning and Swinburne is perhaps a more difficult task than the poets of any age had to face. The first has brought modernity to its acme of lyrical expression. The second has fed the modern soul-dissecting tendency to satiety. The third has sucked all the honey from the flowers.

And two years later he remarks fretfully of his verse-play *Guinevere*, 'It will be another log for the bonfire of unactable minor dramas (minor thoughts and minor poetry). Oh this fearful minor key! This is an age of clipped wings and misty intelligences!'

While he was reading for the Bar he composed profusely:

I rewrote a poem called 'Clytie' about ten times, and I wrote dozens of odes to Venus and Apollo and every deity on earth or in Heaven. I tried most verse-forms, I experimented with blank verse plays on Tristram, Lancelot and other heroes, and later I wrote several times over on the subject of King Cophetua . . . However little I may now have succeeded as a poet, it certainly has not been for lack of early experiment, but perhaps rather through excess of it, for in those days I wrote incessantly, and read too little.[1]

[1] 'How I Began'.

The letters to Browne indicate that in the years from 1901 to 1906 he was reading, had read, or recommended Browne to read: Shakespeare; Spenser, Milton, Cowley; Beattie, Thomson, Byron, Shelley (he was reading him 'from the beginning' in 1903), Keats, Wordsworth, Landor, Hood; Tennyson, Browning, Swinburne, Morris, Emerson, Rossetti, William Watson ('*the only* really known modern poet'); and Dante.

'Have you read H. G. Wells' *Modern Utopia*?' Browne wrote to Monro, from Darjeeling, in 1905. 'If not do so at once . . . It is splendid . . . His idea of the "Samurai" is something incommensurable. I am very anxious to start an order founded on its principles.' Early in 1906, Browne met the young American poet, Arthur Davison Ficke, and was fired by his notion of starting 'a periodical series of little volumes'. These two ideas, united, produced the Samurai Press. The plan originated with Browne, and he remained the moving spirit of the venture, with Monro giving his active support. Monro contributed valuable advice, a certain amount of money, two volumes for publication and a great deal of patience; in return, the Press gave him his first experience of the business of printing and publishing, and introduced him to a number of young writers, who were useful to him later on.

Though Monro was immediately attracted by the ascetic rigours of the Samurai code, and joined Browne in practising moderate forms of vegetarianism, early rising, teetotalism and non-smoking, he was not so easily convinced of the practicality of the publishing scheme. 'We are all practically unknown authors, and are catering for people who *don't want us*,' he wrote to Browne in December 1908, 'I see more and more every day that there is no market for booklets, and E. Mathews, Stockwell and others are doing their best to spoil what little market remains.'

But Browne was not to be restrained by good advice, and the Samurai Press was set up early in 1907, with headquarters at Ranworth Hall, near Norwich. This house belonged to a cousin of

Browne's, and Browne seems to have taken up semi-permanent residence there.

The tone of the prospectus which issued from the Press in 1907 is painfully 'intense': the Samurai authors will be people who 'have an aspiring ideal in life and literature, and seek it earnestly', and 'high seriousness' will characterise their works. This quality was indeed demonstrated in their first publication, *Proposals for a Voluntary Nobility* (January 1907), written jointly by Monro and Browne. It systematised the notions put forward in *A Modern Utopia*: Wells ('perhaps the clearest-sighted idealist in England') had discerned that, in its forward thrust towards perfection, society had already thrown up individuals of exceptional advancement. The Samurai Press would call upon these people to reveal themselves, and they could then proceed to realise Wells's vision of an order of Voluntary Nobles.

Rules for their daily lives were laid down. They were to train with military rigour for a life of ascetic self-control. Indeed, the subjugation of instinct seems to be as much the end as the means of spiritual achievement: 'little pleasures and little emotions impair efficiency, and the control of little emotions will follow on the renunciation of little pleasures'. The Samurai must be healthy—cold baths and daily shaves are obligatory; meat, alcohol, tobacco are condemned, along with unchastity and gambling; on seven days in the year the Samurai must spend the period from sunset to sunrise fasting and meditating in the open air. A footnote reluctantly recognises the existence of women, and admits them to the scheme of things.

The code is absurd in its demands and cruel in its austerity. Nevertheless, Browne recalls, 'the Voluntary Nobles dashed forward, earnest arty-crafty young persons with ideals and pimples. A strangely reluctant Wells was roped in as godfather. At the meetings he would make occasional comments in his high-pitched voice, with a slightly pained expression and distressing detachment.'[1] They were by no means the only group of people who embarrassed Wells by trying to put his ideas into practice.

[1] *Too Late to Lament*, p. 86.

There is no evidence to show that the group took the code very seriously. The Samurai Press began to produce a slim volume a month, but the small group of interested friends certainly did not form a community and seem only to have 'belonged' in the loosest sense. It was, more than anything else, a convenient channel of publication for unknown or little-known authors.

By the time Browne was weary of the venture (after about four months), he had fortunately come across A. K. Sabin,[1] who relieved him of his responsibilities; Browne fled to the Continent. Sabin was a talented and sensible man, a skilled hand-printer and a poet. He took over the management of the concern, moving to Cranleigh, Surrey, near the Monros, who were at Dunsfold. Sabin was provided by James Guthrie[2] with a fine old hand-press, and gave the work a new direction. He saw that, to survive, the Press must take on commissions from the public at large, and by his good management he contrived to keep the business running until early in 1909, when it was dissolved.

It published prose pamphlets devoted to plain living and high thinking (Eustace Miles, the advocate of vegetarianism, contributed *Balanced Life* and *World's Prayer and Creed*, and R. Dimsdale Stocker, *Seership and Prophecy*); and also a quantity of verse most of which is conventional in style and insignificant in sentiment.

Monro's prose pamphlet on *The Evolution of the Soul* was published in 1907. Rejecting alike the materialism of Haeckel[3] which

---

[1] Arthur Knowles Sabin (1879–1959), the son of a Sheffield steel-worker, was largely self-educated. Two volumes of his verse (*The Wayfarers*, 1907, and *Dante and Beatrice*, 1908) were published by the Samurai Press; he later issued further volumes from his own Temple Sheen Press. In 1909 he joined the staff of the Victoria and Albert Museum and was later made responsible for the re-organisation of the Bethnal Green Museum, of which he was Officer-in-Charge 1922–40. His unpublished autobiography, *Pilgrimage*, which is in the hands of his widow, has provided information about Monro's activities in the years preceding the First World War.

[2] James Guthrie (1874–1952), the printer, designer, painter and author. The press which he handed on to the Samurai Press had been in use at his Pear Tree Press at South Harting, Sussex.

[3] Ernst Heinrich Haeckel (1834–1919), a prominent biologist of his day. Monro read his *Die Welträtsel* (1899), in the English translation,

denied that the soul existed, and the Church's teaching that the soul was implanted in man by divine agency, Monro borrowed something from each and produced a Wellsian compromise. Man most certainly had a soul, and it had evolved along with his body. If the individual chose to cultivate his soul during this life, it would survive physical death.

The second part of the pamphlet was headed 'The Soul of Christ'. It presents Jesus as a man of extraordinary spiritual advancement with a message of supreme value to mankind which the Church had wantonly perverted, the first expression in print of Monro's anti-clericalism.

During the same year the press issued Monro's *Judas*, a blank-verse poem of some four hundred and thirty lines, prefaced by the statement:

> I have written this Poem believing in Jesus of Nazareth. I dedicate it to those who, not pausing to impute its heresies to me, shall recognise that my concern has been to see as Judas saw, to understand as he understood, and to disclose his kinship with the money-victims of this and every age.

A dislike of capitalism dovetails with a version of Christianity no doubt more 'rational' than the one he had been taught at Radley.

From the first, says Sabin,[1] Monro and Browne had envisaged a group of poets working towards a common ideal, and had pointed to the Elizabethans, to the Lake poets, and to Yeats and the Irish poets in their support. No such fraternity was formed, but Monro *met* some of the younger writers. In 1908 the Press brought out John Drinkwater's second volume, *Lyrical and other Poems*, and the author visited Cranleigh. Wilfrid Wilson Gibson sent in a pile of manuscripts, and the Press issued three volumes of his work—*Stonefolds* and *On the Threshold* in 1907, and *The Web of Life* in 1908. Young men who knew that the age demanded something new in poetry were impressed by the austerity of his little 'working-class'

[1] In *Pilgrimage* (see note on Sabin, p. 18).

The Riddle of the Universe (1900), and in a letter of August 1904 wrote that it had disturbed him: it was his first contact with a 'rank materialist'.

plays. 'Tennyson was dethroned,' wrote Browne years later, 'Gibson was nominated to succeed him.'[1] Monro never gave unqualified praise to Gibson's work, but he was a colleague and friend in later years.

Through James Guthrie, Monro came into contact with the community of weavers, embroiderers and other craftsmen who inhabited Haslemere at that time, and were trying to conduct their lives on the principles of Ruskin and Morris. He was especially friendly with Romney Green, the designer and carpenter, who made superb tables and chairs out of ponderous baulks of oak, and who later supplied the furniture for the Poetry Bookshop. 'This rugged, fiery, somewhat intractable yet generous creature', Arundel del Re writes, 'loathed all forms of aestheticism and literary cant.'[2] He believed, with Whitman, that art was for the regeneration of man.

There were thus kindred souls of progressive outlook near at hand, and we hear of Monro going to Haslemere to lecture to the Independent Labour Party there. But he was overwrought and gloomy all through the period of the Samurai Press—the attempt to lead the Samurai life may equally well have been a consequence or a cause. In January 1907 he wrote to Browne, 'I have never in my life had an object before me like the present one, and I simply thrill with happiness at it sometimes', and the next day, 'We have plunged too suddenly into our enterprise.'

He struck Sabin as too rigidly set in his ideas. Writing to Mrs. Browne, Maurice's mother, in 1907, Sabin said of Monro:

> He has commenced with certain preconceived notions as to how things should be done—an unqualified and unqualifiable idealism which it is beautiful to have; but alas! in practical life I have found that we cannot meet the world on our own ground.

And in *Pilgrimage* Sabin wrote that at this time Monro was too restless to work in conjunction with anyone. His marriage, which had been growing increasingly troubled, finally broke up:

[1] *Too Late to Lament,* p. 86.

[2] 'Georgian Reminiscences—i', *Studies in English Literature,* University of Tokyo, XII (April 1932), p. 326.

With all the cruel solemnity of high purpose in youth, Harold made himself incapable of sharing Dorothy's natural lightness of heart and happiness in ordinary charming things. . . . He retired with his books more and more into a secluded life of his own, spending the days and often the nights in a little thatched cottage in the garden. . . . So it came about that a year after Maurice went abroad, Harold went also. . . .

The two years abroad were the turning-point of his life. Up to the time he left England nothing had gone right—his marriage and the Samurai Press ventures were failures, the dream of a community of poets had not come true. During the period on the Continent he published two books, one of prose, one of poetry, and these provide direct insight into his state of mind during his voluntary exile.

In the early months of 1909 he took a solitary walking-tour and his account of it, *Chronicle of a Pilgrimage: Paris to Milan on Foot*, was published in the same year. It is the work of a man who has very much enjoyed his excursion, but has not yet learned to write. The style is stilted, and deals death from the start to the intimacy of tone that the subject demands. A loyal follower of Shelley, Monro yields himself up to the emotional stimulus of the Alps, the Simplon Pass and Lake Maggiore. He celebrates his life-long love of the broad highway. The following extract will serve to illustrate both the style and the sentiment of the book:

Tis a madness—the love of the road—that may never be purged from a man's blood till it run cold—and perhaps not then. It will passionately claim him, most often in the Spring, so that he will arise from the ashes of the winter fire, wean himself from the customs of the city and the ways of the household, gird on his strength, wave his lady farewell, and with his pack upon his shoulders and his countenance set high into the new sun, will stride forth amid the scent of opening flowers upon the pathways of the world.

Monro takes occasion to pass judgement on a variety of matters, and reveals a mind that is an amalgam of anti-clericalism, socialism, Utopianism, vegetarianism and faith in the simple life. He looks in vain for evidence of true religion beneath the surface of continental Catholicism; he sees in the poverty of the peasants the evil results of capitalism; he is disgusted by the arrogant English, overeating their way round Europe in motor-cars. Monro took his walk in the spirit of Whitman, Thoreau and Stevenson. Delight in natural things, in things that existed before machines, is the true happiness.

The poems printed in *Before Dawn: Poems and Impressions* (1911) were written while he was on the Continent. They echo faithfully the sentiments of *Chronicle of a Pilgrimage*, pondering the vices of institutional Christianity and questioning man's concepts of God. The dedication reasserts belief in the millennium:

> I dedicate this book to those who, with me, are gazing in delight towards where on the horizon there shall be dawn.
> Henceforth, together, humble though fearless, we must praise, worship and obey the beautiful Future which alone we may call God.

A number of satirical poems indicate a growing feeling, borne out by his letters to Maurice Browne, that poetry should have to do with 'real life'. In addition they expose the reverse side of Monro's high enthusiasm: very many of them are bitter attacks on men who to him represent social evil.

Before Dawn was hand-printed by Arthur Sabin, and published on 15 July 1911. On 19 July Monro wrote to Browne:

> There is a grave fact to face: I am six years too old. The book might be promising at twenty-six. I know too much to go on writing the old sort of stuff and too little to write any new.

When he saw the reviews, Monro was depressed by the suggestion that he might have done better to write in prose. Edward Thomas made this suggestion in a personal letter. Monro wrote unhappily to Browne:

Perhaps I'm not (metrically speaking, at any rate) a poet. And yet why did all those things come to life for me as poetry, and why had I to write them down as such? Perhaps a mere habit of expression from which I shall do best to clear myself for freedom of delivery? . . .

At thirty-two one must either die or be new born. I was thinking something about the latter, but it keeps slipping my memory, and the former never seems attractive for a long enough period together.

It is impossible to follow in detail Monro's movements during the two years from the autumn of 1909 to the autumn of 1911. Most of it was spent abroad, with occasional visits to England. For some of the time he was at Mentone, where his mother went in the winter, and, according to his own account, he stayed in 'various crank settlements'.[1] Arundel del Re describes one as 'a socialist free-love and "reformed clothing" vegetarian German colony at Monte Verita, near Locarno' and another as 'a Tolstoyan one near Stroud in Gloucestershire'.[2] There were at least three stays in Florence, and for a good stretch of time he lived 'absolutely alone in the Swiss mountains'.[3] Restlessness was an inevitable symptom of the process that was taking place in him.

In the early autumn of 1909 Monro paid a visit to London and talked with Sabin. He was still dreaming of forming a group of poets, and he was already forming a plan for a practical means of serving them. 'We discussed the possibility of a monthly publication which might serve to unite the writers of verse and attract and hold the attention of readers as well. But', Sabin acutely added, 'he was not yet ready to settle down to the steady pursuit of such

[1] 'How I Began'.
[2] 'Georgian Reminiscences—i', 328.
This must be Whiteway, a colony set up by S. V. Bracher, a dissident member of J. C. Kenworthy's community at Purleigh, Essex (see W. H. G. Armytage, *Heavens Below, Utopian Experiments in England* (London, 1961), pp. 354–7).
[3] 'How I Began'.

an enterprise. Another journey to Italy was necessary to exhaust his desire for travel.'[1]

In Florence Monro found congenial society, for at this date the city attracted a colony of English writers, artists and art-critics who came regularly in the autumn and spring to work and enjoy themselves. Gordon Craig was publishing his radical views on theatrical production in *The Mask*, and scandalising the sedater members of the English community by his bohemian appearance and alleged loose life. Hellen Bayley, the friend of Yeats and Lady Gregory, came frequently, as did Miss Paget who, as 'Vernon Lee', was a well-known novelist.

Edward Carpenter was a celebrated nonconformist who had expounded his teaching on marriage-reform, vegetarianism, homosexual love and the evils of civilisation in a series of books, of which perhaps the best known was the prose-poem *Towards Democracy* (1883). In 1910 or 1911, says Del Re, he was staying at Settignano with Professor George Herron, who had been obliged to leave his post at an Iowa college for, allegedly, putting into practice his unorthodox ideas on marriage. Monro and Herron had frequent conferences with Carpenter, though Del Re believes that Monro had little faith in the man personally. Be this as it may, Carpenter's brand of idealistic reforming zeal was very congenial to Monro and, as will be seen later, had a considerable influence on his thought. If Carpenter ever told Monro of his meeting with Edward Trelawny, the friend of Shelley (and of Byron), he must have had for Monro an almost charismatic charm.

In Florence, Monro also met Maurice Hewlett, already famous as the author of a stream of successful historical romances, and began a connection which lasted for many years. The story is told by F. S. Flint, with an appositeness that makes one doubt its authenticity, that Monro was lamenting the state of English poetry when Hewlett roused him with the cry, 'If you feel like that, for God's sake go back to England and do something.'[2]

It was through Collingwood Gee, the fan-painter, that Monro

---

[1] *Pilgrimage*, Ch. VIII.
[2] 'Biographical Sketch', *Collected Poems of Harold Monro*, p. viii.

met Arundel del Re,[1] a youth of mixed Italian and English parent-
age, then in his last year but one at the lycée in Florence, and so
enthusiastic about poets and poetry that at first he found his
encounter with Monro a disappointment:

> . . . he seemed such an ordinary mortal, so unlike in his looks,
> dress and hair from what I pictured a poet should be. He wore
> a soft felt hat turned up in front, he had a pleasant oval-
> shaped face with a high forehead and a rather large nose, nice
> eyes and a quiet reasonable personality that at once set me at
> my ease. Gee scampered off and together we slowly and silently
> climbed up to his flat. The study smelt agreeably of tobacco;
> the walls were lined with books; a Bar-lock typewriter . . . lay
> on the desk covered with papers but, so it seemed to me, very
> tidy for that of a poet.[2]

They discussed Keats, Shelley, Carducci and D'Annunzio, and
Monro read some verse aloud. One of the poems he read was his own
'Country Dance in Provence', and, spoken in a 'soft yet clear,
musical voice', Del Re recalls in the same essay, 'it filled me with
a feeling of exquisite peace and rest, as if I were sailing in an en-
chanted boat over a wine-coloured sea to the land of Faery'—
words which are suggestive of the spirit in which Del Re later
accompanied Monro to London.

From this day on, Del Re continues, they met frequently, and
Monro took the boy's poetic education in hand. They discussed the
poetry of the past, but more than this, they discussed the poetry
of the future: the poet, Monro held, had a duty to give expression
to the ideas and feelings of the new age that was dawning, 'an age
in which man must finally cast off worn-out beliefs and meaning-
less traditions and begin to live life more joyously and rationally'.

---

[1] Arundel del Re (1892–) was appointed lecturer in Italian at Oxford
after the First World War, and in 1927 became Professor of English
Literature at Tokyo Imperial University. He was interned during the
Second World War and afterwards took up an appointment at the
University of Wellington, New Zealand, where he is still living.

[2] 'Georgian Reminiscences—i', p. 324.

He may have found in this eager disciple some of the qualities he had found endearing and exasperating in Maurice Browne.

They spent the Christmas of 1910 together in Monro's mill-house at Ascona, above Lake Maggiore, and during the late summer of 1911 took a strenuous hike over the Alps, from Meiringen to Locarno, spending some more time in the mill-house before facing London in September. Monro was an experienced walker, and they made good time, talking little as they went. In a letter to the present writer, Del Re recalls how, sitting outside their wayside inn during the long summer evenings, they discussed the future:

> Monro was a pleasant talker—not a brilliant one but stimulating and convincing, and during those days and our stay at the old Mill House he worked out plans for a review devoted 'exclusively to the study and honest criticism and publication of poetry'.

It was, in fact, the culmination of a period of restlessness and aimlessness. Monro now believed that he had found a practical means of assisting the cause of poetry. With a solemn sense of mission the two men arrived at Victoria on a grey September morning. Del Re had never been to England before; Monro had been away from it for the better part of two years. There is some audacity and a pathetic courage in his resolution to come back and try to serve in a society of men from whom he had been removed for so long. Not surprisingly, London 'seemed to depress Monro who was very silent and thoughtful, obviously not at all pleased to be back. . . .'[1] He and Del Re went to stay for a couple of days at the Strand Palace Hotel, then at Haxell's Hotel just round the corner, and finally joined Dorothy Monro in a house which Monro had newly leased on Hammersmith Mall, in an area favoured by artistic people. It was natural that at this time of good resolutions and fresh starts he should try to repair his married life. His son Nigel, now seven years old and an exceptionally attractive child, had been out to Italy with his governess to stay with him. But the

[1] Arundel del Re, 'Georgian Reminiscences—ii', *Studies in English Literature*, Tokyo (September 1932), p. 460.

division between Monro and his wife was apparently too wide to span, for he very soon left Hammersmith and found rooms in Bloomsbury, moving again later to chambers in South Square, Gray's Inn.

These domestic disturbances were the background to the remarkably rapid fulfilment of his literary plans, and four months after his return to England he issued the first number of *The Poetry Review*. His intentions cannot have been quite unknown, for soon after reaching London he was approached by the Poetry Society with the proposal that he should edit their journal.

2

The Mission Launched: Monro as Editor

1

In launching out upon his hopeful mission, Monro was infected by the spirit of the time. In the years that immediately preceded the First World War hope was in the air, and people concerned with literature and the arts were convinced that changes in the social and moral sphere would soon find aesthetic expression. By 1912 such phrases as 'the new age', 'the new era', 'the boom in poetry' were clichés in the little magazines and in the established literary journals.

Indeed, unless English poetry were to die an ignominious death, it had nothing to do but renew itself.

The Edwardian Age in poetry was the brief lull between the retreat of one wave and the advance of the next. William Watson, Alfred Austin, Stephen Phillips, floated away on the ebb, their poetry, with its decorated rhetoric, a faint ironic echo of the great Victorian thunder. A few poets of original power—Robert Bridges, Thomas Hardy, William Doughty, Thomas Sturge Moore—circled in small eddies of their own, but there was no poet to speak for a generation conscious of living in a changing and exciting world. We may recall Monro, miserably trying to express himself poetically in the year 1905, crying out, 'Oh this fearful minor key! This is an age of clipped wings and misty intelligences!'

It looked as though prose was the language of the new age: Wells, Bennett, Galsworthy and Shaw were vitalised by contemporary life as no poet was, and this tradition went back to the nineties, when the novels of Gissing and Moore and the plays of Ibsen and Shaw confronted life, while poetry went into 'aesthetic' retreat. But the social realism of Wells and Bennett was imaginatively unsatisfying, and a fresh concept of the novel was already taking shape in the minds of D. H. Lawrence, Virginia Woolf and Katherine Mansfield. The time was ripe for a general literary revolt.

The poet's rebellion was to a large extent against their inheritance. The Victorians had prepared for them a vocabulary specially reserved for poetic uses, specially rich in words that combined sensuous beauty with suggestions of spiritual delight, a dialect which did not permit reference to many of the realities of ordinary life. The frameworks of rhyme and metre in which they set their words seemed restricting. The new poet who wanted, in the words of Ford Madox Hueffer, to 'register his own time in terms of his own time,'[1] found his legacy a hindrance rather than a help. The ten years before the outbreak of war saw the emergence of a number of young poets who were striving, with greater or less audacity, to reconcile tradition and their own talents.

Trying to bring Pegasus down to earth, Wilfrid Wilson Gibson turned back to a realism that had its origin in the Wordsworth of the *Lyrical Ballads*, and perhaps in Hardy's novels. His *Stonefolds* (1907) had a hungry welcome from the poets who published it at the Samurai Press. *Daily Bread* followed in 1910, and these collections of stark little verse-dramas of humble life were harbingers of progress to the few who noticed them. Gibson's treatment of working-class life seems sentimental and literary enough to-day: for his contemporaries it pushed back the boundaries of poetry.

The remarkable popular success of John Masefield's 'The Everlasting Mercy' in 1911 showed the way the wind was blowing—the crudeness of its 'realism' ('"You closhy put", "You bloody liar"') was pleasurably shocking to those who expected poetry to be all honey. The facile simplicity of W. H. Davies's lyrics, too, appealed

---

[1] 'Preface', Collected Poems (London, 1916), p. 13.

to poetry-readers weary of pomposity and pretence. The urge to deal honestly and accurately with experience was strong among the poets of the 'new age'. The spontaneity, audacity and *joie de vivre* of Rupert Brooke typify the spirit that was abroad. Defending the 'unpleasant' poems in the 1911 volume—more particularly the description of vomit in 'The Channel Passage', he wrote:

> There are common or sordid things—situations or details— that may suddenly bring all tragedy, or at least the brutality of actual emotions, to you. I rather grasp relievedly at them, after I've beaten vain hands in the rosy mists of poets' experiences. . . . 'Whatever', I declare simply and rather nobly, 'a brother man has thrown up, is food for me.'[1]

Gordon Bottomley's *Chambers of Imagery* (1907) and Lascelles Abercrombie's *Emblems of Love* (1908), works of painstaking integrity and some originality, confirmed the impression that a poetic renewal was imminent.

But history has not been kind to these poets, whose gropings after expression were, in the English fashion, unorganised and haphazard. A group formed rather on the continental pattern, however, gathered round T. E. Hulme in 1909, occupying itself very much with exotic verse-forms. The group included T. E. Hulme, Edward Storer, F. S. Flint, Joseph Campbell, T. D. Fitzgerald and Miss Florence Farr. Ezra Pound, the young American poet, very soon joined them. They were brought together by 'a dissatisfaction with English poetry as it was then . . . being written', F. S. Flint recalled, and went on:

> We proposed at various times to replace it by pure *vers libre*; by the Japanese *tanka* and *haikai*; we all wrote dozens of the latter as an amusement; by poems in a sacred Hebrew form . . . We were very much influenced by modern French symbolist poetry.[2]

[1] Quoted by Christopher Hassall, *Rupert Brooke, A Biography* (London, 1964), p. 294.

[2] 'The History of Imagism', *Egoist*, II (May 1915), p. 70–71.

Their discussion and experiment was dominated by the strong personality and formed philosophic opinions of Hulme, who believed that an age of romanticism was giving way to a new 'classical' period in art, and that this demanded 'absolutely accurate presentation and no verbiage'.[1] The willingness to usher in radical change distinguishes this group, and its cosmopolitan range of experiment makes the innovations of Gibson, Masefield or Brooke look suburban. The Imagist movement, which Pound jockeyed into existence in 1912, had its origin in these discussions: 'there was a lot of talk and practice among us . . . of what we called the Image', says Flint. But in the spring or summer of 1910 Pound left England for a twelvemonth, and the meetings came to an end in the same year.

Monro, from across the Channel, kept a wary eye on poetical developments at home. Had he remained in England, the probability is that he would not have been attracted to Hulme's group: they were too much committed to radical change, too separate from the English tradition, too consciously a *group* to meet his temperamental needs. His task, as he saw it when he landed at Dover in 1911, was to mediate between the poets themselves, and between the poets and the public; to provide a forum where poetry could be seriously discussed, and to restore the public image of poetry, which showed alarming signs of dilapidation.

Criticism of new verse in the newspapers and literary magazines of the first dozen years of this century had reached a very low ebb. The attitude of most poetry-critics to their victims is well expressed in Pope's lines:

> Pretty! in Amber to observe the forms
> Of hairs, or straws, or dirt, or grubs, or worms;
> The things, we know, are neither rich nor rare,
> But wonder how the Devil they got there?[2]

[1] F. S. Flint, op. cit., p. 71.
[2] 'Epistle to Dr. Arbuthnot', II, ll. 169–72.

Lacking any coherent views on poetry—lacking, probably, much interest in it—they found security in an appeal to tradition, or, rather, to the example of the acknowledged masters of verse, and in a quasi-religious reverence for the Art of Poetry, which enabled them to abuse their contemporaries with a clear conscience.

Their lot was unhappy: with no special training for their peculiar task, and uncertain whom they were addressing, they were handed a pile of books to discuss in a very limited space—and too often the books came with a note from the editor, directing them whether to praise or blame. The poor quality of most of the verse printed moved them to condescending praise or to cynical mockery. In either case, one has the impression that they looked on poets as a morbidly introspective, vain and somewhat absurd race, to be endured rather than encouraged. Praise or blame was meted out in lazy clichés, which begged any number of questions and conveyed little or no meaning. Thus, in *The Spectator* for 14 October 1911, we find the critic taking in thirteen books of verse, and a cursory survey of his paragraphs yields 'the true stuff of poetry', 'the charm of complete sincerity', 'a beautiful and rare conception wedded to haunting music', 'passages of lyrical charm', and on the debit side, 'never at any moment does the thought seem to cross the line which separates the poetic from the prosaic'.

This is the kind of review which Edward Thomas in an article on 'Reviewing: an unskilled labour'[1] classified as uninteresting and bad. It was, he claimed, the commonest kind of review, and it depended on 'secondhand words and paralysed, inelectric phrases'. The sublime *insouciance* of the bad reviewer was caught very tellingly by Thomas when he wondered whether the reviewer or anyone else gained by

> ... quoting verses and saying that they show a sense of melody, with a comment that this is the most essential of a poet's gifts, and the aside that though Whitman thought metre of no importance his best lines happened to be metrical.[2]

[1] *Poetry and Drama*, II (March 1914), p. 37.
[2] Ibid, p. 40.

Rupert Brooke suggested the flavour of the newspaper review—and of the bulk of the new verse—in his letter to Frances Cornford:

> *The Daily Chronicle*, or some such, that reviews verse in lumps, will notice thirty-four minor poets in one day, ending with *Thoughts in Verse on many Occasions, by a Person of Great Sensibility* by F. Cornford and *Dead Pansy-Leaves: and other Flowerets* by R. Brooke; and it will say, 'Mr. Cornford has some pretty thoughts; but Miss Brooke is always intolerable.' (They always get the sex wrong.)[1]

Verse crept into the corners of newspapers and popular magazines as a trivial ornament, and generally it deserved no better treatment. But in the serious politico-literary magazine it took a more important place.

A unique prestige attached to *The English Review*, founded by Ford Madox Hueffer in 1908, which offered new work by James, Conrad, Wells, Lawrence and Bennett. But *The English Review* had little to say on poetry, and only in December 1909 did it begin to print sporadic reviews of selected volumes of new verse.

Each number did, however, open with some new poetry, and thus made a generous and ostentatious bow to the dignity of the muse. The choice was eclectic, ranging from Hardy (a major contributor), to Pound, Lawrence, Flint, Masefield ('The Everlasting Mercy'), Binyon and Bridges. It provided the best and most honourable platform for poetry in the years from 1909 to 1911. The prominence accorded to new verse in *The English Review* undoubtedly did a good deal to raise its status in the mind of the serious reading public, but the paper made no attempt, by criticism or discussion, to correct or form taste in poetry.

In A. R. Orage's weekly *The New Age*, poetry was more purposefully handled. Between 1908 and 1912 Holbrook Jackson, J. C. Squire, F. S. Flint and Ezra Pound at various times did poetry-reviewing. Flint, at twenty-three, was given his first chance by Orage. His articles on contemporary French poetry were timely,

---

[1] Quoted by Edward Marsh, 'Memoir', *Collected Poems of Rupert Brooke* (London, 1918), p. L.

and his insight into French work enabled him to urge his English contemporaries to a new directness and economy. Pound's articles were racy and challenging, the work of a man actively engaged in the reform of diction. Arnold Bennett, under the name of Jacob Tonson, wrote vociferously of the literary scene, and sometimes of poets. His virulent abuse of modern poets, whose achievement he found despicable beside that of the mighty dead, was perhaps justifiable, but was hardly helpful in a period of difficult transition. *The New Age* printed verse of uneven quality, and had a tendency to take 'realistic' poems with a social purpose.

Sober periodicals surviving from the nineteenth century—*The Cornhill Magazine, The Athenaeum, The Spectator* and so on—barely noticed new verse, and *The Times Literary Supplement,* though it was a more conscientious critic, showed no greater concern than they seriously to understand or give direction to new poets.

Around 1910 a few magazines of verse struggled to the light, and shortly expired. *The Thrush,* a monthly, ran from December 1909 to May 1910, offering a *mélange* of poetic scraps—the pleasant, totally uninteresting work of people content to turn the handle of the familiar hurdy-gurdy. Douglas Goldring's *The Tramp* combined an interest in literature with an interest in the outdoor life, and ran from March 1910 for about a year.

John Middleton Murry's *Rhythm,* an amply illustrated paper devoted to art and letters, survived longer.[1] *Rhythm* was dedicated to the new spirit in art. It was infused with defiance and optimism. The old gods were dead and the New Thelema was just round the corner. Poetically it leaned towards modernity, printing free verse by Katherine Mansfield, and some poems that were outspoken in sentiment, if conventional in form, by Murry. The chief poetical support was Gibson, but James Stephens and W. H. Davies contributed several poems, and Monro's 'Overheard on a Saltmarsh' first appeared here. But the periodical had nothing vital to say for poetry. Its reviews were undistinguished and at times badly out of

[1] Its fourteen issues appeared between 1911 and 1913. It was replaced by *The Blue Review,* which survived through three issues only.

control, as when Murry declared that James Stephens was not only 'the greatest poet of our day' but one of those 'whom we consider the greatest poets the world has ever known'.[1] *Rhythm*'s circulation was tiny and its effect on contemporary taste was negligible.

In 1919 Henry Newbolt commented:

> The arts have fallen in market value, and poetry has perhaps suffered more heavily than the rest. Writers who only forty years ago would have been enthusiastically praised and followed, perhaps even lavishly rewarded, are now left to each other's sympathy, or informed through the Press that they leave their readers cold, that they are Epigoni, the puny descendants of a great ancestry.[2]

It was, then, with the rarest exceptions, futile for the young poet to look to the critics for understanding or constructive comment: the best he could hope for from the magazines was sporadic and subordinate house-room for a few of his poems.

We have been speaking so far only of the younger poets, whose reputations had yet to be made, or in a few cases more firmly established. There existed also a somewhat faded hierarchy of senior poets who appealed to more conservative tastes, either by writing in the manner of Tennyson, or by extolling the glories of England, or both. These men had a rather suspect eminence, and enjoyed more respectful treatment at the hands of the critics. Among them, William Watson, Alfred Austin, Alfred Noyes and Rudyard Kipling were the most prominent, and they were, in their different degrees, anathema to the young poets. Stephen Phillips, whose speciously 'poetic' dramas caused a stir around the turn of the century, belonged with these men, who included most of the writers ingenious enough to make money out of poetry.

It is a safe assumption that most members of the traditionally

[1] *Rhythm*, II (June 1912), p. 34.
[2] 'A New Study of English Poetry', *English Review*, X (January 1912), p. 286.

minded Poetry Society, formed to foster interest in poets and poetry, and to extend and improve the practice of reading verse aloud, would have confessed to a taste for these authors. The Society was founded in 1909 by Galloway Kyle, who at the age of ninety (he was born on 25 May 1875), is still associated with its work. It concerns us here not because it was of any assistance to young poets, but because of Monro's temporary association with its work, an association surprising enough unless we take into account the naïve hopefulness of his mood at this time.

The first president of the Society was the poetess, Lady Margaret Sackville, who spoke well and to the point at the inauguration, hoping that the Society would 'never become facile or "popular", to turn to a merely trivial gathering of persons amiably interested in the same idea!'[2] Her half-expressed fears were unfortunately fulfilled: the direction in which the Society was heading very soon became obvious—poetry was made an excuse for pleasant social exchanges, for irrelevant snobbery, for the disagreeable consequences of organised association.

A needlessly long and glittering roll of Vice-presidents and Patrons was assembled—when Harold Monro began his connection with the Society's journal in 1912 there were fifty-six Vice-presidents and forty-two Patrons and Honorary Members. The list of their names, ranked in three close columns, fills the best part of a page of the *Gazette*.[1] The Patrons and Honorary Members included the Prince and Princess Alexis Dolgorouki, Miss Marie Corelli, Professor Oscar Browning, Sir L. Alma-Tadema, Lady Mond, the Marchioness of Londonderry, Mr. Theodore Watts-Dutton, Mr. Oscar Asche, and the Rev. Father Benson: an assembly that, in its piquant variety, rivals a Ronald Firbank party-list. The Vice-presidents included many of the more respected poets of the day— Wilfred Blunt, Edmund Gosse, Maurice Hewlett, Thomas Sturge Moore, Henry Newbolt, Alfred Noyes; learning, religion and the

[1] The early history of the Society can be traced in its journals: the inaugural issue, *Journal* (June 1909), *The Poetical* (which ran sporadically from Oct. 1909), and *The Poetical Gazette*, first issued in Feb. 1910, and incorporated in Jan. 1912 with *The Poetry Review*.

[2] *Poetical Gazette*, No. 23, p. 454 [in *Poetry Review*, I (Sept. 1912)].

other arts were represented by such prominent people as Arnold Bennett, G. K. Chesterton, Mme. Melba, Beerbohm Tree, the Bishop of Durham and the Dean of Salisbury.

An event which brought the Society a good deal of press attention, in which it happily basked, was the Poet's Dinner, held on 5 April 1910 in the Royal Venetian Chamber of the Holborn Restaurant. As many lineal descendants of bygone English poets as could be unearthed sat down together, in the chronological order of their poetic ancestry, and contemplated the English flower decorations while the Duke of Norfolk (claiming descent from the poet Surrey) replied to the speech of Lord Coleridge (President of the Society). Afterwards, Lady Strachey read a Keats sonnet, and Rangiuia, a Maori chief, clad in native costume, performed a war-dance, and sang Maori songs at the piano.

During 1912, when the Society's organ, *The Poetical Gazette*, jostled uneasily within the covers of *The Poetry Review*, three events take precedence over the routine readings and lectures held at the centres—the performance of Gilbert Murray's version of Euripides' *Hippolytus* at the Imperial Institute, the pilgrimage to Stratford upon Avon, and the Browning Centenary celebrations. There are remarks in the reports of two of these functions which oblige one at least to smile. Descending from their vestibuled coaches at Stratford upon Avon station, the party made its way to the Town Hall to be welcomed by the Mayor, Councillor Ballance, who 'bears a striking resemblance to the Shakespeare portraits'. This good man made a speech of disarming banality, pointing out how 'Wordsworth's lines on the daffodils and the witchery of the clouds gave an additional interest to people going about the country', and members went on to their ten-and-sixpenny luncheon at the Swan's Nest Hotel. The Browning Centenary was organised by a committee of fifty-eight persons, many of them titled, or if not that, well known, and was held in the Royal Court Theatre. Alfred Noyes supplied a commemorative ode and it was read by Mr. Laurence Irving, the son of Sir Henry; his 'clarion voice reached beyond the sun' according to the Poetry Society's critic. *The Poetical Gazette*, ever fond of reproducing press-notices of its functions, castrates *The Academy*'s review, beginning its quotation *in medias res* with the ominous sentence, 'The latter half, devoted to "In a Balcony" was altogether better, and we must confess to a feeling of surprise.'

At the various centres meetings were held, on an average, once a month. By the end of 1912 there were centres in Central London, in several London suburbs, and in a number of provincial cities— Glasgow, Brighton, Eastbourne, Salisbury, Clifton. Members read and discussed their favourite poems and heard lectures, ladies and clergymen shouldering much of the burden of leadership. The probable character of the meetings is suggested by the choice of subjects: 'Poems on London', 'Poems on Spring', 'An afternoon with Sir Edwin Arnold', 'Modern Poets—Alfred Noyes, Stephen Phillips, W. B. Yeats, W. W. Gibson, Walt Whitman, Poe.' In May 1911 it had been announced that a lady member 'after considerable research' had designed a badge or rosette which the members could wear. It combined three colours: 'the blue is emblematic of the consecration of the intellect to noble service, the orange of intense spirituality, the red of the joy of life, and the three together symbolise pure and noble poetry'. Whether her idea was ever put into effect is impossible to tell: that it could be seriously proposed indicates a good deal.

The Society liked to run poetry competitions, and the winning entries—album verses of no possible merit—are enough in themselves to refute the claim that it took poetry seriously. The lyric competition held in 1911 was won by a trite little essay in the ballad style, and a sonnet entered in the contest won commendation for the lines:

> If joy be void—and with thee joy abiding—
> To me that void were joy, and I would be
> Happy within the hollow shell abiding
> That fancy fills with murmurs of the sea.

2

'THE POETRY REVIEW'

When Mr. Galloway Kyle, the Hon. Director of the Society, asked Monro to take over *The Poetical Gazette*, offering him, for £50, a half-share in the paper, Monro refused, for he realised that 'its traditions would be fatal to any serious new literary venture'.[1] He offered instead to start an independent monthly of his own, which might 'prove of direct benefit' to the members of the Poetry Society. How such a periodical could benefit the Society is not at all clear, for it would be completely autonomous and under the control of a man who had very little concern for the Society's interests. The Hon. Director was right to be 'gravely concerned' at this proposal—but he continued to woo Monro, convinced that he was the best person to run the paper. Of this conviction Monro dryly remarked, 'The Hon. Director evidently misjudged personality.'

But Monro was anxious to begin publishing and, on his own initiative, he suggested a compromise which the Society accepted. The arrangement could have worked only if the parties involved had been in agreement over principle: the periodical was to be conducted by a committee, with the editor, Monro, under its direction. He would accept any censure that the Council of the Society might pass, and proposed that a council-meeting be called at the end of the first year to consider the situation. Monro would defray expenses for that year and hand over any profits to the Society, after receiving interest on his own money. 'I practically sold myself to the Society', he wrote, when he was repenting his decision a year later. In return for an assured market among Poetry Society members ('. . . the chief reason for the alliance', he had written to Browne in November 1911, 'is that they guarantee us 1000 copies a month, tho' they only pay £5 for them.')[2] in return for this, he surrendered

[1] 'Personal Explanation', *PD*, I (March 1913), pp. 8–11.
[2] (10 Nov. 1911) Maurice Browne Collection, University of Michigan.

his right to control the policy of a paper for which he was financially responsible. By the strict terms of the agreement, that is to say, he surrendered his right—in fact, he stood up for his convictions, and from the start there was dissension. The committee could not agree, and almost at once it ceased to meet.

But these problems were pushed aside in the urgent haste to get into print. Confident that he could use the paper to boost the younger poets, Monro had written to Browne: 'The paper is to be the cry of young blood. The Poetry Society is the outer husk, and we shall break through. . . .'

The first number was to appear in January 1912, and at the beginning of November not only had publisher, offices and printers to be found, but material had still to be collected for the first two numbers. 'From that moment', writes Arundel del Re, the paper's sub-editor, 'we were literally haunted by *The Poetry Review*; sleeping, eating, drinking, sitting or walking, the thought of it never left us. . . .'[1]

Fortunately Monro was a good organiser. Dingy offices were found in a corner of the top floor of 93 Chancery Lane. A. K. Sabin, whose business acumen had temporarily salvaged the Samurai Press, came in as 'financial overseer', and they had the help of F. S. Flint, Romney Green, Gilbert Cannan and Cuthbert Wilkinson, the manager of the St. Catherine's Press, which was to publish the *Review*.

Both Monro and Del Re were depressed. It was a dreary winter, and they had embarked on an enterprise foredoomed in the melancholy prophecies of Monro's friends. Tea and crumpets in the 'Wayside Tea-rooms' near by, whose lady-proprietor was happy to let them meet and discuss plans before a warm fire, were a real help. It seems proper to pay tribute to Miss Davies's contribution to the preparation of the *Review*. And then, on Saturdays, when the office was shut up for the week-end, Monro and his sub-editor went and ate a large lunch at the 'Bodega' by Temple Bar, before Monro caught his train into the country, there to look over the manuscripts that had come in during the week.

[1] 'Georgian Reminiscences—iii', p. 30.

Not surprisingly, as that hectic winter rushed away, Monro felt nervous and a little unreal. Sabin writes:

> He frequently begged me to come up to Gray's Inn to meet various people whose interest he sought to evoke in the new publication. 'It all seems less insubstantial when you are with me', he would say. 'When I am alone I can't always believe in myself.'[1]

Yet the first number of *The Poetry Review* appeared in January 1912, only a week late; the printing and production were of the high quality on which Monro always insisted; it was bound in brown paper covers, and cost sixpence.

A literary review is Janus-headed: it has its eyes on readers and contributors alike, and editorial policy decides where most attention is focused. The coterie review exists for the benefit of the contributors, and challenges the public to accept them. The aim of *The Poetry Review* was very different. One of its primary aims was to re-educate a public that had come to misunderstand the uses of poetry.

Monro clung to a loftily idealistic view of the nature of poetry and of its function in society. Poetry was the expression of the ideals of the race, and in a corrupt society could only become corrupted. In 'The Future of Poetry',[2] an article in the opening number, he harks back to a golden age when 'The young nations strode through the world to the clatter and rush of song; it was the natural voice of the spirit.' Civilisation had degraded poetry. Summing up its uses in contemporary society, he wrote:

> Its cultured members expect to find in poetry, if anything, repose from material and nervous anxiety; an apt or chiselled phrase strokes the appetites and tickles the imagination. The more general public merely enjoys its platitudes and truisms

[1] *Pilgrimage*, Ch. X.
[2] *PR*, I (Jan. 1912), pp. 10-13.

jerked on to the understanding in line and rhyme; truth put into metre sounds overwhelmingly true . . .

And, diagnosing the trouble, he asserted:

Poetry is uninteresting to-day in that degree only that it is remote from life. It need not treat necessarily of events, deeds or episodes, but it must be fundamental, vital, innate or nothing at all.

There was a frothy head on Monro's idealism, and he dreamed of a time when

. . . words will indeed be *winged*, and will sweep in flight across the world with the dignity and glorious symmetry of great flocks of birds. . . . Metre will serve substance; form will be one with expression, metaphor with thought; poetry will be the call of spirit to spirit, the very throb of the heart of Nature, as expressed in her ultimate manifestation—man.

Society clearly had to be radically changed before it was fit to receive the poets.

In the preface to the first number, Monro tried to explain his policy in words that reveal at once his hopes and the unformed state of his thoughts:

Time is ripe for the forging of a weapon of criticism, and for an emphatic enunciation of literary standards. Poetry should be, once more, seriously and reverently discussed in its relation to life, and the same tests and criteria be applied to it as to the other arts. This periodical will aim not so much at producing poetry as at stimulating a desire for it. We shall strive to create an atmosphere. We shall attempt to co-ordinate the bases of thought from which poetry at last emerges.[1]

Accordingly, more space was to be given in the *Review* to articles and reviews than to new verse. Harriet Monroe, at this time preparing to launch her magazine, *Poetry* (Chicago) which followed a quite different plan—poetry made up the bulk of it, and criticism

[1] *PR*, I (Jan. 1912), p. 3.

was relegated to the back pages—wrote to him in protest. She clearly felt that he was putting the cart before the horse, but was too polite to say so.

Had she done so, Monro would have pointed out that there was already a spate of new verse. Every year between three and four hundred volumes were issued by publishers ready to oblige the poet who would pay his own expenses. Monro had immediately rejected Galloway Kyle's suggestion that he should undertake to publish books of verse. The young men were already in print, but the public, lacking the guidance of good critics, protected itself from good and bad alike in the only way it could, by ignoring them. 'You cannot expect the public to turn over piles of rubbish to find something for itself', Monro wrote to Miss Monroe, 'It needs, above all, a direction'.[1]

Monro's attitude to the public was benevolent, a little pedagogic. He did not expect a poetic awakening on a grand scale, and very much disliked what he calls 'popularisation'—(he nowhere defines this, but it must imply a lowering of standards for the sake of wider acceptance)—but he believed the English were a poetic race, waiting only to be released from an effete tradition to regain their inheritance. His situation, as the avowed well-wisher of the younger poets, and yet the editor of the Poetry Society's paper, was delicate. He walked warily in the first number, sensing the ambiguity of his position, anxious not to offend his readers. 'Deploring what is, and thundering what might be' he reckoned a waste of energy, and in a sentence described the editorial *persona* he had elected to wear: 'Our attitude is that of the smiling philosopher.'

The affability, critical detachment and impartiality resumed in the phrase 'the smiling philosopher' can be seen, though in a sub-lunary form, in the pages of *The Poetry Review*. Monro was by nature a peacemaker, not a partisan; he was dedicated to the Idea of Poetry, not to any single school. *The Poetry Review*'s thunder was reserved for facile versifiers, for lapses from editorial ethics, and for poets like Kipling and Noyes, who sang a reactionary Imperialism.

[1] Quoted by Harriet Monroe, *A Poet's Life* (New York, 1938), p. 255.

Monro stubbornly resisted the pressure of Pound, who wanted to edge him to the left of centre. Indeed, the whole tenor of Monro's mind is clear when we compare his approach to the poetic situation of 1911 with that of Pound. These two men shared a single-minded and largely disinterested desire to serve poetry, but the resemblance abruptly ceased there.

In the spring or summer of 1911 Pound came back to England from America, set up his lyceum in Church Walk, Kensington, and, a born partisan, energetically began promoting the work of Richard Aldington and H.D., informing them one day in 'a somewhat infernal bun-shop full of English spinsters' that they were 'Imagist' poets.[1] That he and Monro would get on each other's nerves was obvious,[2] and Arundel del Re writes that

> Pound's individualistic and a trifle doctrinaire attitude towards poetry made him sometimes impatient with Monro for wishing to spread the gospel of poetry and for his very Shelleyan conception of the poet's function. . . .[3]

Nevertheless, *The Poetry Review* was the only poetry review in England, and as such it gained Pound's benevolent interest and impatient support.

In spite of their differences, Del Re goes on:

> Pound acted as a powerful stimulus to Monro and together with Flint and, to a lesser extent, Hulme, encouraged and backed the venture as soon as it was started.[4]

[1] Richard Aldington, *Life for Life's Sake* (New York, 1941), p. 134.
[2] According to Aldington, a patronising little poem, 'Amities III', from *Lustra* (1916), is about Monro and Bellotti's, a Soho restaurant which he had recommended:

> But you, *bos amic*, we keep on,
> For to you we owe a real debt:
> In spite of your obvious flaws
> You once discovered a moderate chop-house.

[This is mentioned in a letter from Aldington to Peter Russell (17 Feb. 1952), in the Lockwood Memorial Library, University of Buffalo].
[3] 'Georgian Reminiscences—iii', p. 28.   [4] Ibid.

'Time is ripe for forging a weapon of criticism',[1] Monro wrote martially in the opening number; the *Poetry Review* critics, alas, had no new weapon in their hands, and stumbled along under the aegis of Shelley, Arnold and Croce. Monro's own critical attitude was firmly rooted in respect for the individual—he was, in that sense, always a romantic. In his first preface he defined poetry merely as 'the finer essence of thought, the vivid expression of personality'. 'We admire sincerity more than originality', he wrote, and he sought in poetry the lineaments of a unique personality, sincerely expressed. This criterion is, of course, subjective, and from its judgements there is no appeal: the critic who is unconvinced of the sincerity of a poem has the last word.

Monro himself did his share of reviewing. In the first number he gave a kind appraisal of Edmund Gosse's *Collected Poems*, and showed that the new editor was no firebrand revolutionary. He praised this typical Victorian for his integrity and careful artistry and used him as a stick to beat the voluble poetasters of the day.[2]

But moderation without firm critical policy is not enough. *The Poetry Review* lacked a coherent policy, and lacked first-rate contributors—Monro himself spoke later of 'our inexperience, our ineptitude'.[3] He first looked for contributions from old friends of Samurai Press days—Sabin, Browne, Gibson, Drinkwater and Romney Green; and from Del Re, a devout *protégé* of his own.

There are a few articles of contemporary relevance. Lascelles Abercrombie pointed out, in 'The Function of Poetry in the Drama', that a poetical play was different in *kind* from a prose play, heightening and not imitating experience. Yeats and others had said this, but it needed reiterating in an age grounded in naturalistic prose-drama. In 'Tradition and Technique' John Drinkwater maintained that the real problem of contemporary poets was not what to say, but how to say it. Since Swinburne, he held, creative poets had been driven to one of two courses: either to abandon tradition and with it, form—('These men turned away boldly and went out into the darkness');[4] or to make something new out of

---

[1] *PR*, I (Jan. 1912), p. 4.   [2] *PR*, I (Jan. 1912), pp. 23–25.
[3] *PD*, I (Dec. 1913), p. 386.   [4] *PR*, I (July 1912), p. 299.

traditional materials—('The danger in this choice is certainly greater. Worthily to continue a tradition is at least as difficult as to invent one.')

Drinkwater saw the division as:

> . . . probably the happiest chance that could have befallen poetry. The two schools of technique have exerted an excellent corrective influence on each other, and there are already signs that the new form is to be looked for from their union.

Others who contributed articles to *The Poetry Review* were the aged Victor Plarr, who could speak as one who had *known* Lionel Johnson; and Marsh, whose first adventure in criticism was in the April number: an alert, perspicuous, pedantic appreciation of Rupert Brooke's poems. The young Richard Aldington was asked to read a number of books that, one guesses, no one else wanted to review.

That Ezra Pound was permitted to invade the second number with his captivating strut and bounce and his far more objective canons of criticism, is a tribute to Monro's breadth of mind. Pound supplied a 'Prolegomena' and 'Credo' to introduce and explain a group of his poems.

CREDO

Rhythm   I believe in an 'absolute rhythm', a rhythm, that is, in poetry which corresponds exactly to the emotion or shade of emotion to be expressed. A man's rhythm must be interpretative, it will be, therefore in the end, his own, uncounterfeiting, uncounterfeitable.

Symbols   I believe that the proper and perfect symbol is the natural object, that if a man use 'symbols' he must so use them that their symbolic function does not obtrude; so that *a* sense, and the poetic quality of the passage, is not lost to those who do not understand the symbol as such, to whom, for instance, a hawk is a hawk.

46

Technique   I believe in technique as the test of a man's sincerity; in law when it is ascertainable; in the trampling down of every convention that impedes or obscures the determination of the law, or the precise rendering of the impulse.

Form   I think there is a 'fluid' as well as a 'solid' content, that some poems may have form as a tree has form, some as water poured into a vase. That most symmetrical forms have certain uses. That a vast number of subjects cannot be precisely, and therefore not properly rendered in symmetrical forms.[1]

In a discursive tail-piece he insisted that poetic skill was only acquired by ceaseless practice, 'poetry is an art and not a pastime', 'the mastery of any art is the work of a lifetime', and in this way he justified his 'pawing over the ancients and semi-ancients'.

With none of this would Monro have had any serious quarrel, except with the one challenging statement, 'I believe in technique as the test of a man's sincerity.' This desire for a fixed, objective standard, which Hulme's classicism had helped to form, is a whole world away from Monro's way of thinking. Monro would be inclined to reverse the proposition, and to say, 'I believe in sincerity as the test of a man's technique.'

The most significant single contribution to the *Review*'s pages was F. S. Flint's survey of contemporary French poetry. which filled the best part of the August number. It was the first extended article published in England on the multifarious activity of a generation of poets. Pound mentioned it as 'something which everybody had to get';[2] public demand was heavy and exceeded the supply. (Years later, Monro was chagrined to find that a hoard of copies had been overlooked.)

The article was timely, its enthusiasm infectious, and it did much

---

[1] *PR*, I (Feb. 1912), p. 73.

[2] Letter to Harriet Monroe (28 March 1914), quoted in *Letters of Ezra Pound: 1907–1941*, ed. D. D. Paige (London, 1951), p. 74. (Pound's reference here to *Poetry and Drama* is an obvious error for *The Poetry Review*.)

to enhance the paper's reputation. It ran to fifty-nine pages and was expository rather than critical—Flint's talent was always to exhibit poetry persuasively rather than to criticise it.[1]

He wrote with the eager freshness of a young man describing his hobby, gave frequent examples of the poets' work, and though he was very conscious of 'schools', treated each poet as an interesting individual. Kenneth Cornell, in *The Post-Symbolist Period*[2] compares this essay favourably with attempts by contemporary Frenchmen to see into the poetic tendencies of 1912.

The poets whose work was featured in *The Poetry Review* (whose work, that is, made the sole poetic contribution to a particular issue) were, in sequence, Wilfrid Gibson, Ezra Pound, Maurice Hewlett, John Drinkwater, Katherine Tynan, James Stephens, Emilia Stuart Lorimer, Thomas Sturge Moore and Rupert Brooke. The December number was a miscellany of new verse, and included poets whose work was new to the *Review*'s pages, among them Harold Monro, F. S. Flint, Lascelles Abercrombie, W. H. Davies, Walter de la Mare, James Elroy Flecker, Margaret Sackville, Padraic Colum, Aleister Crowley, and G. K. Chesterton—a good sixpennorth, and a sign at the year's end of growing confidence in the paper. It was a catholic list, and sufficient evidence that Monro was not under the thumb of a reactionary society.

Certain contributions are, for various reasons, interesting enough to deserve special mention. Pound's 'Prolegomena' and 'Credo' introduced a group of poems with titles appropriately recherché— 'Oboes, I, II and III', '*Sub Mare*', '*L'Invitation*, '*Salve Pontifex*', '*Dieu! Qu'il la fait*', and '*Δωρια*'.

The variety and metrical ingenuity displayed in these poems

[1] He glanced back to symbolism and the advent of *vers libre*, and then spoke of Henri Ghéon, Jean Royère, André Spire, the Abbaye; of Paul Castiaux and Theo Varlet, Lucien Rolmer, Jean Thogorma, Florian-Parmentier; of three women-poets, Cécile Périn, Valentine de Saint-Point, and Berthe Reynold; of Tancrède de Visan, Henri Hertz, and lastly of Marinetti. In passing, some fifteen other poets were mentioned.

[2] Yale University Press, 1958.

justifies his experimentation. This Wild Man contributed to the *Review* its most skilfully turned verses:

'*Δωρία*'

Be in me as the eternal moods
of the bleak wind, and not
As transient things are—
gaiety of flowers.
Have me in the strong loneliness
of sunless cliffs
And of grey waters.
Let the gods speak softly of us
In days hereafter.
The shadowy flowers of Orcus
Remember thee.

If Monro was willing to print this classical echo, and the long and less successful '*Salve Pontifex*', it is curious that he printed nothing by Richard Aldington or H.D. From September 1912 onwards Pound was sending his *protégés'* work to Harriet Monroe for *Poetry*, but before that time *The Poetry Review* would have been a suitable outlet for their work.

Rupert Brooke's 'Old Vicarage, Grantchester' was awarded £30, as the best poem printed in *The Poetry Review*, by a weighty and varied panel of judges which Monro assembled. Besides himself, there were Henry Newbolt, Ernest Rhys, Edward Thomas, Victor Plarr, Edward Marsh and T. E. Hulme. 'Mary and Gabriel' earned some votes also; Brooke's other poems were slighter—'Song' ('All suddenly the wind comes soft'), 'Beauty and Beauty' and 'Unfortunate'. The dexterous ease with which these poems are written is instantly attractive, and the refusal to sound quite in earnest is an asset in 'Grantchester', which relies for its effect on the comic exaggeration of a genuine nostalgia. Monro himself was startled by the obliging facility with which Brooke composed poems to order. He went to Grantchester expressly to write for the November number of *The Poetry Review* and 'after a few days sent me a wire which

49

I wish I had kept, because I now can't remember the exact words.
It was to this effect: "Have written four poems. Do you want
more"?[1] Monro mentions the last three poems listed above as
products of this session of work.

Emilia Stuart Lorimer's verse, which interested Pound, has the
attractive power of old spells and riddles, and a remarkable sinewy
strength:

Anger Song

Take from me the little flowers,
And the bright-eyed beasts and birds;
And the babes, oh God, take away;
Hearken my praying-words;
Empty my road of them,
Empty my house and my arm,
For black is my heart with hate,
And I would not these came to harm.

Love Song of the Lady-Lord

II

And I so deep in love with thee
And thou it seems death-hating me.

Ever of thee my heart is thinking
While cup of the fate-store I'm drinking.

Ah dark, dear love, my dreaming'd be,
Could love and hate part thee and me!

Miss Lorimer was the first of a series of introverted female poets
whose work captured Monro's imagination. His comments on her
poetry presage decisions which, as editor and publisher, he made in
later years. 'It is', he says, 'the raw and inevitable product of personality, or nothing. Sometimes it may seem almost ingenuous
through the sheer force of its sincerity.'[2]

---

[1] 'Recollections of Rupert Brooke', '*The Rising Generation*' (Tokyo),
LXIV (Oct. 1930).   [2] *PR*, I (July 1912), p. 312.

Monro's own contributions to the December miscellany, 'Great City' and 'London Interior', show that he had taken a big stride into modernity since *Before Dawn* was published eighteen months before. They reflect the current interest in irregular free verse, and the recording of moment-to-moment impressions and emotions.

The merit of *The Poetry Review* was that it discussed poetry earnestly and conscientiously, and selected it without fear or favour. These qualities were winning for it a measure or respect and confidence which could have been fostered by improved editorship in 1913. One of Monro's plans for the future was to issue the paper quarterly, and thus have more leisure for preparation.

But towards the end of 1912 his conflict with the Poetry Society came to a head. Monro had a high standard of editorial ethics. He stood out against 'log-rolling'—persuading publishers to buy advertising-space by promising their books favourable reviews in the critical columns. He would not compromise his principles for supporters, famous people or friends. He insisted on bad verse being called bad verse, and he objected to the tone of the *Gazette*, and to the irrelevant snobbery of its list of patrons. He objected to a notice, which appeared in the February 1912 issue of the *Gazette* without his authorisation, stating that *for a fee* authoritative criticism could be obtained on manuscripts sent to the Poetry Society. 'By September it had become quite plain to me that the future of the *Review* depended entirely on the degree to which it could be kept clear of the influence of the Poetry Society.'[1]

The Society protested, understandably, at Monro's plan to issue the paper quarterly, for the *Gazette* was a bulletin of current activities. Nevertheless, Monro announced in the October and November numbers that in future the *Review* would be issued quarterly, under the same name, from Devonshire Street. Then on 22 November Monro had a letter informing him that the *Review* was the property of the Society. It was a plain sign that Monro was to be dismissed, and that the Society intended to continue publishing under the old

[1] *PD*, I (March 1913), p. 10.

name—but with a different editor. Indeed, in *The Poetical Gazette* for December appeared the announcement that

> Mr. Harold Monro having decided to enlarge the scope of his periodical by issuing it quarterly under the title POETRY AND DRAMA, THE JOURNAL OF THE POETRY SOCIETY beginning with the next number, January, will be issued under the Editorship of MR. STEPHEN PHILLIPS and a brilliant list of contributors has been secured, including all the principal leaders of modern life and thought and criticism who are associated with poetry. In addition to his editorial functions, the poet-dramatist who thrilled the world with *Paolo and Francesca*, and fascinated us with the rare beauty of *Marpessa, Herod, Ulysses, Nero* will contribute a monthly article on the eternal significance of Poetry.[1]

According to Monro himself, a combination of impatience and expediency drove him to make his odd misalliance with the Poetry Society;[2] but this does not fully explain it, and probably he had a high-minded hope that all might be for the best, that difficulties might be resolved in the service of poetry. Monro shed his illusions the hard way.

Free now of his embarrassing association with a society regarded as hopelessly reactionary, Monro was in a better position to produce the kind of review he wanted. By the spring of 1913, when the first issue of *Poetry and Drama* was offered for sale, Harold Monro had opened the Poetry Bookshop and brought out *Georgian Poetry 1911–1912*, which was having a phenomenal success. In the eighteen months since his arrival in London enthusiasm and hard work had won him a unique position. He had every right to congratulate himself.

---

[1] *PG*, No. 27, p. 563 [in *PR*, I (Dec. 1912)].

[2] A rather similar situation arose when the Imagist group took over *The New Freewoman*, a paper devoted to women's rights, and filled it with *avant garde* literature. But Miss Dora Marsden, the editor, was suffered to have her say on female questions in the opening pages, and since there was no relation between the two parts of the paper, they could co-exist more happily.

3
'POETRY AND DRAMA'

Poetry and Drama, which came out in eight quarterly numbers between March 1913 and December 1914, was issued from 35 Devonshire Street, and cost two-and-sixpence. On the front cover was an engraving of the outside of the Poetry Bookshop; on the back cover was a map of the area, with directions how to find the shop. It was a literary magazine of greatly improved quality. Its interest was extended to include the drama, and it benefited by its freedom from the pressure of monthly publication. Most of all, the good reputation which Monro had earned, and his new independence, enabled him to secure better contributors.

The old foes remained—poetasters, the low morals of publishers, the Poetry Society and all its works. There was a new iconoclastic note: 'I propose to attack here one of the holiest institutions of the Empire',[1] began Algar Thorold temerariously, maintaining that 'God Save the King' was a piece of doggerel with no valid claim to be the national anthem. The Laureateship was under fire from Monro when, on the death of Alfred Austin, he expressed 'a strong hope, based on the conviction that officialdom is incompatible with poetry'[2] that it would be abolished.

Poetry and Drama aimed, like its predecessor, to be mature and impartial, to steer a steady course down the middle of the road, but it teetered inevitably now to one side now to the other.

Two new poetic tendencies called for comment in 1913. Imagism was briefly treated in June. Monro was on friendly terms with the Imagists—Flint was a friend and supporter, Aldington a regular contributor to *The Poetry Review,* Pound offered a bear-like embrace—but his comments on their work are detached and cautious. 'Without taking them too seriously, we cannot but admire their conviction and courage', he wrote. His view of Pound was equivocal. 'Mr. Pound is a stern dictator. He hates dogma. ("Never con-

[1] *PD*, I (March 1913), p. 12.   [2] *PD*, I (Sept. 1913), p. 270.

sider anything as dogma", he writes). Nevertheless, Nietzsche-like, he is himself a dogmatist.' Yet he welcomed Pound's ruthless pruning of bad verse, which made him 'a purging influence in our world'.[1]

Poetry and Drama printed work by several of the poets who figured in the various Imagist anthologies,[2] and in April 1914 Monro went so far as to publish Pound's volume of selections, *Des Imagistes*, under the Bookshop's imprint. A lengthy article in *The Egoist*, the citadel of Imagism, records Monro's mature views on this group's work: 'It will be no use to say that their poetry "does not sing". It is not meant to . . . The test of intellect is more important to them than the test of tradition.'[3] He saw them as serious artists restricted by self-imposed limitations of style, derived from an anti-romantic view of poetry.

Innovations on a more alarming scale had come out of Italy—the *Book of the Futurists* had sold thirty-five thousand copies in Europe, and the fact that it had been 'received with apathy'[4] in Britain did not deter Monro from discussing it, for he was eager to keep up with foreign developments. Monro felt akin to anyone calling himself a Futurist, and at first did not seem to appreciate the ambiguity of the term. He quoted from his essay on 'The Future of Poetry': 'Long ago . . . we conceived the idea to "serve, worship, and obey the beautiful Future",' and he goes on

The first principles of *our* Futurism are:

    i. To forget God, Heaven, Hell, Personal Immortality, and to remember, always, the earth.

    ii. To lift the eyes from a sentimental contemplation of the past, and though dwelling in the present, nevertheless, always, to *live* in the future of the earth.[5]

Futurism had a generous spread in the number for September 1913, which carried Monro's translations of poetry by Marinetti,

[1] *PD*, I (June 1913), p. 128.
[2] Pound, Aldington, Fletcher, Flint, Lawrence, Iris Barry.
[3] 'The Imagists Discussed', *Egoist*, II (May 1915), pp. 77–80.
[4] *PD*, I (Sept. 1913), p. 263.   [5] Ibid, p. 262.

Buzzi and Pallazzeschi, and Del Re's translations of the 'New Futurist Manifesto'.

Monro's temperate nature was fired for a time by the iconoclastic brutalism of these intemperate poets, who in fact extolled the things he detested—violence, war, the machine—and who repudiated the literary past with a disdain which he was far from sharing: '. . . glory to the spirited Marinetti and his disciples for having blared their war-cry, *Futurism*, through every capital in Europe!' he cried.[1]

Marinetti was in England for a few noisy days in November 1913, and spoke at the Poetry Bookshop and elsewhere. In December 1913 *Poetry and Drama* re-assessed Futurism more coolly in the light of his visit, stressing its essentially Italian origin, predicting that it would not gain a foothold in England. Of Marinetti's poems Monro wrote:

> We admire his extraordinary inventiveness; we were enthralled by his declamation; but we do not believe that his present compositions achieve anything more than an advanced form of verbal photography.[2]

In the latter half of 1914 the flood of war-poetry invited comment. Monro was disgusted with the spate of shoddy patriotic jingles in the newspapers and magazines, and praised in comparison the directness and honesty of White Papers and official despatches. In view of the rubbish that the war had produced thus far, he showed remarkable prophetic insight in forecasting that

> A long war would reduce most writers to a condition of elementary candour; there would be so much to express that the tricks and affectations of the past few years would seem as useless as tattered clothes.[3]

Edward Thomas was perhaps the most valuable of *Poetry and Drama*'s acquisitions, for in him Monro secured as a regular

[1] *PD*, I (Sept. 1913), p. 264.
[2] *PD*, I (Dec. 1913), p. 389.   [3] *PD*, II (Sept. 1914), p. 252.

contributor a sensitive and experienced critic of repute. Thomas had begged out of writing for nothing when Monro first approached him in 1911, but by January 1913 he had changed his mind, and decided it was better to write for nothing than not at all. (When Monro did contrive to send him a cheque, he sent it back—grateful, but determined to honour his agreement.) He exposed the fatal facility of Ella Wheeler Wilcox's verse, discussed the 'rusticity' in Hardy's poems and, writing on 'Reviewing, an unskilled labour' he gave a realistic account of the state of journalistic criticism, with special reference to poetry criticism.

The award of the *Poetry Review* prize of £30 for his 'Grant-chester' must have reinforced Rupert Brooke's sympathy for Monro's publications. The 1913 volume of *Poetry and Drama* had two articles by him, one on Webster's adaptation of his source-material, and the other an essay on Donne occasioned by the publication of Grierson's edition. Brooke's method of discussing these authors, whose popularity and influence lay all ahead, was also in advance of his time. He was interested in close textual study and what it could reveal of the inner workings of the poet's mind, an approach which we associate with the 'textual critics' of the twenties.

To discuss *Georgian Poetry 1911–1912*, Monro needed a critic of standing. He found Henry Newbolt, whose long article amply ful-filled the task. He commended 'E.M.'s' initiative:

> The book is a striking one: it has been eagerly bought up, and I believe that it cannot fail to astonish most of its readers, for there are probably but few who have been carefully noting the scattered appearances which together prove the coming of a new breath of poetic emotion.[1]

The article revives the surge of pleasurable excitement that the book engendered. Newbolt found three outstanding qualities in the poems as a whole—poetic imagination ('it would be difficult to point to a time when it has been more suddenly, more widely and more strongly at work than it is at the present moment'),[2] constructive

---

[1] *PD*, I (March 1913), p. 46.   [2] *PD*, I (March 1913), p. 51.

power and truth of diction ('They write as grown men walk, each with his own unconscious gesture').[1] Newbolt, whose own verse remained disappointingly old-fashioned, was, at fifty-one, wholeheartedly in support of the younger poets who were striking out on their own but at the same time keeping close to the familiar shore.

Others who contributed articles and the lustre of their names to the pages of *Poetry and Drama* were Robert Bridges, Ford Madox Hueffer and Remy de Gourmont.

Discussion of the theatre in *Poetry and Drama* showed mingled patience and impatience—impatience with the common run of productions, patient confidence that a few years would produce an '*Annus mirabilis*, when the new theatre will burst into flower and bring with it new action, new decor, new lighting, new criticism'.[2]

Thus wrote Gilbert Cannan, who was responsible for the 'Dramatic Chronicle'. He was a vehement and resolute critic whose articles still make stimulating reading. He was ready to back anyone who would help rid the stage of triviality, ostentation, realism and the cult of the leading actor. William Poel, Granville-Barker, Gordon Craig, and the Repertory Movement—especially John Drinkwater and the Birmingham Repertory Theatre—were among his reasons for optimism. Other writers—among them Basil Dean, Ashley Dukes and William Archer—wrote from a similar standpoint: on drama the paper took a more consistent and more progressive line than on poetry.

The intellectual periodicals of this time took a remarkable interest in developments abroad: just before the cataclysm, English insularity seemed to be suffering a temporary set-back. *Poetry and Drama* was resolutely cosmopolitan. Each number carried F. S. Flint's 'French Chronicle', which, urgent with information and alive with intelligence, maintained the interest aroused by his successful essay in *The Poetry Review*. There were two Chronicles by John Alford on American poetry, and one 'German Chronicle' from T. E. Hulme, which came in June 1914, just in time to escape the war. (The September issue noted, under this head, that 'the

<hr />

[1] Ibid, p. 52. [2] Ibid, p. 75.

principal literary event of the quarter has been the destruction of the Belgian Library at Louvain'.)

The poetry and drama chosen for publication here confirms the impression which *The Poetry Review* has given of Monro's taste and editorial policy. He took work from all kinds of writers, turning his back only on the established public poets who were intent on preserving all they could out of the decay of Victorianism. In a period of confusion and tentative starts, this allowed him a wide latitude.

Contributions from Thomas Hardy ('My spirit will not haunt the mound'), and Robert Bridges ('Flycatchers'), took pride of place in the fourth number, and were a sign of *Poetry and Drama's* improved status. They no doubt galled the officers of the Poetry Society, from whose list of patrons the names of Hardy and the Poet Laureate were conspicuously absent. New poems from Emile Verhaeren and Rabindranath Tagore added distinction to the second number.

Many of the younger writers who were to be 'incarcerated' by Marsh—as one of the Poetry Bookshop's customers put it[1]—in the *Georgian* anthologies were here. But the Anglo-American *avant garde* was well represented, and work by Ernest Rhys, Victor Plarr, Henry Simpson and Lord Dunsany helped to balance the see-saw. Writing to Monro to know if he had decided whether or not to be in the *Catholic Anthology* which was under preparation, Pound remarked (8 July [1914]): 'I don't know that you'll like the company—any more than I occasionally like the company in P & D [*sic*] . . . *ma che* . . . !'

When the war brought *Poetry and Drama* to a close, Monro was arrested in the full flood of a developing enterprise. He was, he wrote, unable to express the reluctance with which he had made the decision to suspend the paper. It was 'slowly gaining for itself a permanent place among the periodicals: a public had been formed; the circulation was steadily increasing; the strength and general quality of the whole was . . . gradually improving'.[2]

[1] Edward Marsh, *A Number of People* (London, 1939), p. 324.
[2] *PD*, II (Dec. 1914), p. 322.

Never again did Monro sit in the editor's chair of a serious literary review. He was not, it is true, made to be an outstanding editor: he was on the one hand too amiably receptive by temperament, too much the kindly husbandman of poets, while, on the other hand (as the following chapter will demonstrate), he was capable of tragic delay in appreciating the merit of new and unfamiliar work. At pains to deny that he was himself a critic, he was not best adapted to head a critical review in a time of experiment and uncertain standards. But the rapid advance of *The Poetry Review* and *Poetry and Drama* was a creditable achievement: in three years Monro had raised himself from the position of seeming hireling of a reactionary Poetry Society to that of editor of a periodical that attracted contributions from the best, and not merely the youngest, talents on both sides of the Atlantic. He had launched *The Poetry Review* in the belief that there was a public for poetry in England and that there were poets, and the growing success of his periodicals was his justification. His idealism took a practical form, and in 1913 the Poetry Bookshop was founded as a kind of *foyer* for poetry, reinforcing the work of *Poetry and Drama*. As the ruling spirit of these two enterprises, Monro had made himself perhaps the most influential figure in English poetry.

3

The Poetry Bookshop

1

THE OPENING OF THE BOOKSHOP

As editor of *The Poetry Review*, Monro had been placed between the poet and the public, in an ideal position to understand the needs of both. He discovered that though the public for poetry was not small—at the lowest estimate he reckoned it at ten thousand[1]—it was 'unorganised, scattered and strangely unguided'.[2] During 1912 his thoughts turned to starting a 'Poetry Shop', and in November he announced to his readers that on 1 January 1913, there would open 'in the heart of London, five minutes' walk from the British Museum', a shop devoted to the sale of poetry, and of all books, pamphlets and periodicals connected with poetry.

The sale of poetry was, he thought, a specialist activity. The new shop was thus not in competition with the recognised booksellers who, with few exceptions, had come to consider poetry unmarketable. The customer who was tired of the shopman's 'out of print', or 'we will try to get it for you', was invited to come to the Poetry Shop. There he could loiter, sit down and examine the books, discuss them with his friends. 'Let us hope that we shall succeed in reviving, at least, the best traits and qualities of so estimable an institution as the pleasant and intimate bookshop of the past.' All this might be bad for business, he admitted, but the circulation of poetry was a 'spiritual, or at the least, an artistic, rather than an economic enterprise'. But even so the well-wishing adventurer was

[1] *PR*, I (Sept. 1912), p. 423.
[2] *PR*, I (Nov. 1912), p. 498.

confident that since a 'depot' for poetry was so obviously needed, it could not fail of support.

The address of the shop was 35 Devonshire Street, Theobalds Road. The British Museum was the most venerable of the centres of culture in the area, but the shop was fairly well situated for students at University College, King's College, the Central School of Art and Craft and other art schools, and for workers in a number of legal and government offices. Monro maintained, according to Arundel del Re, that people interested in literature were more likely to be found in the neighbourhood of the British Museum than in the West End, and that in any case the Poetry Bookshop was primarily for people who cared enough for poetry to come and look for it.[1]

But the street was certainly very obscure. At one end was the decayed elegance of the eighteenth-century Queen Square; at the other, the trams and turbulence of the Theobalds Road as it ran towards the City of London. A slum-area to the south of the Theobalds Road was cleared when Kingsway was cut through to the Strand in 1900–1905, and Devonshire Street seems to have belonged to the same cultural unit. Sir Osbert Sitwell remembers it as 'a narrow street . . . rather dark, but given over to screaming children, lusty small boys armed with catapults, and to leaping flights of eighteenth-century cats';[2] A. K. Sabin describes it as 'a narrow unsavoury thoroughfare'.[3] Maurice Browne, Douglas Goldring, and Arundel del Re call it, bluntly, a slum, and the account which Alida Monro gave, in her talk at the Harvard Summer School in July 1961, supports this. Many of the buildings, she says, were served by one tap on the ground floor, and the passer-by was in constant peril of being hit on the head by kipper-bones and banana-skins falling from the upper windows. Next door to the Bookshop, on the upper floor, lived an unruly family presided over by the grandmother, a very fat old woman who sold flowers at Piccadilly Circus. Her sons were 'race-course toughs' whose

[1] 'Georgian Reminiscences—iii', p. 38.
[2] *Laughter in the Next Room* (London, 1949), p. 35.
[3] *Pilgrimage*, Ch. X.

off-spring, when offered some of the Bookshop's illustrated children's books, tore them up and stamped on them. Mrs. Monro may be harking back to the same experience as Sir Osbert Sitwell, when she recalls him, clad in a bowler, canary-coloured waistcoat and smart grey suit, walking up Devonshire Street pursued by a train of mocking boys.

The street—a fairly short one—boasted, she says, three pubs, and the police always paraded it in pairs. Taking into account the English relish for making fun out of social differences it was clearly a very odd place to put a bookshop, and it was quixotic to put there a shop devoted to the sale of poetry.

It was officially opened on 8 January 1913, by Henry Newbolt. The selection of the proper man to perform this ceremony was a matter of some delicacy. Monro had invited Lascelles Abercrombie to do the job, but he declined it on the ground that the invidious choice of one of the younger men would cause bad feeling. (Yeats even suggested that they get a man who was not a poet at all.) Bridges, Yeats, Gosse and Newbolt were men of sufficient years, who for different reasons stood apart from the faded hierarchy of elderly poets. Newbolt recommended himself rather particularly at that time. The Royal Society of Literature had not long before elected him to its newly-created Chair of Poetry, and in the two lectures he had delivered to the Society in that capacity he had shown an alert sympathy with what the younger generation of poets was about.[1] All that survives of his remarks at the opening

---

[1] Monro had thrown discretion very nearly to the winds in praise of the lectures. They were 'so excellent that, were it not necessary in such matters to maintain a normal English reserve we should feel disposed to assert they were the best pronouncements that had been delivered on poetry for many years'. (*PR*, I (Jan. 1912), p. 151.) Of the younger poets, Professor Newbolt had said: 'They have determined to be no longer unnecessarily hindered by old conventions of diction, of "scanning", of unnatural and ungrammatical inversion: they are bent on getting nearer to the inward melody, on moving more faithfully to the inward rhythm. In this determination I see no lawlessness, no *aischrolatreia*, no cult of the ugly or the eccentric. I see and I desire others to see in it the old and true instinct of the English poets, the belief that formal beauty is begotten not of the hand of the artist, but of the spirit.' ('A New Study

of the Bookshop is his thoughtful wish that it should not become an institution.[1]

The Bookshop had been serving customers for some little time before the formal opening, and had some notice in the newspapers. There was a press of people that afternoon. About three hundred were squeezed in, and given tea.[2]

Edward Marsh was there, sitting, as might be predicted, with the guest of honour, Newbolt. W. H. Davies was there. Robert Frost was there quite by accident, and uninvited. He recalled the day in conversation with Elizabeth Shepley Sergeant in 1949:

> One dark morning, early in the New Year, or maybe it was late in December, I found myself pausing before the window of a shop where a clerk was arranging volumes of current poetry. A notice announced the opening, that night, of Harold Monro's Poetry Bookshop. I went in and asked if I might return for the evening. The assistant told me the guests were 'Invited'. But I might try.[3]

He did return, making his way shyly through the crowd to a seat on a stairway beside a lady who promptly enquired 'Are you a poet?' On the same occasion he met F. S. Flint and through him, later on, Ezra Pound. It was, in addition, an introduction for this isolated foreigner to the world of the Georgian poets, among whom, rather than among the more radical innovators, he was to find congenial companions.

Monro's preference for Georgian London influenced his choice of 35 Devonshire Street,[4] an eighteenth-century building of some

---

[1] *PD*, I (Dec. 1913), p. 387.

[2] Letter to Amy Lowell (24 March 1915), Houghton Library, Harvard College.

[3] *Robert Frost: The Trial by Existence* (New York, 1960), p. 101.

[4] In 1938 the name was altered to Boswell St. No. 35 was destroyed in an air-raid in 1940, and the site is now occupied by Cecil Rhodes House,

of English Poetry', printed in *The English Review*, X (Jan. and March 1912), pp. 285–300, 657–72.)

charm. Charles Ginner's pen-drawing, reproduced in the final number of *The Chapbook*, shows the Monros' stout neighbour sunning herself on the pavement and a substantial policeman casting a wary look around. The three-storied façade is crowned by a classical pediment, with two dormer windows peering over the top. The shop-window is old-fashioned, made up of a quantity of small panes set in wooden slats. Books and rhyme-sheets are placed directly up against the glass. It seems to have been much the same when Amy Lowell, in 1913, was first attracted by the swinging sign, and then by the name of the shop 'in excellently designed, big, black letters over the window'.[1]

The interior fulfilled the promise of the outside. Monro called in Romney Green to provide bookshelves, tables and settles in his characteristic style—massive but finely proportioned furniture hewn from great baulks of oak. It added to the homeliness of the shop, and with its flavour of *rus in urbe* suggested the character of the proprietor. Literary reviews were spread on tables, the bookshelves were unglazed. Amy Lowell calls it 'a room rather than a shop'. A coal fire in winter and, later, the occasional presence of Monro's cat and Mrs. Monro's dogs completed the impression of intimacy and domesticity.

Arundel del Re believes that the peaceful atmosphere which Monro succeeded in giving to the place was the secret of its unexpected success:

> None was hustled or made to feel uncomfortable if he ensconced himself in the corner of a settle with a volume of verse to read all through his luncheon hour.[2]

Even a non-buying patron could ask expert advice of Monro or his assistant and be graciously received.

[1] 'The Poetry Bookshop', *Little Review*, II (May 1915), pp. 19–22.
[2] 'Georgian Poets', a New Zealand Broadcasting Service talk (9 Sept. 1959).

a girls' hostel. Until recently, the gas-lamp, which shone on the heads of the poets and their audiences as they came and went, was still in its original position on the pavement outside. It has been replaced by a modern electric lamp.

Monro's conduct of business is epitomised in an anecdote of Geoffrey Grigson's, which relates to the later period when the shop was in Great Russell Street. His customer should not

'waste all that money on Doughty', said Monro, putting the volumes of *The Dawn in Britain* back on a high shelf, and making me, with his habitual frown of impatience, buy *Grace after Meat* by John Crowe Ransom, introduced by Robert Graves, at a cost of 4s. 6d. instead of 35s. or so.)[1]

What most effectively drew the attention of the public to the 'Georgian' movement and to the Poetry Bookshop, was the publication of the first volume of *Georgian Poetry*, under the Bookshop's auspices, in December 1912.

Favourable reviews began to appear in January 1913, the book became modish, and Devonshire Street for a time shared its glory. The piquant idea of a poetry shop in a slum took people's fancy and, says Arundel del Re, 'the grubby urchins who played hop-scotch in Devonshire Street saw more smart cars than they had ever seen in their lives'.[2] The proprietor was not misled by the short-lived show of enthusiasm. 'Of course', he wrote to Amy Lowell in 1915, 'the novelty of the idea, and the obscurity of the street were the principle of appeal to many of those enthusiastic first customers, who were very soon shaken off. Too many people would have liked to come and smoke their cigarettes here.'[3]

The association between the Poetry Bookshop and the popular *Georgian Poetry* series was pointed out in many of the reviews of the volumes as they appeared—in 1912, 1915, 1917, 1919 and 1922 —and it was due to this, far more than to any other single publication, that the Bookshop's name was made familiar to the poetry-reading public. In March 1916 Monro wrote to Maurice Browne:

The Bookshop is one of the most thriving and appreciated concerns in London at present, I think. People come straight in

---

[1] 'Coming to London—vii', *London Magazine*, III (June 1956), p. 45; in *Coming to London*, ed., J. Lehmann (London, 1957).

[2] 'Georgian Reminiscences—iii', p. 38.

[3] (24 March 1915) Houghton Library, Harvard.

here back from the front, and all the students have found it out.[1]

Even allowing for exaggeration in an account written fourteen years later, it seems from Browne's *Recollections of Rupert Brooke* that 35 Devonshire Street was already, in its first year, a lively meeting-place for a mixed bunch of artistic people. On the night of the first London performance of Stravinsky's *Le Sacre du Printemps* (11 July 1913)

> . . . in the old Georgian house in the murderous slum . . . intellectual and near-intellectual London gathered, mostly from the Ballet. That summer Miss Van Volkenberg, Gibson and I were living under the eaves of the Bookshop, and almost nightly a controversy raged between our visitors and us over Eppstein's [*sic*] *Christ*, of which there was a copy in Monro's living-room downstairs. This night, to Eppstein's new vision had been added Stravinsky's, and their combined onslaught on Philistia pounded to fury those who were set in their artistic ways. . . . The stalls and gallery surged with bitter words up and down the narrow stairs, *Christ* had to be rescued hastily and indiscriminately from his opponents and exponents alike, and I from the sister of an eminent British novelist, lately deceased, who was threatening Stravinsky in my unworthy person with her umbrella.[2]

Such a scene must have gratified Monro, for he wanted the premises to be more than just a shop. The whole building was to be at the service of poets and the public. The 'Poetry House' was planned as the centre of 'an informal Guild'.[3] The first floor housed *The Poetry Review* offices, the second floor was used for some of the early poetry-readings, and on the top floor were two attics, which were made available to needy poets, and others of sympathetic mind, who wanted temporary lodgings at a low rent. The attic which Jacob Epstein occupied was, according to John Cournos, 'barely big enough to contain the bed and with a roof so sloping

---

[1] Maurice Browne Collection, University of Michigan.
[2] (Chicago, 1927), p. 37.   [3] *PR*, I (Nov. 1912), p. 499.

that you could scarcely stand up'.[1] But the rent was only three-and-sixpence a week for a room, and three-and-sixpence for a week's breakfasts.[2] Wilfrid Gibson, John Alford, Robert Frost, Lascelles Abercrombie, Eric Gillett and M. Willson Disher were among those who took advantage of the offer. Epstein and his wife were there for some months in 1913 and 1914. Wilfred Owen had to be turned away, and took a room over a coffee-shop opposite.

In a letter to Sidney Cox in March 1914, Frost explained that he had sold some poetry to *Poetry and Drama*. He proposed to spend a week in London with his family, and instead of accepting a fee to

take it out in room rent in the upper floors of the Poetry Shop. . . . The fellow that runs it and edits the quarterly I speak of is a poet and all about him are the poets my friends and enemies. Gibson had a room there for the year before he married the proprietor's secretary. Epstein, the futurist sculptor, the New York Polish Jew, whose mind runs strangely on the subject of generation whose work is such a stumbling block to the staid and Victorianly but who in spite of all is reckoned one of the greatest living geniuses, will be across the hall from us. All the poets will be in and out there. It will be something that Lesley and the children will be sure to remember.[3]

A. K. Sabin provides an interesting glimpse into Monro's mind as he was developing his plans. In 1911 the two men were revolving large enterprises for the benefit of poetry, and taking twenty-mile walks on a Sunday through Richmond Park to Kingston and on to Hampton Court as they discussed them. Romney Green's advice was called in too.

Experiences of community endeavours had evidently disillusioned Monro. He was not so much interested in setting up a nursery for poets as in bringing poetry to the public, and bringing it in a down-to-earth way. Sabin favoured

---

[1] *Autobiography* (New York, 1935), p. 256.
[2] Eric Gillett, 'The Poetry Bookshop,' a B.B.C. Third Programme talk (28 Sept. 1962).
[3] Quoted by E. S. Sergeant: *Robert Frost*, p. 120.

an academy for poetry on the Alexandrian model, where the Muses should find an actual substantial home. Harold thought that the community had rather be on paper than in the flesh, and if put together would spend most of their time quarrelling with one another. The real thing in these modern days, he opined, would be a crusade on the lines of the Salvation Army: we should spout poetry at the street-corners, in public houses, and even in private houses. *That* was the idea: the poetry circle around the home fire on a winter's night. The bard of the old baronial hall resuscitated in the suburbs.[1]

That was in 1911. Towards the end of 1912 Monro was seized with brief enthusiasm for another, rather similar, idea. 'We've something tremendous on the carpet', he wrote to Drinkwater in November, urging him to come and discuss it at the Poetry House. Drinkwater could not attend, but he had a letter from Monro explaining what it was all about:

> Roughly, the project is to read poetry in villages without formality, payment, pose, condescension, propaganda or parson. You just give it them like the eastern story-tellers, who gather people together at street corners . . . when you hear the whole plan I am sure you will help, later. It will all run very easily. It does not sound much like this, but you should hear me explain it![2]

It was a scheme that could never have had much success under an English heaven, and it was prudently laid aside. But Monro remained convinced that it was necessary to put poetry before the public in a vital way. In *The Poetry Review* he had written: 'The disadvantage under which poetry most suffers is probably that grave one of its inadequate public presentment in some acceptable form.'[3] From this conviction sprang the poetry-readings whose history is the subject of the next pages.

Influences stemming from John Ruskin, William Morris and

[1] *Pilgrimage*, Ch. X.
[2] Letters quoted by John Drinkwater, *Discovery*, pp. 224, 225.
[3] *PR*, I (Sept. 1912), p. 424.

H. G. Wells, and more immediately from Arthur Sabin, Maurice Browne and Romney Green, can be seen in the conception of the Poetry Bookshop. But this does nothing to mar the essential originality of the scheme. It took Monro's peculiar blend of vision, commonsense and perseverence to launch such an enterprise and persist in it until his death.

2

'RECITATION'; CURRENT PRACTICE

'In theory we *must* do what we can to revive (or is it, rather, introduce?) the practice of reading poetry aloud in public: in practice we get the P.R.S. . . . I felt and feel however that if one does not support the P.R.S. one is giving it no chance'.[1] So Monro wrote to Browne in March 1910, half-apologising for joining the Poetry Recital Society (later the Poetry Society), which was then just over a year old.

Four months later, members received notice that:

> Mr. Harold Monro, author of *Judas,* and lecturer to the Poetry Society, will give a reading of his own unpublished work in illustration of the accepted axiom that poetry is written for sound rather than sight reading, at the Holborn Restaurant, on Wednesday July 20, 1910 at 8 p.m. He will explain briefly the principles underlying the experiment for the Poet vocally publishing his own work.

Though he had joined the Society with very qualified enthusiasm, Monro was in general sympathy with its professed aim of encouraging the understanding and speaking of poetry. At the inaugural meeting on 24 February 1909, Lady Margaret Sackville, the first president, spoke constructively, condemning the established methods of recitation in terms which, for an audience of that day, must have had vivid force: elocution, she said, 'differs as much from

---

[1] Maurice Browne Collection, University of Michigan.

the proper rendering of a poem as a gramophone does from a human voice'.

In the multitude of 'reciters' and manuals of elocution put out at this time there is a wealth of information about contemporary precept and practice. Humorous reciters preponderate, while the series edited by Alfred H. Miles with the object of encouraging 'a manly patriotism' was very successful. Special reciters were got out for ladies, for children, for devotees of Scottish, Irish or Welsh verse, as well as any number of collections of general appeal. In selecting poems, the editors were not much interested in literary merit, but in the opportunity afforded for a demonstration of the reciter's art, and hence narrative poetry incorporating strong action, powerful emotion and plenty of dialogue was the most popular *genre*. The authors most favoured, after Shakespeare, were the lesser-known nineteenth-century versifiers, whose works were unscrupulously cut at the discretion of the performer.

The manuals of instruction reduce recitation to a system, and make a parade of science, generally opening with an alarming diagram of the vocal organs and an explanatory rubric which starts with the nose and ends with the gullet. All the sounds of English are practised individually before the student can proceed to the mastery of 'expression', which is concerned with such things as pace, pitch and inflection. Excellent and appropriate as many of the precepts are, they live in a strange vacuum, unrelated to a particular poem, uninspired by a particular need, and could too easily betray the reciter into a mechanical, self-conscious or affected delivery.

The use of gesture is invariably advocated to assist expression, and exercises are given which will bring the necessary suppleness to hands and arms. Carrington Willis, in *The Elocutionist's Handbook*, gives a simple outline of the use of gesture:

The hands may express much, and should never be covered with gloves by the reciter when gesturing, or they will be powerless to convey any passion or sentiment. The palm of the hand is turned *upwards or towards the body* when approbation,

70

The Poetry Bookshop, 35 Devonshire Street, Theobald's Road,
London, W.C. (Drawing by Joanna C. Webb based on contemporary engravings)

Alida Monro

affirmation, joy, love or any pleasing passion is expressed, but *downwards or away from the body* when negation, sorrow, hate or any disagreeable passion is depicted. In gestures of hearing they move to and from the ear and the place whence the sound is heard. In gestures of feeling (Love, Hate, etc.) they move between the seat of affection, i.e. the heart, and the object of love, hatred, etc. In gestures of thought one hand approaches the brain, the fingers sometimes passing over the forehead lightly, and at times, though rarely, both hands may approach the brain.[1]

Rose I. Patry, in her *Practical Handbook on Elucution*, explains how to suit the action to the word:

(i) *Illustrate an Appeal to Heaven.*
Arm to be held high above the head and slightly curved. First finger to be curved and to point upwards. Head and eyes to be raised.
Example: 'God alone knows that I speak the truth'.
(ii) *Illustrate Supplication.*
Body bent forward. Arms extended in front, Hands raised and clasped.
Example: 'Oh, have mercy—spare me!'[2]

The exponent of this technique was self-consciously displaying himself, and *using* a poem for the purpose. The anthologies were full of 'reciters' pieces' which lent themselves admirably to such treatment—verses of little subtlety and little sincerity, which could be satisfactorily rendered by a technique equally facile and insincere.

A desire to rid the speaking of verse of this deadly conventionality grew alongside the desire of poets to be rid of outworn conventions of composition. What success the Poetry Recital Society had in breaking down the convention, what standard its members aimed at, is very hard to judge. A great deal of recitation went on in a

---

[1] Second edition (London, 1904), p. 68.
[2] Ibid. (1909), pp. 201–2.

great many drawing-rooms from Glasgow to South Australia. One suspects that many of the members were already experienced in the old methods, and glad of the opportunity of another audience.

In 1912, though the Society's name had been changed, it was still putting strong emphasis on recitation. Mr. Sturge Moore was speaking at the centres on the reading of poetry, Dr. H. H. Hulbert ('lecturer in verse-speaking at the University of London') on the uses of the voice. One piece of machinery breeds another, and in the course of 1912 a foray was made upon the schools, and a junior order set up, each member undertaking to read at least ten lines of Poetry and to try to appreciate it each week. A member of the Society would come in and start the ball rolling, for a fee of one guinea to cover her travelling expenses. In addition, the Society set up a system for the examination of both amateur and profes- sional reciters, and the certificates of proficiency would have, the Society promised, a high professional rating. The remarks made by Mr. Forbes-Robertson after examining candidates of 1912 in the Throne Room of the Holborn Restaurant were the subject of a leading article in *The Times*. He welcomed the improvements which the efforts of the Society had brought about, but still found cause for complaint in the excessive use of gesture and the affected accents of some candidates.

Outside the pale of the Poetry Society, isolated and praiseworthy endeavours were going on. On one of the rare occasions when Monro contributed to the pages of *The Poetical Gazette*, it was to praise the work of his friend, the actor Cecil Duncan-Jones, who had given a series of poetical causeries at Claridge's Hotel, and was holding drawing-room readings at Heathfield, Sussex. He was demonstrating that modern poetry could enthral audiences when it was delivered 'without the gestures and affectations of the modern reciter'—could even enthral audiences that were 'under the peculiar disadvantage of having been gathered together for a special purpose'.[1] Basil Watt was another friend of Monro's, and his views on the reading of poetry were contained in an article, 'The Poet Articulate', which was printed in *The Poetry Review*. He

[1] *PG*, No. 18, p. 141 [in *PR*, I (March, 1912)].

too demonstrated his theories in drawing-room recitals, and Arundel del Re remarks on the quality of his performance.

Monro notes with disapproval the attempt of Miss Beatrice Irwin to combine theatrical effects with poetry in her performance at Crosby Hall, 'all her ringing of gongs and tricks with hideous limelight fell flat—as they should'.[1] But he gives high praise to Miss Florence Farr's recitations to the psaltery. He hoped that people would learn 'sufficient restraint and self-surrender to submit themselves, after her manner, to the cadence and rhythms of poetry, becoming . . . rhapsodist rather than exponent, instrument rather than representative'.[2] Miss Farr's technique had greatly impressed Yeats when he first heard her perform.

Yeats himself was the only poet whose renderings of his own work were well known. His lecture-recital in London in 1901 had demonstrated his way of rhythmically chanting poetry, which forcibly asserted its lyrical quality. His innovation had been debated in the press, and his occasional public recitals from that time were attended by an eager and devout following.

But the public generally was quite unaccustomed to hearing poets read their own work. John Masefield was already aware of the need for the revival of poetry as *sound*, but his ideas did not take a practical form until he and his wife started the Oxford Recitations after the First World War. In his autobiography he points out that, in the early years of this century, many readers were not aware that poetry had an existence off the printed page. The concept of 'eye-rhymes' could still influence the poet's choice of a word—'blood' would be a perfect rhyme for 'wood'.[3] Eye-rhymes can be demanded only when pattern in poetry is very largely a visual rather than an aural experience.

Monro was struggling against this attitude when he began to hold public readings at the Bookshop. 'We are absolutely certain that the proper values of poetry can only be conveyed through its vocal interpretation by a sympathetic and qualified reader', he wrote. 'Indeed so obvious does this appear that we regard the books on

[1] *PR*, I (June 1912), p. 250.   [2] *PR*, I (Sept. 1912), p. 424.
[3] *So Long to Learn* (London, 1952), pp. 134–5.

sale in the shop merely as printed scores for the convenience of refreshing the memory in hours of study or of indolence. The transplantation of poetry out of the common ways of life into the study is an abuse not to be tolerated.'[1]

This conviction of Monro's led him into some strange scenes. Sabin describes a prosyletising visit which Monro paid to a girls' school in Hampstead, where thirty-five of the older girls, protected by one of the older mistresses, assembled to hear him. The prudent headmistress had stipulated that he should only read from the 'safe' poets, and the audience showed little response until the last two poems were given—Tennyson's 'The Sisters', and 'Fatima'. Monro read 'The Sisters' 'with considerable dramatic force'. The poem relates how a girl lures to her bed her sister's seducer and there stabs him to death. 'The girls thrilled; the mistress looked a little bewildered.' Monro proceeded to 'Fatima':

> ... one could almost feel the itchings of delight that stirred among the girls as this golden music of insidious dream was poured into their ears, and the mistress becoming frozen with horror at the enormity of the thing.

> O Love, o fire! once he drew
> With one long kiss my whole soul thro'
> My lips, as sunlight draweth dew.
>
> .   .   .   .
>
> I *will* possess him or will die.
> I will grow round him in his place,
> Grow, live, die looking on his face,
> Die, dying clasp'd in his embrace.

'Thank you, Mr. Monro', said the mistress icily, rising the moment he had done. 'Come, girls.'

'These girls have realised for the first time within their narrow lives that poetry can be worth listening to', Monro remarked with satisfaction.[2]

---

[1] *PD*, I (Dec. 1913), p. 387.   [2] *Pilgrimage*, Ch. X.

His zeal for the cause led him to high hopes for the future: 'At present there can be scarcely a hundred first-class readers of poetry in England, the demand for them having almost ceased. But we are on the way to altering all this. We hope that Poetry Bookshops will eventually be established in all the principal towns of England —not as institutions, but as houses of enjoyment.'[1]

His hopes for a proliferation of Poetry Bookshops were disappointed (though one did open in Hull in 1919 in direct imitation on Monro's shop),[2] but his solitary venture was doing something to satisfy an obvious need. Poetry here would be free from the trammels of affected recitation, and the poet would have a place in which he could present his own work.

3

POETRY-READING AT THE BOOKSHOP

The poetry-readings were a prominent and characteristic part of the Bookshop's work for twenty-three years, but they began in a desultory way—at first five or six people would come and listen in a room upstairs, then ten or fifteen would attend readings in the offices behind the shop; by the end of 1913, at seventy readings held, the average attendance was twenty-seven; in March 1915, after two hundred readings, Monro estimated that the attendance had averaged about thirty-five.[3]

The historic reading-room, to this day a vivid memory for a number of people, was first used in March 1913. It was a happy

[1] *PD*, I (Dec. 1913), p. 387.

[2] The Poetry Shop, Pryme Street, Hull, opened by Mrs. Priestley Cooper in partnership with Miss Kathleen Wright, and with the assistance of Harold Monro, It was a converted cobbler's shop, with a curtained recess at one end for the poetry-readings; Monro, Miss Klemantaski, De la Mare and Lord Dunsany were among the first readers. It closed in 1937 for lack of support.

[3] Details of attendance taken from a letter from Monro to Amy Lowell (24 March 1915), in the Houghton Library, Harvard.

accident that at the back of the premises, but separate from the shop, was an old out-house, formerly a goldbeaters' workshop,[1] large enough to seat an audience of sixty or seventy.

The atmosphere of these meetings is recalled in the accounts of some of the people who attended them. Much depended on the relationship which Monro set up between himself, his readers and the public through his unobtrusiveness, his obvious sincerity, and his courteous but shy manner.

Dr. B. G. Brooks has described the readings given before the First World War. The audience, he wrote, collected in the Bookshop:

> One looked over the walls with their rough rime sheets nailed up (they were decorated with antiquarian woodcuts), one fingered the books on the shelves: or else one just fidgeted about till the hour struck.
>
> Half by accident, so it seemed, one became aware that the presiding genius—Mr. Harold Monro—had pushed aside the curtains at the rear and was standing there with stiff little soldierly bows and a slight wave of the hand—just the faintest suspicion of a smile working round the corners of his impassive,

[1] Goldbeaters still worked next door, and Mrs. Monro records that 'from early morning to evening the thud-thud of the goldbeating hammers was an undercurrent in our lives'. [B.B.C. talk (1955).]
Wilfrid Gibson, one of the earliest tenants, described the effect that the goldbeating had on him, in a poem in *Friends* (1916).

Gold

All day the mallet thudded, far below
My garret, in an old ramshackle shed
Where, ceaselessly, with stiffly nodding head
And rigid motions ever to and fro,
A figure like a puppet in a show
Before the window moved till day was dead,
Beating out gold to earn his daily bread,
Beating out thin fine gold-leaf blow on blow.

And I within my garret all day long
To that unceasing thudding tuned my song,
Beating out golden words in tune and time
To that dull thudding, rhyme on golden rhyme:
But in my dreams all night in that dark shed
With aching arms I beat fine gold for bread.

swarthy, as it were half-oriental face—standing there, inviting entrance into the sanctum. People passed under the curtain, beyond a crooked corner, and along a passage with white-washed plaster walls. Then I think there was another turn— and this time, under a part of the ceiling open to the sky (one felt a few drops of rain in wet weather, anyway), and so up the narrow staircase, out of the candlelight into the reading room.

There was something like a small village meeting-house in its ensemble,—the seats arranged in rows,—the windows cur-tained with green[1]—and the white plaster walls broken by diagonals of black beams. All was in semi-darkness, lit only by a shaded lamp over against the reading-table, in a little space set in the far end of the room. The seats would fill rapidly . . . There was a short pause. . . . Then the person who was to read came up the 'middle aisle', took his or her place at the desk, and so started.[2]

On summer evenings the curtains were drawn to reduce the light pouring in through the large windows, and the reading-room was illuminated as softly as possible. By the glow of the green-shaded oil-lamp the reader's face was only half-lit, and Mrs. Monro recollects the 'peculiar light'[3] the lamp cast on the paper. Electricity was installed later on, but there was a time when the reading was done by candlelight.

Arundel del Re writes evocatively of the occasion of Yeats's reading:

I can still vividly remember the time Yeats read at the Poetry Bookshop. Spring was in the air, and the lady in front of me—I

---

[1] According to Mrs. Monro and Dr. del Re, curtains of dark blue serge covered the three windows on one side of the room. Del Re says that they extended behind the reading-desk.

[2] From an unpublished article on 'The Poetry Bookshop', written when the shop closed down in 1936. This article, of which Dr. Brooks has provided me with a copy, incorporated material from a previous article which he had published, probably in 1917, in *The Londinian*, the magazine of the London Day Training College. It refers to the period 1914–1916.

[3] 'The Poetry Bookshop', a B.B.C. Third Programme talk (21 Feb. 1955).

think she was young—anyhow she had a large bunch of sweet-smelling purple violets. The dark curtains were drawn across the windows and the room was in darkness except for the golden light shed on the reader's table from the two slender oak candle-sticks. From the workshop next door came the muffled beat of the gold-beaters' mallets. A ripple of expectation ran through the packed audience, then a deep expectant hush as the poet stood silent for a moment framed in the candlelight against the dark curtain, a tall dark romantic figure with a dreamy inward look on his pale face. He began softly, almost chanting, 'The Hosting of the Sidhe', his silvery voice gradually swelling up to the solemn finale. No one moved, waiting for him to continue. I cannot remember how long he read—all lyrics—some sad, some gay, some tragic, varying the pitch and tone of his voice to suit the mood, weaving a spell over his listeners. And when he concluded with the Fairy Child's song from *The Land of Heart's Desire*, we were drawn back with a start into ourselves, as if we too had been wandering with Yeats in that land:

> Where the faeries dance in a place apart,
> Shaking their milk-white feet in a ring,
> Tossing their milk-white arms in the air;
> For they hear the wind laugh and murmur and sing
> Of a land where even the old are fair,
> And even the wise are merry of tongue.[1]

Harriet Monroe, writing in 1923, likened the reading-room to a temple:

> For seven days and nights, in the holy reserve of silence and emptiness, it gathers a faintly perfumed atmosphere for the weekly rite. And when I heard Mr. Monro read there a few poems by Rupert Brooke, the beauty of his voice and the priestly authority of his presence made a ritual—a ritual enriched by overtones from the voices of many other poets who

[1] 'Georgian Poets', N.Z.B.S. talk (1959).

had stood on the little platform, some of them never to be heard again.[1]

The meetings began at 5.30 or 6.0 p.m. and were short. Monro discovered by experience that people could not listen in comfort for more than forty minutes, and the readings were timed to last for about thirty-five. They were held twice weekly, on Tuesdays and Thursdays, until 1915, and from then on once a week, on Thursdays only, except during the summer months. They were not advertised in the press—the public was trained to expect that something would be on each Thursday, and details could be had at the shop. In this way Monro helped to preserve the informality of the readings, and avoided institutionalising them. As far as was possible, he wanted them to have the character of spontaneous reading among a group of friends:

> Official societies for the collective enjoyment or promotion of poetry must always be failures. Here we have simply a few people gathered together, and, since the English climate is bad, a house—otherwise a field or a beach might have done. We make a regular practice of reading poetry aloud, and anyone who wishes to stroll in may do so.[2]

For Ford Madox Hueffer, Yeats and De la Mare, and for other speakers of unusual interest, a larger hall was hired. The neighbourhood offered several, but the favourite was the Artificers' Guild Hall in Queen Square. Marinetti, the Italian futurist, spoke under the auspices of the Poetry Bookshop in Clifford's Inn;[3] when Henry Ainley gave a reading he attracted an audience of three hundred.

The entrance fee was at first threepence, but was later raised to sixpence; for meetings outside the shop the charge was a shilling. At a time when funds were low, an attempt was made to put the

---

[1] 'The Editor in England', *Poetry*, XXIII (Oct. 1923), p. 35.

[2] *PD*, I (Dec. 1913), p. 387.

[3] Three lectures also were given there during 1912: Harold Monro on 'Modern Poetry' (May); Darrell Figgis on 'The Sanction of Poetry' (June); T. E. Hulme on 'The New Philosophy of Art as Illustrated in Poetry' (July).

ordinary fee at a shilling, but the audience was loth to pay so much
and the old price was restored.

Monro's deepest purpose in creating the Poetry Bookshop was to
convince people that poetry was written by men alive to their own
time. The most effective way of doing this is to put the poets in
front of the public in person, to induce them to read their work
aloud in informal surroundings. Yet Monro knew the dangers of
doing this: he might attract a public more interested in 'personali-
ties' than in poetry. 'In my work at the Poetry Bookshop', he
wrote in notes for a lecture on 'The Youngest Poets' prepared
before the First World War, 'from the very beginning, I have
striven to suppress the curiosity about poets, and to stimulate an
interest in reading poetry, and its appreciation, and above all in
listening with full and concentrated attention to verse read aloud.'

Monro and his wife were frequent readers. Every autumn, at the
start of the new season, Monro would read Shelley's 'Hymn to
Intellectual Beauty'. It was a poem, says Mrs. Monro, that was
'ever-present in his mind',[1] and it served as an appropriate invocation.

It was customary from the start for writers to come and read
their own work at the Bookshop. The poets felt under some
obligation to give readings, and did so, with the exception of a few
who would have found it a private agony. Ford Madox Hueffer's
reading, like Yeats's, was an important event, well described by
Dr. B. G. Brooks from the moment when he saw

> his great round flabby, slightly moustached face rising up the
> stairway behind us into the immediate light of the candle at its
> head. Monro, I observed, was very obsequious to him ... he
> plainly regarded the visit as a high favour: and Hueffer, one
> felt, took unto himself the air of a wise uncle encouraging the
> efforts of his green and inexperienced nephew.

He read 'Heaven':

[1] Talk given at the Harvard Summer School (1961).

He went through it in a hurried panting manner, starting each tirade high in the voice, pouncing heavily on the irregular and unexpected rimes, and finishing off fairly low down. After he had done this a few times, he asked, as if in parenthesis, if he were not reading too fast. He was answered he was not (by Monro from the stairhead).[1]

Rupert Brooke gave two readings. He was a warm supporter of Monro's work, and during his trip abroad he sent letters and postcards from all over the world with hints on publicity, and suggestions of poets with whom Monro could make contact. He came many times to the Poetry Bookshop, wearing the broad squash hat which made some people take him for an Australian, but inspired the Devonshire Street urchins to run after him, calling out 'Buffalo Bill!' Sabin remembered him 'beautiful as an annunciating angel'. He would sit on the corner of a table, swinging a leg to and fro as he listened to the admirers who crowded round him.[2]

Brooke's first reading, on 28 January 1913, was from Swinburne and Donne, and was attended by six people; at the second, in July 1914, he read his own poems to a packed house of sixty or seventy, who craned their necks to hear him, for he had a prodigious cold. Eric Gillett, who was living in the Bookshop at that time, says, 'He came in and gave me his hand and told me he dreaded the thought of having to perform. After he had read a line or two in a low voice, an old lady in the front row who carried an ear-trumpet exploded, "Speak up, young man".'[3] This reading was attended by Amy Lowell, and her account of it and its aftermath is given on a later page.

The last sight we have of Brooke at the Poetry Bookshop is in Monro's description of a visit he paid after the expedition to Antwerp. He was completely changed, and sat 'mostly on the corner of the table, in his new uniform, looking haggard and discouraged. and talking almost entirely about the war'.[4]

[1] See note on p. 77 above.   [2] *Pilgrimage*, Ch. X.
[3] 'The Poetry Bookshop', B.B.C. talk (1962).
[4] 'Notes and News from England', *Rising Generation*, Tokyo, LXIV (Oct. 1930).

Sabin recalls that Drinkwater was willing to read endlessly (he was, after all, an actor); that Wilfrid Gibson murdered his work by reading it at great length in a monotone; that Hodgson was unwilling to read at all. This seems most probable, for Mrs. Monro says that he could not tolerate so much as a mention of his poetry.[1]

On leading Sturge Moore to the foot of the steps outside the reading-room, she was disconcerted to hear him say in his high falsetto that he had 'forgotten his *Wings of the Air*'. W. H. Davies read 'most beautifully', but suffered badly from stage-fright, only dispelled by her reminding him of 'the large whisky afterwards'.

In selecting readers, Monro was up against a problem which touched him in several ways. He wrote to John Drinkwater in 1924:

> Personally, I have always endeavoured in my capacity of Proprietor of the Poetry Bookshop to represent it as a public institution independent of my private views and judgments. . . . The question has been brought rather forcibly before me several times as to whether my various remarks in writing about my contemporaries were compatible with my activities in the shop, but I have decided that the two capacities should remain independent. . . .
>
> Many people, with whom I am not entirely in sympathy, have given readings and lectures here. Alfred Noyes, who certainly has much cause for grievance against me, is reading his own poems this Thursday. People so far apart as Marinetti and J. C. Squire have both participated, though the latter I admit not lately. Robert Bridges has read and De la Mare and Davies and Yeats and Newbolt and Abercrombie. Gibson is coming again next month and Gosse has read two or three times, but then I have also had Ford Madox Hueffer several times. If, in issuing invitations to read, I allowed my own private judgements to influence me, I should be doing an injustice to the shop, to the audience, and to the poets. The general standard, of course, has to be kept as high as possible, but that is another thing.

[1] Harvard Summer School talk (1961).

Among others who came to read were T. S. Eliot, Ezra Pound, Edith Sitwell, Robert Graves, Roy Campbell, Harriet Monroe, Francis Meynell, Margaret L. Woods, Emile Verhaeren, Humbert Wolfe and Anna Wickham.

Monro's own reading style was founded on the submission of the personality to the poem. His views are explained in *Poetry and Drama*, and in notes for a broadcast talk. He wanted the reader to be an instrument and not a person: for this two things were required—a sensitive understanding of the poem, and an instinct for verbal rhythm. He disliked histrionic tricks—the 'tea-pot attitude' (one arm outstretched and the other posed on the hip), and the unnatural emphasis and declamatory manner that went with it. A clear voice, correct pronunciation and proper breathing were all that was needed.

His range was limited, according to Dr. Brooks, by a rather light and quiet voice in which some people detected a slight lisp. But he read with perfect tact and delicacy, and with a marked sense of rhythm. Arundel del Re praises 'the perfect simplicity of his manner'.[1]

Dr. Brooks's remark that 'in reading, he often struck one as being overheard rather than heard' suggests that he had successfully overcome selfconsciousness. He was, however, reluctant to read his own unpublished work aloud, and his wife read many of his new poems for him, as she did for Charlotte Mew, who was also shy of reading her work.

In the summer of 1961, Mrs. Monro spoke at the Harvard Summer School about her husband's work, and her talk, which included readings from his poetry, was recorded. She was regarded in her day as an excellent reader, and it is delightful to hear this strong and vibrant alto voice which was, in a small way, famous. The voice has power, the pronunciation is clear and unaffected; the manner comes as a slight surprise, for though it is very far from formal declamation, it is emphatic by present-day standards. We have become used to the casual, half-apologetic reading of poetry which tends to blur meaning. Mrs. Monro's style consciously clarifies meaning.

[1] Georgian Reminiscences—i', p. 328.

Unlike her husband, she is aware of her audience, and is making an effort to transmit her material to them.

Notes of the contents of readings given by Harold Monro and his wife during the post-war period have been preserved among his papers. They show a wide-ranging taste, and at the same time a preference for presenting modern work. The eighteenth century was illustrated by 'lyrics and trivia', and by a selection from Blake. Byron had a reading to himself, and Shelley had two. In one of these part of *Prometheus Unbound*, *The Cenci* and *Queen Mab*, and selected lyrics were given.

Separate readings were given of Mathew Arnold, John Davidson and Arthur Symons, which, jointly, must have thrown unfamiliar light on the later Victorians. There was also a programme of the poetry of the 'nineties. Extracts from Stephen Phillips's *Paolo and Francesca*, and from William Watson were read, which indicates the breadth of Monro's tolerance. One evening was given over to the *Georgian* anthologies, and another, on the war poets, offered seven poems by C. H. Sorley, five by Wilfrid Owen, and Jeffery Day's poem about flying, 'On the Wings of the Morning'.

At one meeting the respectable lineage of free verse was established by quotations from *Samson Agonistes* and 'The Strayed Reveller', and its extension into modern times illustrated from the work of Pound, H.D., Hueffer, and Philip Henderson. In a 'reading according to three periods' Bridges represents the earliest, Brooke, Flecker, Masefield, De la Mare, Lawrence and Sassoon the middle, and Huxley and Eliot ('The Waste Land')—with a glance back at Hopkins—the most recent phase of twentieth-century poetry.

New American poetry was twice represented. Work by Carl Sandberg, Cummings, McLeish, Aiken, Frost, H.D., Robinson and Fletcher was read. On the second occasion a memorandum noted 'no Fletcher. He coming to read', and 'no Eliot—English and coming to read'.

There is a record of Alida Monro's reading from her husband's work. On another day they offered a remarkable miscellany of

twentieth-century writers, with a flavour all Monro's own: John
Masefield, James Joyce, Eleanor Farjeon, Charlotte Mew, Douglas
Pepler, D. H. Lawrence, Anna Wickham, Walter de la Mare and
Harold Monro.

Something of Monro's hopes and fears for the readings can be
gathered from an interesting exchange between him and Amy
Lowell. In 'A Letter from London', dated 28 August 1914 and
printed in *The Little Review*, she described the atmosphere of false
security that had prevailed in the city only a month before the
outbreak of war. One of its most pathetic manifestations had been
the meeting she attended in Devonshire Street:

> A month ago I toiled up the narrow stairs of a little outhouse
> behind the Poetry Bookshop, and in an atmosphere of over-
> whelming sentimentality, listened to Mr. Rupert Brooke whis-
> pering his poems. To himself, it seemed, as nobody else could
> hear him. It was all artificial and precious. One longed to shout,
> to chuck up one's hat in the street when one got outside . . .[1]

Monro wrote to say that the article had 'surprised and shocked'
him. A little conversation with him would have corrected her mis-
apprehensions about the readings. She had attended an unrepresen-
tative meeting, and had no right, on so slight evidence, to alienate
'a limited but very critical American public' from the work of the
Bookshop. The letter mounts to a peak of emotion as he points out
that he is well aware of the danger of preciosity:

> Don't you think I have been fighting from the very start
> against the horror you depict? Haven't I gone out like you into
> the street to chuck up my hat? Haven't I wanted to blow up
> the Reading Room? *Haven't I realised the War?* I've nearly
> chucked it all up three times and gone as a dispatch rider. You
> depict us as a little effete group clinging on in a dark corner
> to the sentimental, artificial, precious. Oh! sentimental! Have
> you talked to me? Evidently not.

[1] *Little Review*, I (Sept. 1914), p. 6.

I am so disgusted, I can't restrain myself . . . you accuse the Bookshop of suffering from a disease so putrid that if I suspected you were right I would shake the dust of it from my feet today.[1]

In a letter of regret for the pain her article had caused, Amy Lowell wrote, 'I know that you are honest, absolutely sincere, hardworking, faithful, and of an idealism which takes a practical form',[2] and offered to write an article for *The Little Review*, giving the history of the Poetry Bookshop if he would send her the facts. Monro, mollified, sent a six-hundred-word account, from which I have already largely quoted, and Miss Lowell's kind words were printed in *The Little Review* not long afterwards.[3]

Monro and his Bookshop were in an exceedingly vulnerable position. Like the proprietor of a newly opened restaurant, he must have lurked apprehensively behind his door, dreading invasion and occupation by undesirables. Dr. Brooks was clearly aware of the creeping menace when he wrote that the audience for the readings were made up of 'people of all sorts. There was nothing remarkable about them—no such extravagance of garb or demeanour as our national comic papers seemed to have instituted for what one might call the guild uniform of the poetry enthusiast. I may faithfully assert that I never saw one head of hair abnormally long: nor was the peculiar shortness of hair prescribed for the bohemienne anywhere in evidence.'[4]

4

MONRO'S WAR-SERVICE AND MARRIAGE WITH
ALIDA KLEMANTASKI

The outbreak of war in September 1914 was only a temporary setback for the shop's business, but it put Harold Monro in a dilemma.

[1] (22 Oct. 1914) Houghton Library, Harvard.
[2] (3 Nov. 1914), Houghton Library, Harvard.
[3] *Little Review*, II (May 1915), pp. 19–22.
[4] See note on p. 77 above.

RHYME SHEET: [Second Series]

FOR THE BAPTIST

The last and greatest Herald of Heaven's King,
Girt with rough skins, hies to the deserts wild
Among that savage brood the woods forth bring,
Which he than Man more harmless found and mild.
His food was blossoms, and what young doth spring,
With honey that from virgin hives distill'd ;
Parch'd body, hollow eyes, some uncouth thing
Made him appear, long since from earth exiled.
There burst he forth : " All ye, whose hopes rely
On God, with me amidst these deserts mourn ;
Repent, repent, and from old errors turn ! "
—Who listen'd to his voice, obey'd his cry ?
    Only the echoes, which he made relent,
    Rung from their marble caves " Repent ! Repent ! "

POEM by WILLIAM DRUMMOND. DECORATIONS by CHARLES WINZER.

Rhyme sheet decorated by Charles Winzer (actual size $7\frac{1}{4}'' \times 14''$)

I

She has the porter's room; the plush is mildewed,

~~For the apartment heavy with cigarette plush~~

Old Clients have left their photos there to perish.

She waits behind green shutters; those who press

~~To~~ ~~reach~~

unconsciousness

Licking

And ~~she will lick~~ her thin magenta varnished lips,

~~Picking~~ her foretooth with a pointed nail,

She ~~looks~~ leans out

~~Watches,~~ orders to admit them, or

~~them (to what fate~~ in torture at

~~Leave~~ grovelling ~~at~~ the door.

II

Heat has locked the ~~afternoon~~ heavy earth,

Given strength to every sound.

He ~~Where~~ his life still holds him to the ground,

Drowsy with morphia, groaning for rebirth,

at the door ~~Because~~ Inside the house there is dull flutter;

a Lackey; giggling from behind the shutter.

Facsimile of part of MS of 'Bitter Sanctuary'

In later years he stubbornly referred to the conflict as the 'Big' and not the 'Great' War, and from the start adopted an attitude common among the liberal intelligentsia of the day: that the war was an alien thing, thrust upon them by soldiers and politicians, in which they had no duty to engage.

Early on, he did make an effort to join 'the motor-cyclists' (he had previous experience with these machines, having fallen off one and seriously injured himself in 1906), but, he wrote to Edward Marsh in August 1914, 'I realised it would be best for me to hold on here, unless there is later urgent need for every man available to take an active part.' For Monro, war service was an irritating interruption to his career as it was getting under way, but he managed to spend it in England, and much of the time was in easy reach of the Poetry Bookshop.

On 6 December 1915 he was still a free man, anticipating call-up, but, he told Marsh, hoping to get 'some job of a subsidiary kind that will permit my staying in London and keeping my eye on the shop. My doctor who has known me since childhood says I'm not fit for active service, as I also know myself by general experience.'[1] Monro's life was indeed dogged by ill-health, but although he was complaining of a severe abscess a month or so before, he was called up early in June 1916, and in July was gazetted—second lieutenant in the Royal Garrison Artillery, a section of the Royal Artillery. His first month was spent in training at Handel Street barracks, only ten minutes' walk from the Bookshop. He slept at home, but as the Army claimed him from 5 a.m. to 6 p.m. and the shop's hours were 11.0 to 4.30, he was a frustrated man.

By October 1916 he was in command of an anti-aircraft station at Newton Heath, Manchester, glad to have time on his hands, but wishing he was nearer London. Still unsatisfied, he wrote to Marsh on 11 April 1917 from 'an odious spot in Kent' (he was at Abbey Wood, near Woolwich) that he was trying to get a job with the Intelligence Branch on the strength of his languages. After some months stationed at the Waterworks, Putney Heath, he did indeed spend the rest of his service in London, working in the Intelligence

[1] Berg Collection, New York Public Library.

Department of the War Office at Watergate House, Adlephi, where he was as near Devonshire Street as he could decently expect to be.

There was in any case no need for anxiety about the shop, for it was in the capable hands of Miss Alida Klemantaski. He had first come to know her in March 1913, shortly after the Bookshop was opened—a gifted and beautiful girl of Polish descent, seventeen years his junior, who was looking for a worthwhile way of life. F. S. Flint says she meant to become a doctor and to spend her life rescuing prostitutes; she has mentioned to me that she thought of going on the stage. Monro discovered in her an idealism and a love of poetry that went well with his own, and in addition a fine speaking-voice and a gift for reading verse. She quickly became one of his regular readers, and when his secretary, Miss Gertrude Townsend, left to marry Wilfrid Gibson late in 1913, she took over her duties, and ran the business single-handed after Monro was called up. She kept the shop open throughout the war, ran weekly poetry-readings, took over the complex finances of *Georgian Poetry I* and *II*, and was solely responsible for the publication and distribution of *Georgian Poetry III*. Christopher Hassall relates that without clerical assistance she invoiced and despatched the orders and, helped by a friend who shared her enthusiasm, hired hand-barrows and pushed her parcels to the carrier in the Goswell Road.[1] In spite of ill-health and over-work she carried on, and preserved the continuity of Monro's work through the war years. When plans for *Georgian Poetry III* were under discussion, Monro wrote to Marsh, 'Don't fear of course that it will suffer through my absence and inattention to business, as Miss Klemantaski is just splendid and understands everything.'

Monro was divorced from his first wife in 1916. Romance had turned to rancour long before. They seem to have been a genuinely incompatible pair, and the intensity of Monro's revulsion from Dorothy may be gauged from an anecdote (related 'so amusingly'

[1] See C. Hassall, *Edward Marsh*, p. 412.

by Monro himself) which is retold by Conrad Aiken. It describes an encounter at the ballet between the divorced couple:

How long since they had seen each other? A long time—enough, it appeared, for the rancors to have been dissipated; they were glad, they were delighted, to see each other again, and began to talk animatedly, just as if it were a first meeting, or even a flirtation. But then, Arnault had said, a curious thing began to happen: in the space of something like half an hour, they had begun to disagree, then to wrangle, then to look at each other with mounting dislike and distrust, in an accelerated recapitulation of the whole marriage, the long years of marriage: and suddenly they had again reached identically the same end in identically the same silence of hatred, the long hard look of hatred: and realising that he still had more than an hour to sit beside this terrible woman, he had got up abruptly during the next curtain, the next interval, and departed without another word.[1]

Monro's poem 'Natural History' is no doubt the product of this encounter:

> The vixen woman,
> Long gone away,
> Came to haunt me
> Yesterday.
>
> I sit and faint
> Through year on year,
> Was it yesterday
> I thought her dear?
>
> .   .   .   .
>
> Now that again
> I see your eyes
> I do forget
> I have grown wise.

[1] *Ushant, An Essay*, pp. 259–60.

Your argument
Has claim and poise,
But there's a vixen
In your voice.

Nightmare! O hard
To understand!—
She tried to give me
Her bright hand.

I sit and faint
Through year on year.
Was it yesterday
I thought her dear?

The traditional Christian notion of marriage Monro found intolerable for both parties, and at a later date he vented his feelings in 'Holy Matrimony':

The dark doors close
Upon the sky.
They shall be locked within
Till they do die.

His ideal was an unpossessive relationship, a species of friendship, in which each partner was free, and for a man of Monro's constitution this was probably the best solution. Sabin provides fuller insight into his emotional complexities than anyone else:

He possessed a wide circle of friends, but he needed also one specially intimate and sympathetic associate on whom he could depend and bestow his devotion. He asked for a friend where another man perhaps would have sought a lover . . . He wanted close intellectual companionship rather than physical sympathy, and a sexual appeal without this had little hold on him . . . Of intimate friends who answered his need for a while, I saw the succession of Maurice Browne, his wife Dorothy . . .

myself, Arundel del Re, and lastly, Alida Klemantaski, his second wife.[1]

Monro and Miss Klemantaski were married in 1920. There were no children, and Mrs. Monro (who was still known as 'Miss Klemantaski') shared wholeheartedly in Monro's work. There are many tributes to her charm and beauty, but Del Re remembers her contribution to the running of the shop:

> Calm, business-like and neat, she was just the person needed to keep the Poetry Bookshop going during the difficult war days and afterwards. But infinitely more valuable than all her secretarial accomplishments were her sympathy, her sound literary judgement and her unselfish devotion to the cause of poetry and to Monro personally that made their friendship and their married life one of the finest and happiest examples of literary collaboration. It was mainly due to her that Monro was relieved of the most soul-destroying practical details connected with the running of the Bookshop. . . .[2]

[1] *Pilgrimage*, Ch. X.   [2] 'Georgian Reminiscences—iii', p. 41.

4

The Poetry Bookshop Publications

1

GEORGIAN POETRY

A publishing-house intending to specialise in poetry (almost by definition a doomed concern) could hardly hope to commence operations with a greater *éclat* than attended the Poetry Bookshop's first undertaking, *Georgian Poetry 1911–12*. The commission came Monro's way very easily. On the evening of 19 September 1912, Rupert Brooke and Edward Marsh were seized with a flurry of excitement at the plan they had conceived: to publish in a single volume a selection of the best recent verse, chiefly by the younger poets. With the coronation fresh in the memory, a title for the volume came readily into Marsh's mind—'my proud ambiguous adjective "Georgian"'.[1]

Early the next morning Monro received a phone-call from Marsh inviting him to lunch, and it would scarcely have been polite of Monro to claim for himself the happy invention of the adjective, which, according to A. K. Sabin, he had coined over fifteen months before:

> ... we walked along Brompton Road to Harrods, and went up in the lift to their newly decorated refreshment rooms. 'Georgian Restaurant', shouted the lift-boy, as we reached the top floor. Hundreds of people were seated at lunch. 'It ought to be called the *Gorgean* Restaurant', said Harold, with one of his rare touches of slightly sardonic humour. As we followed

[1] *A Number of People*, p. 321.

92

an attendant to a vacant table, he continued reflectively: 'This is the first time since my return that I have been reminded we are living in a new Georgian era—and, by Jove, Arthur, we are the new Georgian poets!'[1]

This event took place, Sabin writes, on or about 7 June 1911, and Del Re's account shows that Monro did indeed visit England in the 'late spring' of that year; Harrod's archives confirm that in 1911 a new restaurant was opened on the fourth floor, 'an oak-panelled and beamed room with gas chandeliers', originally to be called the Tudor Restaurant. The advent of the new sovereign suggested a more topical if less appropriate name.

If Marsh was the father of *Georgian Poetry*, Monro was the responsible midwife, and had some right to help name the child. He took the financial burden, Mrs. Monro has told me, and stood to lose on the cost of production if the book failed. All he stood to gain if the book succeeded was the ordinary bookseller's commission of 10 per cent on each copy sold (in 1919 this was raised to 15 per cent), together with his share of the profits as a contributor. The profits were divided equally between the contributors to each volume, regardless of the size of their contributions. It was decided to publish 500 copies before Christmas, at 3s. 6d. a copy.

Monro's sympathetic co-operation was of great practical assistance, for though Marsh took the task of selection into his own hands, he depended heavily on Monro's knowledge of printing and publishing, and Marsh goes so far as to say that, but for Monro, *Georgian Poetry* 'could not have come into being'.[2] His rooms were close by, on the other side of Gray's Inn, his offices were in Chancery Lane, his printers, the St. Catherine's Press,[3] were in the Strand.

They had been in contact before when, through the good offices of Francis Meynell, Marsh had written an appreciation of his friend Rupert Brooke's *Poems* for *The Poetry Review*, though at that time Marsh had half-apologised for appreciating Brooke in 'the organ of

---

[1] *Pilgrimage*, Ch. X.
[2] *A Number of People*, p. 325.
[3] *Georgian Poetry* was in fact printed at the Arden Press, Letchworth.

the Poetry Reciters—I am afraid it is rather an absurd publication . . .'[1] The paper's reputation was healthier in September than it had been in February, and no apologies were now needed for publishing under its imprint.

Monro promptly agreed to the plan. Though he no doubt wished he could do the editing himself, Marsh meant to include writers as diverse as Housman and Pound (though in fact neither of these poets contributed), so that the *Review*'s reputation for impartiality would not be compromised. Edward Marsh, now forty years old, was Secretary to the First Lord of the Admiralty, Winston Churchill, and one of the most sought-after and influential young men in London. He exerted his influence—Arundel del Re remembers that he sent over a hundred copies to friends—and *before Christmas*, when Rupert Brooke called in on Monro, all the copies of the anthology had been sold. 'The most extraordinary people keep looking in and spending immense sums.'[2] The surprising demand for *Georgian Poetry* was splendid advance publicity for the Bookship, due to open in January 1913.

With Monro and Pound, Edward Marsh now became the third rallying-point for poetic talent in the London of 1913. Marsh's interest in poets and poetry came to life through his devotion to Rupert Brooke, and it remained a permanent feature of his days. Five volumes of *Georgian Poetry* appeared, in 1912, 1915, 1917, 1919 and 1922, a vast labour of love, for which his reward was the friendship of his Georgians. No. 5 Raymond Buildings, Gray's Inn, became a place of resort for writers of a certain complexion, who enjoyed his urbane hospitality; the bed in his spare-room often cradled a country poet at week-ends. His thoughtful and timely disposal of his 'murder-money' for the relief of writers in Queer Street helped to establish him as a patron of poets, a patron of decided and rather limited views. Monro was never an intimate member of the Georgian social group that circled round Marsh—

[1] Letter of 4 Feb. 1912, quoted by C. Hassall, *Edward Marsh*, p. 182.

[2] Letter from Brooke to Marsh, quoted in C. Hassall, *Edward Marsh*, p. 203.

perhaps his own business, perhaps an aversion from cliques, perhaps an imperfect sympathy between himself and Marsh, kept him away. We learn that in 1912 Monro did not accompany Del Re to Marsh's 'breakfasts'—'he did not much care for them';[1] and, more significant probably (for social gatherings at 8.0 a.m. do not appeal to everyone), when Marsh gave his dinner in 1919 to re-unite the Georgian brotherhood after the war, and to celebrate the success of Brooke's *Collected Poems*, Monro was not among the seven dinner-guests, but came in for coffee with the newcomers—Shanks, Squire, Turner and Sassoon.

Monro's letter to him (in May 1914) when *Poetry and Drama* was in financial straits suggests that Marsh was taking little active interest in that paper:

> We never see you here now. The Bookshop is fairly healthy. *Poetry and Drama*, however, will enter upon a rather critical stage after the next number. Hewlett and other supporters are anxious for me to call a meeting the week after next to consider ways and means. Do you feel sufficiently interested to attend, if you have time?[2]

When the meeting was eventually held, Marsh was delayed at Downing Street, and Monro never benefited from Marsh's patronage, which had been extended to the editors of other periodicals. Marsh had generously lavished money, meals and kindness on Middleton Murry and Katherine Mansfield, while they struggled to keep *Rhythm* and *The Blue Review* in existence; and he took a strong protective interest in *New Numbers*, the quarterly produced in Gloucestershire by Abercrombie and Gibson to propagate their own work and that of Drinkwater and Brooke.

Their correspondence shows Monro a conscientious but harassed publisher generally late with his accounts, blaming the confusion on his clerks, who seem to have been exceptionally incompetent. The following is a rather typical explosion:

[1] 'Georgian Reminiscences—ii', p. 463.
[2] In the Berg Collection, New York Public Library.

The excellent cashier I have here now has been trying hard to get the muddle straight created by the last three hopeless fools who succeeded each other after Collins left. . . .[1]

But the trouble with clerks was endemic, and five years later he was complaining of the shortcomings of another clerk, now sacked: the new one was, again, 'quite different'.

The correspondence also records Monro's changing attitude to the series. The phenomenal success of the 1911–12 volume, which went into its ninth thousand by the end of 1913, seemed to justify his conviction that the public would receive modern poetry, and it furthered his plans in a variety of practical ways. It swelled the audiences for the twice-weekly readings at the newly opened Bookshop; the sales commission on so successful an undertaking was a very pleasant windfall; as their publisher, Monro strengthened his connection with the poets who were the mainstay of the first two volumes. As their devoted well-wisher, he was no doubt gratified that Marsh had engaged the interest of critics, writers and the fashionable in these young contemporaries, however dubiously he welcomed 'the most extraordinary people' to the rugged simplicities of the Bookshop. Some of the verses in *Before Dawn* profess a per-fervid distaste for wealth and fashion, and it was disconcerting to have them come looking for him in his humble shop. Monro may have looked askance at the débutantes who sold his chapbooks at the Georgian Matinée at His Majesty's Theatre on 19 May 1917—though long before this the vogue for the slum-bookshop had passed.

At all events, he was very willing to bring out a second volume, and thought it in retrospect the best of the series. The first two volumes are alike in their unassuming sincerity of purpose, their effort to deal honestly with experience, and to talk without ex-aggeration of small as well as great things.

In reply to Marsh's suggestion that they bring out a third volume in 1917, Monro wrote that it was 'an unexpected but quite pleasant proposition',[2] though he urged haste in getting the book printed,

[1] (19 Aug. 1914) Berg Collection, New York Public Library.
[2] (22 Aug 1917) Berg Collection.

as costs were continually rising. Neither Monro nor any of the contributors had a significant say in the selection of poems—Marsh was an autocratic editor, Monro merely his publisher—and when he saw the draft of the contents of the new volume, Monro was disturbed. His main objection was to Maurice Baring's 'In Memoriam, A.H.', which seemed far too Tennysonian. It would convey 'a wrong impression with all its Victorian language and images, its forced or obvious rhymes. It is not only not "Georgian" poetry to my mind, but it is definitely bad poetry.' Needless to say, 'In Memoriam, A.H.' was retained. Monro most strongly urged Charlotte Mew's 'Farmer's Bride' which the Poetry Bookshop had published in 1916, and put it 'among the dozen best poems of the last year'. The imaginative world of Charlotte Mew was beyond the range of Marsh's sympathy, her style too idiosyncratic to please him, and he rejected her work now, and again in 1922 when Monro made a second bid for its inclusion.

'I don't think I'm naturally keen on advertising myself,' Monro went on, 'but I'm sure, in the case of *GP*, I shall feel rather bitter if I have provided the material and it is not fully represented . . .' On the strength of this plea, Monro had more pages to himself in the third volume than any of the original Georgians. From *Strange Meetings* Marsh chose two short pieces from the title-poem, with 'Every Thing', 'Solitude', 'The Bird at Dawn' and the sonnet-sequence, 'Week-end'. The title of the last was pounced on as a handy pejorative epithet by the detractors of *Georgian Poetry*, who now began to be heard.

The characteristic features of Georgianism in its later phase—a vacuous nature-worship, a false *naïveté*, the resurgence of a 'romantic' vocabulary—were apparent in the third volume, and inescapable in the two that followed. Monro's confidence in the series progressively declined. When a fourth volume was mooted, he was doubtful if the time was ripe for it, and when it was printed and selling well, he wrote, 'I am sure that I think it the worst *GP*'.[1] He advised the three-year interval before attempting another volume. Marsh agreed, and then found that some poets were not

[1] (13 Dec. 1914) Berg Collection.

anxious to be seen in a series that had a name for tameness and insincerity. Monro dissimulated a little, 'I had thought it might be better to leave me out this time',[1] but he let Marsh have three poems from *Real Property.* One of them, 'Unknown Country', was unalloyed 'week-end' poetry, and Monro was uneasy about it: 'I feel somehow that "Unknown Country" is almost too *Georgian* even for *GP*!' As Christopher Hassall suggests, this may be the first time that 'Georgian' was used as an opprobrious epithet.

Monro's final action, in suggesting a sixth volume in the series, is impressive in its awful tactlessness. He suggested that it might be an idea to

> . . . round off the series by suggesting new directions. This view, I know, is not entirely compatible with your original objects. Nevertheless, circumstances alter continually with the progress of the years, and the original motives for *GP* are now slightly obscured, or have become diverted, by subsequent developments. I very much hope you will be sympathetic with my scheme. Alida Klemantaski (an individual of most clear and careful judgement) would undertake to select a sixth volume, or, rather should I say, would undertake at once to investigate the matter and find out whether my impression that a sixth volume might be possible has really any warrant, and then would either decide in the negative, or would draw up a scheme, and submit it to you, or not, as you like. No *GP* is quite imaginable without your production. Even if you had to cavil, or to object, or to question, or to doubt, would you at any rate undertake to introduce such a volume into the world?[2]

Few men possess the detachment and self-abnegation for such a gesture, and Monro seems oddly obtuse in suggesting it to Marsh, whose *Georgian Poetry* had been a cherished personal creation, and his Georgian poets a close corporation of friends. Monro, who thought poetry more important than poets and would follow the

---

[1] (6 July 1922) Berg Collection.
[2] (8 June 1925) Berg Collection.

will-o'-the-wisp wherever it led, was crediting Marsh with his own kind of devotion.

2

IMAGISM

With the publication of *Georgian Poetry* there came a hardening of the division between radicals and moderates. Pound was the focus of the one group, criticising their efforts, and sending them off to Harriet Monroe in Chicago with persuasive covering letters. A leader who throve on opposition, he did not find it in Monro: during 1912 *The Poetry Review* was hospitable to both groups of poets, and in 1913 the Poetry Bookshop opened its doors, a kind of club with *fay ce que vouldras* inscribed metaphorically over the door.

The emergence of Marsh provided a third focal point, however. His anthology was moderate-to-conservative in tendency, and was sufficiently exclusive to provoke the rumour of bad feeling. On 22 June 1913, when *Georgian Poetry* was already in its sixth edition, Marsh wrote to Brooke, 'Wilfrid tells me there's a movement for a "Post-Georgian" Anthology, of the Pound–Flint–Hulme school, who don't like being out of *GP*, but I don't think it will come off.'[1]

Nearly a year passed before the scheme did 'come off'—*The Glebe*, Alfred Kreymborg's New York periodical, published Pound's anthology, *Des Imagistes*,[2] in February 1914. They reproduced it in book form in April of the same year, simultaneously with its British publication by Monro. Even if, as Aldington declares, Monro's decision to handle the book was made 'after a good deal of hesitation and misgiving', he could have given no more striking evidence of his independence of spirit and disregard of cliques than to

---

[1] Quoted in C. Hassall, *Edward Marsh*, p. 229.

[2] Eleven authors contributed to the main body of *Des Imagistes*: Richard Aldington, H.D., F. S. Flint, Skipwith Cannell, Amy Lowell, W. C. Williams, James Joyce, Ezra Pound, Ford Madox Hueffer, Allan Upward and John Cournos.

publish it hard on the heels of *Georgian Poetry*.[1] *Des Imagistes* was widely reviewed in America, but hardly noticed here, and few copies were sold. Richard Aldington relates that 'one copy was angrily returned from the Savoy Hotel by an American, and an old gentleman came into the shop and made a row'.[2]

The book was, in some sense, intended to cock a snook at the Georgian anthology, and naturally no Georgian was included. On stylistic grounds, D. H. Lawrence would certainly have been eligible. But Monro's known readiness to commit what Pound calls 'acts of independence', and his stylistic development away from the rest of the Georgians are implied in Pound's obituary article in *The Criterion*. Speaking of the omission of Monro's work from *Des Imagistes*, he says:

> Why he wasn't in it, I can not at this time remember, unless it was that I had called him a blithering idiot or because he had clung to an adjective. Either at that time or later he certainly wrote poems that measured up to that standard or at any rate without reconstructing the standard or re-examining the actual text, one remembers them as attaining the level desired. It may have been that I was strict, at that time, to the point of fanaticism.[3]

A prudent publisher, comparing the sales records of *Georgian Poetry* and *Des Imagistes*, would have washed his hands of Imagists for ever, but Monro, in December 1915, brought out Richard Aldington's *Images*, his first volume to get into print, and F. S. Flint's *Cadences*, both in chapbook form.

Aldington's poems exhibit the imaginative limitations which Monro found in Imagist poetry. Prefaced with the warning '*non canimus surdis*', they are skilful exercises in the new technique. Part I is full of conscious aestheticism, which still provided one way of escape from Victorian moralising. Part II is more down-to-earth, taking subjects from London life—the tube, the cinema, Hampstead Heath—but a certain preciosity of technique, and the devis-

[1] Only one slim volume, John Alford's *Poems* (1913), separated the two volumes.
[2] *Life for Life's Sake*, p. 147.   [3] *Criterion*, XI (July 1932), p. 586.

ing of *récherché* images, makes them ring slightly false. It was a minor 'act of independence' to publish these poems, and a mark of Monro's respect for the serious craftsmanship of a young poet whose work he did not very much enjoy.

The qualities of personality and sincerity which he prized are far more characteristic of Flint, who had his own interpretation of Imagism, more relaxed than that of either Aldington or H.D. As a writer of free verse he was early in the field in this country and *Cadences* exhibits his growing mastery of the form. His poetry will be discussed in greater detail later in this chapter, for it is among the most interesting work published by Monro. There was a long-standing friendship between the two men, and Flint's example probably eased Monro's half-grudging acceptance of 'modernity'.

3

REJECTION OF T. S. ELIOT AND EDWARD THOMAS: RELATIONS WITH WILFRED OWEN

Monro's decision to publish these *avant garde* volumes is interesting in the light of another decision, which he made a few months later, and which, wrote Conrad Aiken, 'always embarrassed him'.[1] This was his rejection of work by T. S. Eliot when it was offered him for *Poetry and Drama*.[2]

Aiken was introduced to Monro by Rupert Brooke in the summer of 1914 at 'a poetry "Squash" in Devonshire Street', and later offered him 'The Love Song of J. Alfred Prufrock', which he was endeavouring to place for his Harvard friend, who was then living in London. Monro returned it to Aiken saying that it was

> absolutely insane, or words to that effect, in giving it back to me. Later, at a party, during a discussion of symbolism, with

[1] *Ushant*, p. 258.

[2] Letters from Mr. Aiken to me correct and expand the account given in Charles Norman's *Ezra Pound* (New York, 1960). Mr. Eliot has written to me (3 April 1963) confirming that the account corresponds with his memories of Mr. Aiken's report of the affair at the time.

H.M. and Flint, and thinking of the pertinence of 'La Figlia', a copy of which was in my pocket, I produced it, only to have Harold thrust it back at me, with the remark 'O I can't be bothered with this.' He so obviously thought I was seizing the opportunity for showing something of *my own* that I put things right the next day by sending it to him, with Eliot's address in Germany and—of course that too was rejected.[1]

Aiken then took Eliot's poems to Pound, who persuaded Harriet Monroe to print 'Prufrock' in *Poetry* in June 1915, and seven further poems, including 'La Figlia che Piange', in the September and October issues. It seems that at the time Pound was unaware of the offer of 'Prufrock' to Monro, for on 25 September 1915 he wrote to Miss Monroe: 'Monro discovered "Prufrock" on his unaided own and asked me about the author when I saw him last night. I consider that Harold is dawning. He was very glad to hear that T.S.E. was in the forefront of our [Catholic] *Anthology*.'[2]

Monro's wariness of extremes, his love of tradition and his natural caution were, no doubt, all alerted by work which had so little apparent relation to any of the main trends of contemporary verse. The apparent inconsequentialness of 'Prufrock' with its calculated *montage* effects and its sophisticated employment of literary allusion, must have bewildered a reader in days before the exegetes had set to work and explained them. Monro was not the only editor to reject Eliot's early work, and Pound had to wait from October 1914 until June 1915 for Harriet Monroe to print 'Prufrock'.

Monro's mind, there is no denying, adapted itself rather slowly to what was new—though it adapted itself in the end. The time-lag involved was intensely irritating to Pound, who was always beforehand with the world, and he continually reverts to this theme in his *Criterion* obituary:

> During those early years I doubt if he ever received an idea clean at first go, or ever gripped it at once by the handle. He was one of those exasperating editors who seem more or less

[1] Letter to the author, 31 Oct. 1962.
[2] *Letters of Ezra Pound, 1907–1941*, p. 108.

to comprehend what they are told but who are two hours later told something else.[1]

Pound's comments on other people need, generally, to be tempered with a dash of moderation, and to be understood in the light of his aggressive personality. A policy of anything-for-the-sake-of-peace-and-quiet may underlie the behaviour of editors who seemed 'more or less to comprehend' what they were 'told' by Pound.

Pound refers later in the article to Monro's halting progress to the light, 'He certainly did not die in his errors, or at least in the errors that had been his in an earlier period.' We know that, in the case of Eliot's work, by the time rather more than a year had passed Monro had modified his views, for Pound wrote to Harriet Monroe:

> You can take Hueffer's commendation of Eliot to back up mine, if it is of any use to you. Even Monro's Devonshire Street occiput has been pierced.[2]

Stella Bowen, who frequented the Poetry Bookshop readings, recalled her friend Phyllis Reid reading 'Prufrock' there. Miss Reid's 'flattered pleasure when T. S. Eliot turned up, with his gentle and benevolent smile and a black satin chest-protector, at some of our beer-and-gramophone parties' suggests that Eliot may have witnessed the reading.[3]

There is no mention of Eliot in Monro's *Some Contemporary Posts* (*1920*). In the introduction to his anthology, *Twentieth Century Poetry* (1929), however, he discusses the importance of Eliot:

> To-day we have each our 'Waste Land', and the strong influence of Mr. T. S. Eliot, and a few other poets, chiefly unacknowledged in Georgian circles, is more indicative of future tendencies than any other recognisable Signpost. I should say that just as A. E. Housman and Rupert Brooke were very powerful up to 1929, so Eliot will be up to 1940.

Monro contributed to *The Criterion*, and was on terms of personal friendship with its editor, which led to Eliot's generous critical

---

[1] *Criterion*, XI (July 1932), p. 583.
[2] *Letters of Ezra Pound, 1907–1941*, p. 109.
[3] *Drawn from Life* (London, 1941), p. 61.

note in the collected edition of Monro's poems. We can discount, I think, all but a vestigial, humanly-inevitable residue of sour grapes in Monro's limited enthusiasm for Eliot's work. In *Ushant,* Conrad Aiken introduces Monro as

> Arnault—stubborn, crotchety, perverse and difficult Arnault, down from his bookshop for the week-end, with his latest kinky poem, and the latest news of the Tsetse's quarterly, or of the Tsetse himself, and ready for the libations of Bristol Milk and the stubborn rearguard defence of Georgian Poetry—or some of it, anyway, he would say belligerantly: for though in the course of time he had come to acknowledge the Tsetse's genius, it was usually with reservations. . . . Even the famous Blick ins Chaos, wasn't it destined—he said—to become a twentieth-century Kubla Khan, with the same sort of romantic and talismanic glitter, but fragmented or fragmentary, and perhaps without final profundity in scale or idea, a broken bundle of mirrors, an anthology of vivid reflections, a tantivy of vivid scenes—and therefore minor?[1]

The rejection of Eliot's work in the summer of 1914 was followed in the winter of the same year by a second decision which history has shown to be an error of judgement. Shortly before Christmas, Edward Thomas discussed his poetry in a letter to Eleanor Farjeon:

> I sent what I had to Monro asking for secrecy. He kept it 4 days and then said he hadn't had time to read it, so that I took it back rather crestfallen . . .[2]

Early in 1915, Thomas told Miss Farjeon, he again sent Monro 'a lot of verses in hopes he would make a book of them. He won't. He doesn't like them at all. Nor does Ellis. . . .'[3]

Thomas's reply to Monro's rejection showed pain and disappoint-

[1] p. 258.
[2] Quoted in Eleanor Farjeon, *Edward Thomas, The Last Four Years* (London, 1958), p. 104.
[3] Ibid., p. 133.

ment. Monro's knowledge of the poet's circumstances, and his obligation to Thomas for work for *Poetry and Drama* must have made his decision difficult, and Thomas's request that no explanation be given made a refusal seem more unkind. We are in a better position than Monro to understand how vulnerable Thomas's feelings were in regard to his poetry. When he met Robert Frost in 1913, Thomas was in a mood of despair, and in his friend's genius discovered his own, opening the floodgates on the pent-up creativeness of years.

Monro, one would think, was the very man to appreciate work so unassuming, so near to the bone, so natural in its language and rhythms, so acutely observant of nature—the apotheosis of Georgian poetry. The poems he rejected were presumably among those in *Poems* (1917). Thomas sent 'a lot' of poems in hopes that Monro would make a book of them, so his decision was not based on inadequate evidence of the poet's skill.

It would be invidious to seek to justify Monro's mistake, but no honour is lost in attempting to explain it.

Thomas's is probably the most diffident and self-effacing charm in the whole of English poetry, and his ruminatory, conversational tone (more intimate than Frost's colloquialism) is too easily dismissed as flat, and his matter as dull. After Thomas's death, Monro revised his opinion. He wrote to Mrs. Helen Thomas offering to bring out an edition of his poems, and acknowledging his mistake. But, in an undated reply, she said that she was already under obligation to another publisher. She very much wished that Monro had accepted Thomas's poems when they were first shown to him, and well remembered his hurt when they were refused. She regretted that her husband's poems had not had the advertisement they would have had 'coming from the Poetry Bookshop'.[1]

At precisely the time when Thomas was offering work that was the fruit of maturity, Monro was making contact with a young and untried writer whose work showed promise, but was raw still. In

[1] Letters in the Lockwood Memorial Library, University of Buffalo.

November 1915 Wilfred Owen wrote to his mother from a boarding-house in Tavistock Square that he was about to move his quarters:

> I found a room at 5/6 per week, right opposite the Poetry Bookshop!! A plain enough affair—candlelight—no bath—and so on; but there is a coffee-shop underneath. . . .[1]

The same letter describes how he 'clamp-clump-clamp-clumped' into the Poetry Bookshop, to the surprise of the 'poetic ladies' assembled for a reading from Rabindranath Tagore. His reference to Monro suggests that they already knew each other: 'I could not speak to Monro, but he smiled sadly at my khaki', and, as if to explain Monro's sad smile, he goes on to quote three verses from 'Youth in Arms', where Monro had pointed out that in war old men exploited the gallantry and bravado of the young. Mrs. Monro has remarked that Owen often came into the shop to read books, and, finally, as appears from a letter to his mother, he solicited Monro's opinion of his verse:

> I thought I should never see Monro; but last night at eleven o'clock, when I had strewn about my goods preparatory to sorting and packing, up comes Monro to my room, with my MSS! So we sit down, and I have the time of my life. For he was 'very struck' with these sonnets. He went over the things in detail and he told me what was fresh and clever, and what was second-hand and banal; and what Keatsian, and what 'modern'. He summed up their value as far above that of the 'Little Book of Georgian Verse'. The curious part is that he applauded precisely those phrases which Prof. Morley condemned!
>
> So then, I have gained his esteem and a (first) handshake! I need not say that he is a peculiar being; and I doubt whether ever we shall become 'Friends'. For my own part I should prefer a Business Relation, and I believe it possible—when he restarts his journal 'Poetry & Drama', now checked by the War.[2]

[1] Letter in the possession of Mr. Harold Owen.
[2] Letter dated only 'Saturday', but according to Mr. Harold Owen, probably written 5 March 1916.

Up to this time, Owen had had little opportunity of discussing his work with literary people—Miss Edith Morley of the English Department at University College, Reading, had gone over his poems with him, and he had a stimulating friendship with Laurent Tailhade during his stay in Bordeaux in 1913. But Monro was the first potential publisher to whom he had shown his work. The excited pleasure which he took in the discussion and his boyish respect for Monro's opinion recall his timid approaches to Siegfried Sassoon at Craiglockhart Hospital in 1917. 'Short, dark-haired and shyly hesitant', Sassoon wrote, '. . . He had a charming honest smile, and his manners—he stood at my elbow rather as though conferring with a superior officer—were modest and ingratiating. . . . In fact my first view of him was as a rather ordinary young man, perceptibly provincial, though unobtrusively ardent in his responses to my lordly dictums about poetry.'[1] It is quite impossible, according to Mr. Harold Owen, the poet's brother, to establish which sonnets were shown to Monro, but their character can be confidently deduced by studying Owen's work before he entered his great and final phase.

Sassoon recalls himself as 'censuring the over-lush writing in his immature pieces. . . . But it was the emotional element even more than its verbal expression, which seemed to need refinement. . . . There was an almost embarrassing sweetness in the sentiment of some of his work, though it showed skill in rich and melodious combinations of words.'[2]

Strongly tinctured with emotional romanticism, owing a large debt to Keats, and sharing in his sensuousness, it nevertheless suggests a poet with a distinct personality who is still in the chrysalis stage. Monro's early work had been similarly derivative, and he was well qualified to discriminate about work of this kind.

He was right to encourage the 'fresh', 'clever' and 'modern' elements in Owen's poetry—in strengthening, that is, Owen's original genius. The value of Miss Morley's judgement is called in question when we hear that it was the reverse of Monro's, and

[1] *Siegfried's Journey* (London, 1945), p. 58.
[2] Ibid., p. 59.

Owen's *naïveté* once again revealed in his surprise that the two 'authorities' should disagree.

4

CHAPBOOKS, BROADSIDES AND RHYMESHEETS

The last issue of *Poetry and Drama* announced the forthcoming publication of a series of 'chapbooks and broadsides', partly intended to bridge the gap until it was possible to issue a regular periodical again after the war.

They derived ultimately from the wares of seventeenth- and eighteenth-century pedlars, but more directly from the practice of Claud Lovat Fraser, Holbrook Jackson and Ralph Hodgson who during 1913 had set up the Flying Fame Press at Fraser's home at 45 Roland Gardens, S.W. They issued a series of broadsides and tiny booklets, using verses chiefly by Hodgson, and other pleasant and rather juvenile little pieces that lent themselves to this homely treatment. The character of their wares was rough and ready, the paper was quite coarse, and the woodcut illustrations by Fraser were bold and heedlessly coloured.[1]

In 1914 the Poetry Bookshop took over the Flying Press publications, and began issuing similar productions under its own imprint. Monro's admiration for the honest, the plain, the home-brewed attracted him to this sort of publication. Poetry in this humble form, he told his readers, could be 'sold anywhere and everywhere, carried in the pocket, read at any spare moment, left in the train, or committed to the memory and passed on'. In a letter to Amy Lowell he added: 'Briefly they are supposed to be good poetry (not

---

[1] Miss E. C. Yeats and Jack Yeats had engaged in a rather similar enterprise at the Cuala Press, Dundrum, Co. Dublin. They issued a monthly series of Irish ballads from June 1908, calling them inaccurately 'broadsides'. The Flying Fame Press and the Poetry Bookshop were equally inaccurate: strictly speaking, a broadside is a sheet printed on one side only, suitable for use as a poster, and these were folded and printed on three sides, and should more properly be called single sheets.

too much of it because no one ever writes much good poetry) with cheap production. Anyone who will is supposed to be able to buy them. They're not the final form of production, but something between the periodical and the collected volume.'[1] This was no doubt a more startling idea in a period which knew no cheap paperback editions.

The outbreak of war occasioned quantities of rabble-rousing verse which could be suitably produced in this way. Maurice Hewlett's *Singsongs of the War* went into a chapbook in November 1914 —nine crude and homely jingles in the traditional manner of gutter-poetry. Ford Madox Hueffer's 'Antwerp', a rambling celebration of the heroic Belgian resistance to invasion, followed in 1915. Flecker's new and improved version of 'God Save the King' was perhaps a slightly ambiguous gesture of patriotism; Newbolt's 'King's Highway' was a rousing lyric, set to music, about the glories of the navy; and Hewlett's 'Ballad of "The Gloster" and "The Goeben"' told a topical tale of German cowardice and British heroism.

Owing to rising production costs, Monro published only one chapbook in the spring of 1916—Robert Graves's first volume, *Over the Brazier*. Edward Marsh was behind the undertaking, and it is clear that he was more taken with young Graves's work than was Monro. 'I'm afraid I'm not keen on the poems,' Monro wrote, 'but that doesn't matter. They are too consciously *young*.'

The conscious deployment of youth to which he objects comes out in Part II of *Over the Brazier*. Part I is made up of poems written at Charterhouse; they are of no importance whatsoever—cheerful little *facetiae* for the most part, the rumble-tumble verse of a schoolboy, with a certain careless mastery of rhythm. Part II takes this boy to the war. It was a commonplace of war-poetry to compare the horrors of the present with an idealised past, and for Graves who was, and felt himself to be, very much a boy still, the comparison is often with childhood. A series of three poems, 'Nursery Memories', ironically contrasts childhood experiences with incidents in the trenches. The sight of his first corpse hanging on

[1] (24 March 1915) Houghton Library, Harvard.

the German wires reminds him of a dead dog which he and another
child had found and buried:

> The whole field was so smelly;
> We smelt the poor dog first:
> His horrid swollen belly
> Looked just like going burst.

Marsh, it seems, was becoming acclimatised to 'unpleasant'
poetry!

> *The Trenches* (*Heard in the Ranks*)
> Scratches in the dirt?
> No, that sounds much too nice.
> Oh, far too nice.
> Seams, rather, of a Greyback shirt,
> And we're the little lice
> Wriggling about in them a week or two,
> Till one day, suddenly, from the blue
> Something bloody and big will come
> Like—watch this fingernail and thumb!—
> Squash! and he needs no twice.

The poems are honest and free of cant, but Graves was too young
and inexperienced to touch the fringes of his mighty and squalid
theme. To publish the collection was an act of avuncular faith,
more Marsh's than Monro's.

In 1919 Monro followed his own inclination and published *Mag-
pies in Picardy*, the work of a young officer killed in France in 1918.
But his judgement erred—T. Cameron Wilson's verses have the
adventitious pathos of war-poetry, but nothing in them lends
weight to Monro's sanguine hope (expressed in the Introduction)
that, had he lived, Wilson would have been 'among the most
original poets of the time'. His 'Sportsmen in Paradise' is a charming period-piece, and perhaps deserves quoting for that reason:

> They left the fury of the fight,
> And they were very tired.

The gates of Heaven were open, quite
Unguarded, and unwired.
There was no sound of any gun;
The land was still and green:
Wide hills lay silent in the sun,
Blue valleys slept between.
They saw far off a little wood
Stand up against the sky.
Knee-deep in grass a great tree stood . . .
Some lazy cows went by . . .
There were some rooks sailed overhead—
And once a church-bell pealed.
'God! but it's England', someone said,
'And there's a cricket field!'

Monro was unfortunate in failing to secure for himself any of the best war-poetry.

The issue of rhymesheets, which the Poetry Bookshop maintained over many years, was probably as effective as any of its other devices for spreading the gospel of poetry. The first series, a dozen sheets, began to appear in 1914. They measured twenty-three by eight inches, and their size made them, as Holbrook Jackson wrote in *T.P.'s Weekly*, 'eminently suitable for hanging on a wall much as the Japanese hang their *kakemonos*'.[1] The earliest sheets were offered at the traditional price of a penny plain and tuppence coloured, though in course of time the prices rose to as much as sixpence. The plain sheets were withdrawn early on, for they were clearly inferior as decoration. A second series of twenty-four sheets was issued after the war, and a third series, called *The New Broadside*, came out later.[2]

[1] *T.P.'s Weekly*, XXIII (5 June 1914), p. 719.
[2] Particulars of publication are not consistently given on the sheets, making it impossible to give a fully detailed account of their issue from the press. The last fifteen of the second series bears British Museum

The poems used had to be short and direct, with instant appeal, and the decoration bold. There is no doubt that Monro achieved a peculiar and calculated aesthetic effect with these productions. Their presentation took the humbug out of poetry-reading. The danger was, indeed, that avoiding one kind of preciosity they might fall into another: taking poetry out of the holy of holies and putting it in the lavatory was inviting false simplicity and whimsy.

On the whole the rhymesheets succeed—even to-day, when the fashion for conscious simplicity is not with us. The authors who figure there range from Pope to Pound, Herrick to Hodgson, Dryden to De la Mare. The selections is always from the most readily intelligible of the authors' poems. Dryden, for example, is represented by an operatic lyric 'Thamesis' Song', and Byron by 'We'll go no more a-roving'. Osbert Sitwell provided 'Winter the Huntsman' and Pound 'An Immortality'. Sacheverell Sitwell's contribution was an extract from ' "*Psittachus Eois Imitatrix Ales ab Indis*" Ovid':

> The parrot's voice snaps out—
> No good to contradict—
> What he says he'll say again:
> Dry facts, like biscuits.

Not all poems reach this standard, and too many pleasant, vapid verses with a strong hint of childishness were included, like this by Claud Lovat Fraser:

The Wind

> When the wind spoke to me
> He spoke of the sea
> And of deserts and plains
> And of Devonshire lanes
> And of harebells of blue
> That he slips his hands through—
> *Now is that what the wind has spoken to you?*

stamps dating from Nov. 1919–May 1924. The British Museum has twenty-three in the third series, bearing dates from Dec. 1923 to Nov. 1931.

The decorations are an important part of the rhymesheets' appeal—in most cases they are placed at the head and the foot of the text, and executed in one, two or three colours. Claud Lovat Fraser was responsible for many of the designs for the first and second series, but there is work too by John Nash, Charles Winzer, James Guthrie, Paul Nash, Thomas Sturge Moore and others. *The New Broadside*, which came out after Fraser's death, employed sixteen artists, among whom the brothers Nash, David Jones, E. McKnight Kauffer, Albert Rutherston and Edward Bawden are the best known. Monro thus obtained work from many of the best graphic designers of the day.

He undoubtedly admired Fraser's work, beguiled by its seeming simplicity.[1] Claud Lovat Fraser, a self-taught draughtsman, achieved a considerable reputation, especially with his designs for *The Beggar's Opera* in 1921. His style was in conscious revolt against pomposity and academism, but it has grown very dated: he drew a Cloudcuckoo-Land of a past, where figures in 'period costume' have the quaint appeal of the inhabitants of Lilliput—we cannot take them seriously as humans. This has an unfortunate effect when they are placed as auxiliaries to such poems as Drayton's 'Since there's no help, come let us kiss and part', or even to 'There is a lady sweet and kind' (both poems occur as Rhymesheets). His interpretation of rural scenes was equally sentimental: gingerbread cots are embowered in clumps of elms without, and furnished with four-poster beds within.

Fraser's dilettantism influenced some of the early numbers of *The Chapbook*—'Poems Newly Decorated' includes seven of his decorations; 'Rhymes for Children' illustrates nineteenth-century rhymes with contemporary woodcuts, and may have owed its suggestion to him; 'Old Broadside Ballads' gives facsimiles of sheets

---

[1] In 1922, shortly after Fraser's death, the Poetry Bookshop published *Poems from the Works of Charles Cotton Newly Decorated by Claud Lovat Fraser*, which reproduces a personal selection which he had compiled in a manuscript notebook, and adorned with seventy-five drawings. It is a well-produced book, and the illustrations, mawkish as they are, lend it charm. Four of them are reproduced in this chapter, one at the end of Chapter 8.

from the seventeenth to the nineteenth century, and had a useful introductory note by Fraser. This final contribution represents the valuable side of his hobby. It only became vicious when in his designs he misguidedly attempted to recreate a 'period atmosphere'. There is no doubt that, in his work for Monro, Fraser showed himself as a trivial artist, responsible in part for the cult of the 'crinoline lady' which still has its devotees.

5

FURTHER SLIM VOLUMES AND THEIR AUTHORS

Admiration for the simplicities of a by-gone age produced not only the Rhymesheets and Broadsides. Many of Edward Shanks's *Songs*, published as a sixpenny chapbook in 1915, had the quality of rhymesheet verses; well-turned, clear, simple little ballads, which, though they lack the vigour and passion of genuine folk-poetry, have a faint derivative charm. 'The Great Child' is typical.

> I heard a young girl singing
> Under the summer sun:
> For burning love of a young man
> Her heart was all foredone.
> 'This is my child and lover,

114

My lover when he's strong.
But when he's spent with loving
My child the whole day long.

I nurse him on my bosom,
So dear a weight he is
And sooth his weary eyelids
With a half-perceivèd kiss.'
And I saw in them together,
Amid the grasses wild,
The maiden with her lover,
The mother with her child.

A number of books intended specifically for children deal in a
different kind of ingenuousness. *Nurse Lovechild's Legacy, being a
mighty fine collection of the most noble, memorable and veracious
Nursery Rhymes*, decorated by Fraser, caught the Christmas market in 1916. In 1924 parents could choose between an anthology,
For Your Delight, edited by Ethel L. Fowler, and two books by
Eleanor Farjeon—*A Town Child's Alphabet*, and *A Country Child's
Alphabet*, the first decorated by David Jones, and the second
adorned with bold and humorous drawings by Michael Rothenstein, then a boy of sixteen, and undertaking his first commission.

Many of the poems in Frances Cornford's *Spring Morning* (Poetry
Bookshop, 1915) were written for a juvenile public. Some of them
have a rather more adult appeal—like the well-known 'To a Fat
Lady seen from a Train', which has caught the eye of the anthologists, perhaps because of the surprising way in which it expresses
an adult thought in childish language. Mrs. Cornford's work hovers
somewhere between true and false simplicity, according to your
taste. In 1923 the Poetry Bookshop re-issued *Spring Morning* along
with a second volume of her verse, *Autumn Midnight*. This finely
produced book was hand-printed at S. Dominic's Press, Ditchling,
and adorned with decorated capitals and other wood-carvings by
Eric Gill. Mrs. Cornford was moving now towards her poetic
maturity, when under the watchful guidance of Edward Marsh, and

within the strictest limits of subject and form, she produced fresh, impeccable, charming poems. Hers was the work of a sweet-natured, domesticated woman bred among men of culture from whom she had learnt discrimination. It was a creditable, but quite uncontroversial addition to the Poetry Bookshop's list.

Charlotte Mew, F. S. Flint and Anna Wickham were the three most considerable authors published by the Poetry Bookshop, and the discussion of their work is delayed until the end of the chapter. Mary Morison Webster, H. H. Abbott and 'Michael Field' remain. Of these, the first two are discussed in Chapter 5, in connection with *The Chapbook* to which they were contributors. Harold Monro's conviction of the value of 'Michael Field's' work remains to be discussed here.

'Michael Field' was the pseudonym of an aunt and niece, Katharine Bradley and Edith Cooper, who had published prolifically since the eighteen-eighties. Their work was initially received with enthusiasm, but soon sank into obscurity, though they were comforted by the approval and friendship of such men as Robert Browning, Thomas Sturge Moore and Gordon Bottomley. The two women died in successive years, of cancer—the niece in 1913, the aunt in 1914—and in 1918 the Poetry Bookshop brought out, in one volume, three of their unpublished plays; *Deirdre, A Question of Memory*[1] and

[1] *A Question of Memory* was published by Elkin Mathews and John Lane in a small edition in 1893, but had subsequently been entirely re-modelled.

Ras Byzance; a single unpublished play, *In the Name of Time*, followed in 1919. In *Poetry and Drama* (March 1914) Thomas Sturge Moore had written an enthusiastic note on their poetry, and in 1923 he completed and introduced *A Selection from the Poems of Michael Field*, a work which Mary Sturgeon had undertaken but had been forced to leave unfinished. In his 'Preface', Sturge Moore stated his opinion that 'the study and enthusiasm contributed by Mr. Harold Monro and Miss Klemantaski, of The Poetry Bookshop, by which the present volume has been greatly enriched' was an omen of the 'vital worth' of Michael Field's poetry. A list on the fly-leaf mentioned fourteen of the poets' publications which could be had at the Poetry Bookshop.

Monro's esteem for the work of these dedicated ladies is not very easy to understand—the passion which their biography persuades us they put into their work was reduced in the act of composition to the smoothness of a well-tended lawn. Their lyrics are tasteful, elevated, limpid, well controlled—but dull. They lack spontaneity and individuality, and Professor Saintsbury was right in describing them, from the historical standpoint, as not much more than 'the half machine-made verse which usually comes late in great periods of poetry'.[1] The standard of their dramas, as he suggests, is not much above the general standard of nineteenth-century closet drama.

Following *Cadences* (1915), Monro published a second volume of Flint's poems, *Otherworld*, in 1920. Frank Stewart Flint (1895–1960) was for many years a personal friend of Monro's, an executor

[1] 'Lesser Poets of the Middle and Later Nineteenth Century', *Cambridge History of English Literature*, XIII (1953), p. 181.

of his will, and the author of the 'Biographical Sketch' in the *Collected Poems*. None of Monro's contemporaries was as close to him in style and feeling as Flint. Without going into the slippery question of who influenced whom, we may conclude that Flint encouraged Monro's reading of foreign, especially French, poetry.

Flint had little formal education, but an enthusiasm for literature and an unusual gift for languages (he was finally able to read thirteen languages and to speak and write nine) gained him a foothold in the literary world as *The New Age*'s correspondent on French poetry. As a writer of free verse he was early in the field in this country, and a good deal of his work appeared in *The English Review*. He was an important contributor to *Des Imagistes*, to Amy Lowell's three anthologies, *Some Imagist Poets*, and to Pound's *Catholic Anthology*. His work had the promise of interesting development, but for personal reasons he almost ceased writing from 1920 onwards, and devoted himself, in the intervals of working for the Civil Service, to translating and reviewing.

In his first book of verse, *In the Net of the Stars* (1909), desire outran performance: he wanted, he said, to follow his ear and his heart, but he was burdened with old poetic conventions. In *Cadences* he moves with much more confidence. *Cadences* is a chapbook with a bold, brightly coloured woodcut on the front cover, where a swan sails down a woodland stream towards a red-brick bridge. This cheerful wrapper opens on twenty-two lyrics. One poem is in metrical form; the rest are in 'unrhymed cadence', the synonym for free verse which Flint preferred.

Candidness is Flint's most endearing personal quality, and it regulates his verse. Many of his best poems, with disarming frankness, discover the shadow-side of his personality, showing him in moods of anxiety and dejection. In 'Malady' and 'Hallucination' he explores, in a manner close to Monro's, the territory 'inside the skull', noting the blurred impressions of the mind reduced by illness or by a half-sleeping, half-waking dream:

> I know this room,
> And there are corridors:

the pictures I have seen before:
the statues and those gems in cases,
I have wandered by before,—
stood there silent and lonely
in a dream of years ago.

I know the dark of night is all around me;
my eyes are closed, and I am half asleep;
my wife breathes gently at my side.

But once again this old dream is within me;
and I am on a threshold waiting,
wondering, pleased, and fearful.
Where do those doors lead,
what rooms lie beyond them?
I venture . . .

But baby moves and tosses
from side to side,
and her need calls me to her.

Now I stand awake, unseeing,
in the dark,
and I move towards her cot . . .
I shall not reach her . . . There is no direction . . .
I shall walk on . . .

Self-pity can have a morbidly softening effect on his poems, and
'Otherworld', in the 1920 volume, is a heartbreaking comparison
between Flint's real life as a city-pent wage-slave and his dream
life as a leisured writer in a country home. There is a suggestive
coincidence of feeling and imagery between his hatred of routine
and Monro's, though Flint puts his misery down to economic
necessity, and Monro blames the human condition:

To-morrow I shall wake up tired and heavy-minded
With a bitter mouth and bleared eyes.

Sluggishly, reluctantly, I shall pull myself from my bed.

I shall thrust on my shabby clothes and wash my face and hands;

Put on a collar and tie, a waistcoat, all in haste,

Drink a cup of hot tea, eat a few mouthfuls of bread and butter;

Then, with a hurried kiss to wife and children,

Run down the stairs into the miserable street,

All I meet are shabby, all go one way,

Drawn by the same magnet, urged by the same demon.

We are the respectable; and, behind us, though we do not see him,

Driving us with his goad, is hunger—the first law in our land.

Flint tends to see life as a very doubtful benefit, and death as a bleak conclusion, though he is able to take refuge in a deep domestic happiness, and in a fresh and happy eroticism which Monro did not know.

In *Poetry and Drama* for June 1914, there was a group of poems by Anna Wickham, and in 1915 Monro published a chapbook of her work, *The Contemplative Quarry*. *The Man with a Hammer* (Grant Richards, 1916) followed, and the Poetry Bookshop issued a further volume, *The Little Old House* in 1921. These last were published in one volume in the United States, where her name became better known than it ever was in England. She figured in Richards' *Shilling Selections from Edwardian Poets* (1936), but to Monro belongs the credit of perceiving and fostering her uncouth talent, of giving her confidence in work which she wrote because she had to, and which she believed could earn no praise. It was, in fact, the urgency of her need to write that gave her work its power.

Anna Wickham was the pen-name of Edith Alice Mary Harper. She was born in Wimbledon in 1884, and was taken to Australia at the age of six, where she grew up. As a small girl she took to her pen, and at eighteen published some verse-plays written for performance by the pupils of her mother, who taught elocution. At twenty-one she came to Europe to study singing, but gave up her career a year later to marry Patrick Hepburn, a solicitor by profession and an amateur astronomer of some note, at one time president of the Royal Astronomical Society. With him she spent a stormy married life in London, mostly in Hampstead. She had four sons, and her poems reflect a constant conflict between domestic duties and her desire to write. She was a woman of tremendous energy. subject to uncontrollable bursts of creative activity, when she would completely neglect household tasks.

Anna Wickham was a termagant, a gipsy and a bohemian, wedded to a correct and conventional husband whose dilemma she partly appreciates in 'The Tired Man':

> I am a quiet gentleman,
> And I would sit and dream;
> But my wife is out on the hillside,
> Wild as a hill-stream.
>
> I am a quiet gentleman,
> And I would sit and think;
> But my wife is walking the whirlwind
> Through night as black as ink.
>
> O, give me a woman of my race
> As well controlled as I,
> And let us sit by the fire,
> Patient till we die!

In a less sympathetic mood she wrote:

> I married a man of the Croydon class
> When I was twenty-two,
> And I vex him, and he bores me
> Till we don't know what to do!

Her best poetry is in *The Contemplative Quarry* and *The Man with a Hammer*, and is notably free from both prettiness and measure. *The Little Old House* (1921) is marred by an excess of these virtues, and is mawkish. One would be tempted to conclude that contact with Monro had enervated her style (for these poems were written

121

after she came under his influence), were it not that in *Some Contemporary Poets* (*1920*), he praises her work for its ability 'to shock those mild beings who delight in the thrill of a good shock'.[1] He obviously enjoyed the irregularity of her measures, appreciated her feminist attitude, admired her 'power of condensing a troublesome problem of social psychology into the form of a lyric', and relished her 'wild moods of anger or lust'. Comparing her poems with those of D. H. Lawrence, he finds in the latter

> The querulous chaotic despair, or tired aimlessness of the man who seeks warm pleasure among women, but whose intellect interferes with the freedom of the senses; but in Anna Wickham, frank sensuality. . . .

In her best poetry she does indeed wrest and rend her innocent couplets and quatrains with the ferocity of her passions.

> If I had peace to sit and sing,
> Then I could make a lovely thing;
> But I am stung with goads and whips,
> So I build songs like iron ships.
> Let it be something for my song,
> If it is sometimes swift and strong.

She can generate an amazing amount of energy in a small space, as in 'Sehnsucht':

> Because of body's hunger we are born,
> And by controlling hunger are we fed;
> Because of hunger is our work well done;
> And so are songs well sung, and things well said.
> Desire and hunger are the whips of God—
> God save us all from death when we are fed.

She can build up to an explosive climax:

> For love he offered me his perfect world,
> This world was so constricted, and so small,

[1] pp. 197–8.

It has no sort of loveliness at all,
And I flung back the little silly ball.
At that cold moralist I hotly hurled,
His perfect pure symmetrical small world.

'Gift to a Jade'.

Or, as in 'Sailing near Shoals', she can arrest attention with the force of an opening couplet:

I have been so misused by chaste men with one wife
That I would live with satyrs all my life.

The power of her verses derives from deep-seated conflicts in her personality. In 'Self-Analysis' she writes:

The tumult of my fretted mind
Gives me expression of a kind;
But it is faulty, harsh not plain—
My work has the incompetence of pain.

She was, she wrote, grateful to Monro because he did not think her verses 'symptoms of a disordered mind'.[1] With an abundance of inspiration, she lacked the discipline of art, and her poetry remains interesting and eccentric minor verse.

Of the poets whose work was published by the Poetry Bookshop, Charlotte Mew was probably the finest, certainly the most delicate flower. *The Farmer's Bride* came out in 1916 and was re-issued with eleven additional poems in 1921; a posthumous volume, *The Rambling Sailor*, appeared in 1929, and these two books contained the bulk of Charlotte Mew's output and were combined in the *Collected Poems* published by Duckworth in 1953.

Alida Monro's memoir in the collected edition describes her first encounter with Charlotte Mew's poetry in the pages of *The Nation*.

[1] From Anna Wickham's unpublished autobiography, in the possession of her son, Mr. George Hepburn.

Here she found 'The Farmer's Bride', was deeply struck by it, learnt it by heart, and a year or two later repeated it to Harold Monro. He suggested that they approach the poet to discover whether she had sufficient work to make up a volume. Miss Mew sent a self-deprecating reply, enclosing 'The Changeling', which Alida decided to give, with 'The Farmer's Bride', at a forthcoming poetry-reading. Miss Mew was invited, and came:

> At about five minutes to six the swing-door of the shop was pushed open and into the room stalked Charlotte Mew. Such a word best describes her walk. She was very small, only about four feet ten inches, very slight, with square shoulders and tiny hands and feet. She always wore a long double-breasted top-coat of tweed with a velvet collar inset. She usually carried a horn-handled umbrella, unrolled, under her arm, as if it were psychologically necessary to her, a weapon against the world. . . . The whole time she was speaking she kept her head cocked at a defiant angle. When she came into the shop she was asked: 'Are you Charlotte Mew?' and her reply, delivered characteristically with a slight smile of amusement, was: 'I am sorry to say I am.'[1]

From that evening, a close friendship between her and Alida Monro developed.

Short stories and poems by Charlotte Mew had been appearing for many years in various periodicals, but *The Farmer's Bride* was her first publication in book form. It secured few reviews, and sold badly (only five hundred copies were printed, at a shilling each, and they took years to sell out). Writing to Monro in July 1916, Miss Mew expressed her disappointment; though she was 'simply not the person' to angle for notice, she did think that 'the 1 or 2 more or less influential people who have used all sorts of adjectives about *The Farmer's Bride* would have put same into print'.[2]

She was born in 1869, and her life from the age of twenty-nine,

---

[1] 'Charlotte Mew—a Memoir', *Collected Poems of Charlotte Mew* (London, 1953), p. viii.

[2] In the Lockwood Memorial Library, University of Buffalo.

when her father died, was spent in genteel poverty with her mother and sister. An inherited strain of mental illness confined their younger brother and sister in mental asylums, and made the two girls resolve not to marry. Her sister's death was quickly followed by that of her mother, and Charlotte Mew went into a nursing-home for rest and medical supervision. On what was to be her last visit, Alida Monro was handed one of her friend's most prized possessions—a copy of her poem 'Fin de Fête', transcribed by Thomas Hardy. The next morning, 24 March 1928, she went out, bought a bottle of disinfectant, and committed suicide.

Her prose-writing came to an end in 1916, and her poetry dwindled: few of the poems in the posthumous volume were written after that year. She spoke of 'stacks of MSS. salted away in trunks',[1] but after her death very little was found. If the stacks of manuscripts ever existed, she had very possibly destroyed them —Mrs. Monro recalls her explaining as she sat making spills, that she was burning up her work 'for she didn't know what else to do with it'.

Harold Monro was her warm advocate. He was unsuccessful in persuading Edward Marsh to include her among the Georgians, but he gave her generous representation in *Twentieth Century Poetry*. 'The Recorder' (Alida Monro) in *Chapbook* No. 12 (June 1920) rated her as 'Undoubtedly one of the best poets of the century'. In *Some Contemporary Poets* Harold Monro gave her ex-tended praise—for the condensation of her style, for her originality, for her imaginative power. Charlotte Mew's apprehension of life was a highly individual one, and the core of her achievement, for Monro, was that she found an individual way of expressing it. As so often, his admiration came back to the enjoyment of intimacy with an unusual mind:

> She writes with the naturalness of one whom real passion has excited; her diction is free from artificial conceits, is inspired by the force of her subject, and creates its own direct intel-lectual contact with the reader.[2]

[1] 'Charlotte Mew—A Memoir', p. xx.　　　　[2] p. 82.

And he perceptively commented, 'She does not tire you with her personality; but continually interests you in its strange reflections.'[1]

Stylistically, her work shows a tension between traditional metrical and verbal usage and the demands of a free spirit. She found a large freedom in an original handling of old forms, and never adopted the fashionable conventions of 'modern' verse. 'The Farmer's Bride', the poem which attracted the attention of Alida Klemantaski and Harold Monro, is in the folk-tradition, and could, on a cursory examination, be passed over as just another fake ballad. It tells of a union between a farmer and a maid who turns out to be fey, farouche, unamenable to marriage, perhaps not quite human. This interesting ambiguity, and the intense but muted passion in the poem make it into a rarity:

> She sleeps up in the attic there
> Alone, poor maid. 'Tis but a stair
> Betwixt us. Oh! my God! the down,
> The soft young down of her, the brown,
> The brown of her—her eyes, her hair, her hair!

Charlotte Mew's poetry, like Monro's, was the product of a 'tortured human consciousness'. It hung, one senses, too near the edge of sanity for comfort. Mrs. Monro, in her memoir, speaks of a dichotomy within her, of which she was unaware, between her emotional nature and her moral sense, which made her censorious of the lapses of others. Yet in other respects she was her own psychoanalyst, writing, for example, in 'Fame' with great candour of her odd persona—of what Mrs. Monro describes as 'her rather strident voice and her *méfiant* manner'.[2] Of this poem she wrote to a friend, 'I am glad you like "Fame" which I personally prefer to anything I have done although I don't know why . . .'[3]

The poem has a rather premature, red and raw look, that look of exposed 'personality' which Monro preferred, and I quote it as evidence of her quality and desert:

[1] p. 77.
[2] 'Charlotte Mew—A Memoir', p. xiii.
[3] Quoted in the above memoir, p. xvii.

Sometimes in the over-heated house, but not for long,
Smirking and speaking rather loud,
I see myself among the crowd,
Where no one fits the singer to his song,
Or sifts the unpainted from the painted faces
Of the people who are always on my stair;
They were not with me when I walked in heavenly places;
    But could I spare
In the blind Earth's great silences and spaces,
    The din, the scuffle, the long stare
    If I went back and it was not there?
Back to the old known things that are the new,

The folded glory of the gorse, the sweet-briar air,
To the larks that cannot praise us, knowing nothing of
                      what we do,
And the divine, wise trees that do not care.
Yet, to leave Fame, still with such eyes and that bright hair!
God! If I might! And before I go hence
    Take in her stead
    To our tossed bed
One little dream, no matter how small, how wild.
Just now, I think I found it in a field, under a fence—
A frail, dead, new-born lamb, ghostly and pitiful and white,
    A blot upon the night,
The moon's dropped child!

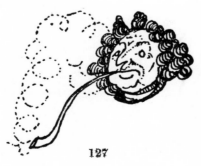

The publishing activity of the Poetry Bookshop is steeped in an atmosphere of happy amateurishness: it is desultory and highly idiosyncratic, and money-making is clearly not a serious motive. The volumes of *Georgian Poetry* are to some extent exceptions on all three counts, but it is very obvious that but for the shaping spirit of Edward Marsh, they could not have taken the form they did.

It is in his work as a publisher that Monro's limitations as a critic of new poetry show to worst advantage. There was a time, before the First World War, when, had he possessed the insight and initiative to seize his chance, Monro might have found himself the publisher of most of the most interesting and progressive new verse available in this country. Had he accepted Eliot, had he accepted Thomas, and been responsible for establishing their poetic reputations, the prestige of the Poetry Bookshop as a publishing house would have been enormously enlarged. As it was, the liveliest young talents of the post-war years went elsewhere.

Charlotte Mew, F. S. Flint and Anna Wickham were talents well worth fostering, but it is probably as a Cheap Jack that Monro made his most distinctive mark—in encouraging the notion that verse-reading and verse-buying could happen without solemnity, in the course of every day.

5

The Post-war Years

'SOME CONTEMPORARY POETS (1920)'
THE POETIC SCENE

Harold Monro's amiability towards writers of all complexions enabled him, when the war was over and his military commitments
came to an end,[1] to play a significant part in repairing a literary
society that had been shattered and dispersed.

Douglas Goldring wrote:

> Early in 1919 Harold Monro gave a series of 'stag parties' in
> his beautiful Georgian house in Devonshire Street, Theobalds
> Road, to which all his old contributors and all the younger
> generation of war poets were invited. At these reunions, with
> the aid of unlimited supplies of drinkable and not very intoxi-
> cating white wine, we got to know one another, exchanged
> experiences, and discussed plans for Monro's new monthly
> miscellany, *The Chapbook*.
>
> I look back on those Poetry Bookshop gatherings, after six-
> teen years, with the warmest emotion of gratitude to Monro
> for having organised them. No one else in London at the time
> could possibly have collected together so many poets and
> writers under such friendly and informal conditions. I suppose
> I have been, in my life, to some hundreds if not thousands of
> literary parties, but I cannot recall any which I enjoyed as
> much and at which I made so many friends.[2]

[1] He was released in 1919, and relinquished his commission in April
1920.   [2] *Odd Man Out* (London, 1935), p. 233.

Frank Morley was 'one of those who appreciated browsing in the bookshop in the twenties', and in a letter to the present writer recalls being invited upstairs after dinner:

> It was I think John Gould Fletcher who got me into that evening and I remember that Conrad Aiken was there and Eliot had been expected, and perhaps had been there and left early. . . . It was a contentious period and not even Harold and Alida could expect many men of letters to get on together in perfect amity. I don't think Harold was very perceptive (Alida more so) that people could be of different breeds: I think he felt that all who 'served poetry' should love one another. He was distressed if they didn't. I remember that evening because among the few of us an argument developed between attackers of some of the 'new' poets and defenders— Eliot must have gone by that time for I seemed sometimes to be the only (and how unworthy) defender of various expressions made by Eliot and Read. . . . I instance this dispute only because Harold was upset at there being *any* dispute. It was his sweet nature that lamb and lion should together lie down.

And Sir Osbert Sitwell writes of these gatherings:

> Sometimes there would be battle, but always one heard the literary news and was told of small incidents which, though the world's foundations have been shaken since those days, continue even now to come back to the mind . . . Whatever outbreaks had taken place, one left Harold Monro's parties enlivened, and grateful to him: for he was an excellent host.[1]

Monro's ideal—the peaceful commonwealth of poets—was not easy of attainment in the post-war years. While enjoying Monro's hospitality the poets may sometimes have appeared docile enough, but his influence could not prevent them carrying on a petty civil war which made the pre-war contention between Georgians and Imagists look like happy cameraderie.

In *Some Contemporary Poets (1920)*, Monro expressed his feelings

[1] *Laughter in the Next Room* (London, 1949), p. 34.

about the changed literary scene.[1] The whole drift of his complaint
shows how much the scene had shifted since 1912—then, the poets
were starving for lack of attention, now, they are being corrupted
by too much. Monro describes a new generation of bright young
men and women, their work readily accepted by newspapers and
magazines, their eyes firmly glued to the main chance, keenly com-
petitive, worldly, professional and insincere. Success depends on
knowing the right people, and the poet, 'if obliged to admit that he
has not actually met Mr. H., Mr. N., or Sir S. G., must be able to
imply skilfully that he will probably be dining with them next
week'. If he is wise he will join a 'group', which will enable him to
lay claim to a secret unknown to those outside it, will keep him
au fait with the latest artistic chit-chat, and give him space in its
'little magazine'. The group is

> . . . a support to individuals not strong enough to stand alone.
> It is at the same time a useful school for young poets. The cus-
> tom has been imported from Paris with its factional acri-
> monies, jealousies and scandal-mongerings, but without its
> pleasant and private inner qualities. Most French groups are
> societies of friends, not Unions of Professional Poets. The
> members of English Cliques meet less at supper than in periodi-
> cals, less in private than in public.

He recognised that poets of genuine quality might derive something
from the group

> . . . by learning to avoid the vices of their colleagues, or by
> imitating their virtues. Thus it may happen, and it generally
> does, that one, two, or more persons emerge out of a move-
> ment of several, stronger by reason of collaboration. They will
> 'rise o'er stepping-stones of their dead' *confrères,* who, con-
> tinuing inevitably to imitate themselves or each other, will
> sink out of a temporary limelight into the literary obscurity to
> which they were predestined.

But this was not offered in justification for the existence of groups
—only in partial excuse. Monro remained firmly set against the

[1] pp. 11 ff.

ganging-up of poets, as he observed it in post-war London. His attack on groups was general—he named no names, though he was doubtless primed, willy-nilly, with all the gossip as it passed, and fully aware of the changing patterns of association.

Broadly speaking, there were two contending factions: the Georgians, who declared themselves, some of them reluctantly, in two further anthologies in 1919 and 1922; and the modernists. As the anthologies came under increasingly heavy critical fire, the best poets among the Georgians—De la Mare, Sassoon and Graves, for example—were unwilling to be identified with the group. The advent in November 1919, however, of J. C. Squire's *London Mercury* with its resolute advocacy of the 'Squirearchy'—Edward Shanks, W. J. Turner, John Freeman and Squire himself, among others—gave fresh solidarity to the poets who represented the Georgian decline. From this citadel Squire and his supporters strafed the foe.

The London Mercury was a self-confessedly conservative organ, disapproving of unbridled experiment, taking its stand on common-sense. In June 1924 Squire defined the new poetry (through the mouth of a fictional character) as

> . . . a kind of hideous little underworld; the sort of thing you see when you lift up a large stone and see disgusting insects, beetles and centipedes scuttling about. They dislike the daylight too. . . . The second-rate have discovered the trick of incomprehensibility in our time; the trick of bogus audacity has always been known.[1]

The circulation figures of *The London Mercury*—ten thousand in its first year, rising to twenty thousand—indicate its nice adjustment to contemporary taste.

A sharpening of critical hostility to experimental verse dates from the appearance of *Wheels*, which ran annually from 1916 to 1920, and was dominated by the Sitwells and their friends. Associated with this group to the extent that they sought bold new

[1] 'The Man who wrote Free Verse', *London Mercury*, X (June 1924), p. 128.

horizons in poetry, and enjoyed with them the disfavour of *The London Mercury*, were such writers as T. S. Eliot, Ezra Pound, Wyndham Lewis, Herbert Read, Aldous Huxley and Richard Aldington.

Armed with his publisher's assurance that 'the Author does not belong to any clique of professional critics, nor does he share the prejudices of any particular school of poetry',[1] Monro entered upon this thorny ground in Part III of *Some Contemporary Poets (1920)*— the section of the book which was provocatively entitled 'Poets and Poetasters of our Time'. Sketchy, hasty and ill-digested though his remarks were, they were made without fear or favour, and what they lack in grace they made up in honesty. The inspirational, quasi-religious notion of poetry which Monro formerly held had gone, and his attitude was now rather that of a craftsman austerely reviewing another man's pots.

There was a marked falling-off in his faith in some of his old friends and contributors. 'Lascelles Abercrombie is almost without lyrical impulse. A turgid blank verse is his medium.' Gibson is 'more facile than most of his contemporaries, but his mind has not sufficient range to justify that facility'. In Drinkwater he discovered a 'speciously noble manner'. On the other hand, his faith in the value of Pound's work had increased, though he saw that 'The recognition of his genius will be gradual and tardy, its qualities being, few of them, apparent on the surface.'

He pointed out the deterioration within the Georgian movement: its 'fortuitous and informal' quality was lost when 'the poets subsequently included in the anthologies devoted much energy to narrowing and hardening what began as a spontaneous co-operative effort'. This was remarkably candid, when he had just issued the fourth and was later to publish the final volume, and his guileless action would seem to justify his protest (in 1922) to Herbert Palmer, who had accused him of favouring Georgians:

[1] 'List of New and Forthcoming Publications' appended to *Some Contemporary Poets (1920)*.

I think you must be wrong in attributing any prejudice to me in favour of one school or another or one kind of verse or another. By temperament I am perhaps too impartial. . . . As regards the volumes of *Georgian Poetry* I am merely their publisher, but not otherwise particularly their supporter or apologist.[1]

Determined to give a balanced judgement, he found kind things to say of the leading late-Georgians. Equally, they were the objects of his irony or condemnation. 'In J. C. Squire we have an interesting example of the modern professional poet,' whose serious poems were 'labours of conscious brain, supported by encyclopaedic investigation'. 'Turner has suffered from the disadvantage of learning the "tricks of the trade" in the neo-Georgian school . . .' 'Much of Shanks's poetry is what reviewers might call "worthy of Keats". In this respect he resembles several other of the writers discussed in this section. Most of them, therefore, have still to prove that they are worthy of themselves.' Of Robert Nichols's weighty collected edition of 1917:

> . . . the principal amusement to be derived from the greater part of the books is merely the pastime of puzzling how these verses have been put together, and trying constantly to recall from which particular passages of English poetry they happen to be derived.

His remarks on a long-standing bugbear opened and closed thus: 'Of Alfred Noyes nothing can be written in extenuation.' 'He has been universally praised by reviewers.'

T. S. Eliot was not mentioned. Of the *enfants terribles*, Aldous Huxley won highest praise, for originality, dexterity and modernity. The Sitwells came in for some guarded encomiums:

> Though his [Osbert Sitwell's] mind works in a painted overheated atmosphere, it has a considerable power of feeling its way back into the past or peering into the psychology of the present.

[1] (11 Sept. 1922) Lockwood Memorial Library, University of Buffalo.

Of Sacheverell he wrote: 'The long hard training of civilisation has staled a Sitwell mind', and he found that Edith moved 'with comparative comfort among the shrill flowers of hell.'

He showed tolerance of experiment, however extreme, quoting poems by John Rodker and by Max Weber, the Cubist poet. While condemning them, he urged his readers to believe that

> . . . their spirit is more representative of modern civilisations than ever the studied rhymes of those young bloods who follow closely on the traditions of the best poetry, ignoring the trend of real life. Unsuccessful experiment is far more interesting than successful imitation.

For all its occasional insights, *Some Contemporary Poets* is a rather colourless book. Monro's cautious spirit and his desire for fair play (along with his publisher's requirements) combined to produce a survey rather than an evaluation. T. S. Eliot's comment on the book, though it overstates the case, is partly justified:

> Some of the poets whom Mr. Monro chats about are dull, some immature, some are slight, some are downright bad: Mr. Monro's effect is to make them all seem dull, immature, slight, and bad.[1]

2

'THE CHAPBOOK':

In working towards his ideal—peace among poets—Monro was not content with the roles of host, bookseller, sponsor of verse-recitals and occasional critic. In December 1914 *Poetry and Drama* had closed with the assurance that it would reappear after the war; and in July 1919 Monro emerged again as an editor, but this time he was directing a periodical of a very different character.

Though *Poetry and Drama*'s development had been prematurely arrested, its intention was plain: to establish itself, within its

[1] *Dial* (New York), LXX (1921), p. 449.

chosen limits of poetry and theatre, as an authoritative critical quarterly of moderate-to-progressive views; to provide documentation of current publications and tendencies at home and abroad; and to publish new verse by poets of varied types. It was, if not a heavy-weight, at least a medium-heavy-weight paper.

An obvious reason why Monro decided not to revive the magazine was that its functions had been taken over by other periodicals. *The New Freewoman*, having come under the influence of Pound and the Imagists in 1913, had continued publication throughout the war under its new title, *The Egoist*. As Imagism broadened down and lost its character as a militant movement, so *The Egoist* lost its Imagist limitations. It published work by the Anglo-American *avant garde* in general, and was interested in developments on the Continent. Richard Aldington, H.D. and T. S. Eliot were at different times assistant editors. During Eliot's term of office (June 1917–December 1919) the critical standard was specially high.

With John Middleton Murry as editor (April 1919–February 1921) *The Athenaeum* was transformed from a moribund monthly into a lively and up-to-date publication of post-war character. Such writers as Leonard and Virginia Woolf, Aldous Huxley, E. M. Forster, Irving Babbitt, Conrad Aiken and T. S. Eliot supplied book-reviews, and there were articles from contributors of equal distinction. Among the poets whose work was printed, the modernists were much in evidence.

If these papers favoured advanced writing, Holbrook Jackson's *To-day* (March 1917–December 1923) joined *The Bookman* in catering for middle-brow tastes; and *The London Mercury*, though pitched in a higher intellectual key, was acceptable also to the mighty army of conservatively minded readers. Though *The London Mercury* did not begin publication until four months after *The Chapbook*, Monro would certainly have been aware of its proposed scope and character. 'So well was the ground prepared', writes Patrick Howarth, 'that thousands of people agreed to subscribe for a year before they had seen a copy of the paper.'[1] Monro thus found

[1] *Squire: Most Generous of Men* (London, 1963), p. 122.

the critical middle-ground which he had, in *Poetry and Drama*, claimed for his own, sub-divided and parcelled out amongst others.

A number of little magazines whose main intention was to carry new writing, or new writing and art combined, had sprung up around the end of the war, following in the wake of *New Numbers*, *Blast*, *Rhythm*, *The Blue Review* and similar ventures. *Wheels* came early, with its provocative eccentricities of style. *Form*, *Art and Letters*, *The Owl*, *Voices* and *Coterie* lived and died, some very briefly, during the years between 1916 and 1922, offering poets the chance to see themselves in print.

Into this active scene Monro entered with yet another little magazine, *The Monthly Chapbook* (later re-named *The Chapbook*),[1] which commenced publication in July 1919. As their name implies, the *Chapbooks* were miniature volumes (averaging about thirty-two pages), bound in paper covers, and economically priced.[2] They are unpretentious in appearance and yet attractive, with gay and simple cover-designs by a notable series of graphic artists.[3] The quality of the paper and printing was high, and many issues were embellished with designs on the backs of the covers or in the body of the text.

For all that their charm was unobtrusive, each number brought

[1] The periodical ran as *The Monthly Chapbook* from July to December 1919; it was thereafter re-named *The Chapbook*, and continued monthly publication until June 1921. The next two numbers appeared in February and May 1922, but monthly publication was resumed in July 1922, and continued until June 1923. Two larger annual volumes (No. 39, published in October 1924, and No. 40 in October 1925) concluded the series. Of No. 39 there was a larger paper edition, issued by Jonathan Cape, as well as an ordinary one.

[2] The first three issues were priced at one shilling, and the next twenty-one at one-and-sixpence. Thereafter the price was reduced to a shilling.

[3] These included Claud Lovat Fraser, Albert Rutherston, Ethelbert White, Paul Nash, E. McKnight Kauffer, E. Gordon Craig and Jean de Bosschère. Decorations on the backs of covers or in the body of the text were by John Nash, Wyndham Lewis, Charles Ginner and David Jones among others.

something different from the last, each number had the lure of the unexpected, and dropped from the press like the first lamb of spring. They were pretty enough to preserve, but free from the solemnity of the 'art magazine'.

The first issue announced that

> Each number of *The Monthly Chapbook* will be of separate interest, and complete in itself. At the same time, a definite continuity will be preserved so that the six issues for any half-year will form a volume combining a record of that half-year's production in poetry and drama, a critical survey of contemporary literature, and numerous examples of the creative work of the present period. . . . Former subscribers to *Poetry and Drama* will find *The Monthly Chapbook* as useful from the student's point of view, and more entertaining from the point of view of the general reader.

Monro, then, was not willing entirely to abnegate his critical function—to produce simply a miscellany of new writing. Yet the mere size of *The Chapbook* and the diversity of its range disqualified it from competing with papers like *The Athenaeum* or *The London Mercury*. The paper was a rather light-weight production, presenting new verse, new verse-drama or criticism, in convenient, bite-size portions; and the plan announced at the outset—of producing a full critical and bibliographic survey of each six months' work—was quietly shelved. The casualness and freedom that resulted was one of *The Chapbook*'s attractive qualities.

The first number provided a variety of talent never secured again. The inclusion of De la Mare and W. H. Davies harked back to the first Georgian anthology, and Thomas Sturge Moore and Charlotte Mew hailed from an even greater distance; the old pre-war *avant garde* was represented by Aldington, H.D., F. S. Flint and D. H. Lawrence: Siegfried Sassoon, W. P. R. Kerr, W. J. Turner and Robert Nichols were Georgians of the war-time generation, while the three Sitwells, Aldous Huxley and Herbert Read were in the very firing-line of post-war poetry. Monro contributed 'Underworld'. *The Chapbook* was plainly interested in experiment of every kind, and issued incongruously from the house that, a few months later, produced *Georgian Poetry 1918–1919*.

John o' London, under the heading 'Incoherent and Freakish', confessed himself mystified by many of the poems. Had the war, he asked, left the poets 'seeing sights and thinking thoughts that are unintelligible to the ordinary mind'?[1] He singled out Herbert Read and the Sitwells for special condemnation.

An intelligent reading of Read's *'Étude'* did demand a considerable effort of concentration:

> That white hand poised
> Above the ivory keys
> Will soon descend to
> Shatter
> The equable surface of my reverie.
>
> To what abortion
> Will the silence give birth?
>
> *Noon of moist heat, and the moan*
> *Of raping bees,*
> *And light like a sluice of molten gold*
> *On the satiate, petitioning leaves.*
>
> *In yellow fields*
> *The mute agony of reapers.*
>
> Does the hard horizon give release?
>
> Well, higher,
>> against the wider void the immaculate
>> angels of lust
> lean
>> on the swanbreasts of heaven.

'"The mute agony of reapers" leaves me blank and questioning', says John o' London, unusually obtuse. '"The mute agony of reapers?" No, I cannot solve it.'

---

[1] *John o' London's Weekly*, I, XXII (6 Sept. 1919).

Osbert Sitwell's '*De Luxe* (*Nursery Rhyme*)' was sophisticated cosmopolitan satire in the manner of Eliot:

> The dusky king of Malabar
> Is chief of Eastern potentates;
> Yet he wears no clothes, except
> The jewels that decency dictates.
>
> A thousand Malabaric wives
> Roam beneath green-crested palms;
> Revel in the vileness
> That Bishop Heber psalms.
>
> . . . .
>
> But Mrs. Freudenthal, in furs,
> From Brioche dreams to mild surprise
> Awakes; the music throbs and purrs.
> The 'cellist with Albino eyes
>
> Rivets attention. . . .

The opening verse of Sacheverell Sitwell's 'Church and Stage' had the new cynicism, and (for most readers) the new obscurity:

> *Terra feros partus immania monstra gigantas*
> *Edidit ausuros in Jovis ire domum,*
> Beating the marble floor with well-drilled, giddy precision,
> The host of aspirants are on the safest road to Heaven.

And Edith Sitwell's 'Interlude' perversely juggled with sense-data:

> Amid this hot green glowing gloom
> A word falls like a raindrop's boom . . .
>
> Like baskets of ripe fruit in air
> The bird-songs seem, suspended where
>
> Those goldfinches—the ripe warm lights
> Peck slyly at them—take quick flights. . . .

Beside this, the exquisite Imagist 'Coastline' of F. S. Flint was agreeably old-fashioned:

> Here the wind
> winnows the sand
> as it sifts
> through the grass-wrack,
> and the grains beat,
> needlepoints,
> against the skin.
>
> Here the sea
> knaws the long coast,
> churning the shingle
> over the beach,
> and the waves,
> wind-driven,
> whiten and topple
> over our bodies.
>
> Wind and sea
> and the print of naked foot.

Several of the poems in this opening number would not have seemed out of place in *Georgian Poetry*—Rose Macaulay's 'Driving Sheep', De la Mare's 'To Lucy', or W. J. Turner's Miltonic sonnet 'To Stars'. Sturge Moore's Shakespearean sonnet, 'On Shakespeare's Sonnets' carries a warning for scholars who search those poems for biographical data:

> . . . not bloom to fruit,
> Meal to moth's wing, sight to blind eye is less
> Recoverable! Time treads life underfoot;
> These dead black words can warm us but as coal;
> Once, forest leaves, they murmured round his soul.

An entirely different note was struck by Douglas Goldring's 'A Triumphal Ode', a jejune satire on contemporary poets and men of letters, which ended with a general malediction:

> Of all the Georgian and Edwardian potes,
> Of all the Mile End Yidds in velvet coats,
> Of all the sects, the circles and the cliques
> Who boost each other's works in their critiques,
> Of all on whom E.M. has ever smiled;
> Of all whom Galloway has ever kyled;
> Of 'marvellous boys', and of youth's soulful loom—
> > Sing Boom!
> > Sing Boom!
> > Sing Boom!

The issue closed on a more rewarding note with Charlotte Mew's 'Sea Love'.

This first number presented a conspectus of the poetic activity of the day, and displayed—partly, no doubt, deliberately—the catholicity of the editor. It turned out to be *The Chapbook*'s most brilliant moment, for its promise was not fulfilled, though *Chapbook* No. 13, with Charlotte Mew's 'I have been through the gates', Edna St. Vincent Millay's 'Spring', Edith Sitwell's '*En Famille*', and work by Ford Madox Hueffer, Wilfrid Gibson, Harold Monro, Richard Aldington, John Freeman, and Thomas Sturge Moore, was a good second best.

Monro succeeded in getting copy from an overwhelming majority of the poets active in the first half of the 'twenties.[1] He approached J. C. Squire for material, and had an illuminating reply:

[1] Poems from the Sitwells, W. H. Davies, Siegfried Sassoon, Walter de la Mare, Herbert Read, Padraic Colum, John Gould Fletcher, Conrad Aiken, Edna St. Vincent Millay, H.D., Richard Aldington, Charlotte Mew, Anna Wickham, Humbert Wolfe, L. A. G. Strong, Thomas Sturge Moore, John Redwood Anderson, A. E. Coppard and Lascelles Abercombie occur, and there are single contributions from T. S. Eliot, Aldous Huxley, Edgell Rickword, F. S. Flint, John Freeman, W. J. Turner and Robert Graves.

Alas I have nothing. I had only heard vaguely of the scheme before. My Muse has run dry for the time being. But if you are having all the contending factions in I don't think I'd feel entirely comfortable. Isn't it like trying to make a church out of Catholics, Jews and Atheists? Anyhow I'll hear about it when we meet. Meanwhile good luck to it. Yrs. ever, J.C.S.

In an undated letter Ezra Pound made a rather similar point:

Bring your blood [*sic*] C.B. to Paris, and try to collect a real team of contributors and perhaps something might be done about it.

Only *HELL*—you never had a programme—you've always dragged in Aberbubble and Siphon, and Wobblebery and wanted to exploit the necropolis. Eliot may be in the act of sinking beneath the Londonian slough—but after all he has worried the [?], and been associated with some form of activity. Blast, Little Review, etc.

One always suspects you of having (and knows you have had) sympathy with a lot of second-rate lopp—and never knows when the ancient sin will break out again.

A rumble-tumble satire on the Georgians by Osbert Sitwell in the issue of September 1922 brought out the curious ambiguity of Monro's position. 'The Jolly Old Squire or Way-down in Georgia' had for its heroes 'J**k C*ll**gs Sq**re, Poet and Journalist. Editor of the *English Hermes*. Ed**rd Sh**ks, Journalist and Poet. Contributor to the *English Hermes*'. The presiding deity was the goddess Mediocrity, and the villain who sought the heroes' overthrow was Satan, to be impersonated at the first performance (a footnote tells us) by 'Mr. H*r*ld M*nro'. This was an unexpected role for the publisher of the Georgian anthologies, whose work appeared regularly therein; who from time to time printed a full-page advertisement for *The London Mercury* in his *Chapbook*; and who was on friendly enough terms with Squire to be asked to join his literary cricket-team.

Odder still, two of Monro's poems were among those pilloried in the course of the 'Prologue' (which is all that is, in fact, offered of

143

the proposed drama). The Georgians have a predilection for birds and they 'teach the nightingale to sing quite near a house', Sitwell points out, in an obvious reference to Monro's 'Nightingale near the House', whose 'indifferent success' he alludes to in a footnote. We are taken to Chiswick, the home of Squire:

> Yes—Here dwells He: in yonder den he made
> 'Moon', 'Trees', and 'Rivers', on this blotting pad.

and a footnote archly explains, of 'Trees':

> I apologise for my negligence in overlooking the fact that this particular poem is not by Mr. Sq**re. I cannot, at the moment, alter, and destroy, the scansion of my line. Indeed, I could not feel sure, anyway, to which of the two particular poets concerned I should be paying a compliment by attempting a revision.

and, later, after including Monro's 'Trees' once more in a list of Squire's productions, Sitwell notes 'I am in confusion again. Shall I retract "Trees"? Is it by Mr. Sq**re or by whom? Alas, my ignorance!'

Osbert Sitwell, by thus putting him on the side of the devils and of the angels at once, draws attention to the ambivalence of Monro's position, and Monro himself renders his see-saw balance more precarious by publishing Sitwell's satire in his own *Chapbook*. The only thing that emerges unambiguously from the affair is the quality of Monro's sense of humour—his willingness to accept a joke at his own expense, and, even, to publish it.

Chapbook No. 26 (May 1922) noted that readers had asked for more frequent issues of poetry, and Monro's policy thereafter reflected their preference. Altogether, fifteen issues were devoted entirely to new verse, and the annual volumes for 1924 and 1925 each contained new poetry in abundance. Monro complained here and there in his correspondence about the conventionality and imitativeness of most of the material sent to him, and he must be congratulated for keeping the standard as high as it is. We must sympathise with him too, for he was a sitting target for manuscripts from poets and poetasters of every age and sex.

In *Some Contemporary Poets* (*1920*), he analysed the stock-in-trade of the typical young poet:

> He has read most of Keats, some Shelley, a little Wordsworth and a certain amount of Byron. He knows the *Shropshire Lad* rather too well. Walter de la Mare's rhythm also handicaps his freedom. He can understand French, has looked through Baudelaire and Verlaine, and is able to talk with respect of almost anyone who wrote, or writes, *vers libre*. He likes Donne, but Chaucer, Milton and Campion he is still meaning to study. Long poems he hates—or imitates.
>
> Here and there, in cursory moments, he has picked up tags of Darwin. These he employs occasionally, in his psychological stuff, as aids to cynicism; with a touch of Rubert Brooke added they are invaluable to him.[1]

With this interesting *pot pourri*, blending romantic and late-romantic influences with twentieth-century fashions in thought and poetry, Monro was bound to be over-familiar. The tone of his letters to would-be contributors was distinctly blunt and autocratic. If a poem did not 'please' him, that was clearly that; and he would indicate the precise textual alterations that he wished to see made before he would accept work. Arundel del Re has noted that he never failed to enclose a personal note with a returned manuscript. 'Far from resenting criticism', wrote Narcisse Wood in 1921, 'I am only too glad to have it. So many publishers and editors give out nothing but the bare bone of rejection, that it is comforting to find anyone who takes enough interest to offer suggestions.' And later she wrote again in the same vein: 'I am always most grateful for and amazed at your kind and careful criticism as one gets so little elsewhere.'

To Geoffrey Wells, Monro wrote:

> It is plain that you are trying experiments in style, but you have not succeeded in pleasing me personally except in one of

[1] p. 12.

the cases where you have used the conventional style, namely, 'At Morning Prayer'. The observation and descriptive power seem to me both good in this fragment, except when I come to the last line but three. Then I am pulled up with a violent jerk by the word 'o'er', which is quite incongruous. If you could alter this line to your satisfaction and to mine, I should be glad to print the poem. . . . I think 'The Park Concert' is the next in interest and the most successful passage of it is the third one, in brackets. 'The Ideal Sanctuary' is slight [*sic*] reminiscent of the style of Rupert Brooke and 'Grey Dusk' perhaps still more so.

H. Cedric Hopegood was given detailed advice on how to improve his poem 'Vigil':

In line 9 surely the word 'now' would read much better than 'do'. The latter has an archaic sound which is incompatible with the general tone of the poem and makes the line halt unnecessarily. I should like to suggest leaving out altogether lines 11, 12 and 13. In any case, I think the line you have substituted for the typewritten one, namely, 'Shuddering voices ride, their gruesome guests to entertain' is weak, particularly the inversion at the end. Perhaps you will have some view about these three lines.

Mr. Hopegood wrote two letters in reply, the second even more obliging than the first, but 'Vigil' was never printed in *The Chapbook*.

And to another would-be contributor Monro wrote:

Thank you for your letter. I do not think you ought to wish that the influence of Rupert Brooke had been stronger.

It will be illuminating to consider here two poets whose volumes were issued by the Poetry Bookshop in the post-war period. Their discussion here is only partly in parenthesis, for both authors contributed to *The Chapbook* before their volumes appeared, and each opportunely represents the bevy of small and unknown poets who sent copy to Monro, and who, if they were lucky, figured in *The Chapbook*'s pages.

H. H. Abbott was a man of very limited poetic gift, but he is interesting for another reason. In 1922 Monro published *Black and White*, a small collection of his work, which included ten poems previously printed in *The Chapbook*.

Mud on his boots, Abbott wrote blank-verse bucolics about English farm-life:

> The road rises and winds: at its crest
> The farm still stands, and Beaumains is its name—
> They call it Beemans: if you look upon
> Its great square chimney-stack you'll see the date—
> Sixteen hundred and eight—upon its bricks.　　('Farm')

He also wrote poems that were echoes of traditional ballads, and in a series of three poems about cricket tried his hand at verbal impressionism:

> The sun beats down upon my head;
> I fix my gaze upon the yellow shiny stump.
> Slim white figures, ghostly figures, stand
> In the distance thin white lines and red dots
> 　　Cross and intercross
> Slowly the bowler glides to the wickets,
>
> 　The sun beats down.
> 　My head swims. . . .　　('Umpire')

In 'Fact' he challenged scientific cynicism in sharp dialectic:

> 'Enamelled plumes of birds and butterflies,
> Clashing antlers and hairy manes,
> Songs and callings—'　　'Sex-appeal.'
>
> 'Claspings and soft syllables,
> Tender looks and playfulness,
> Hands conjoining—'　　'Urge of Life.'

147

'Well,

There's nothing to be ashamed of, is there?'

It is surprising to find, three pages later in the book, a poem on 'Medea' which opens:

> Lithe savage mystery-woman,
> No blue Symplegades again for thee
> Or clear-cut Corinth. Exile on the shores
> Of Greece, what shouldst thou find in love but grief?

H. H. Abbott dabbled, and the result is a gallimaufry of samples —verses which illustrate some of the alternatives open to the traditionalist who wanted to seem a little modern.

> Here's sly Monro with *Chapbook* under arm,
> And fair aspirants round him in a swarm.

Thus wrote Douglas Goldring in his 'Triumphal Ode' ironically celebrating contemporary poets in *Chapbook* No. 1. The fair aspirant who had most success with Monro was Mary Morison Webster, whom he never actually met, but whose work figured in four issues of *The Chapbook*, and filled three volumes published by the Poetry Bookshop: *Tomorrow* (1922), *The Silver Flute* (1931), and *Alien Guest* (1933). In a letter to the present writer Miss Webster recalls that, in 1920, 'Monro was quite excited about my poetry and wrote entreating me not to go to South Adfrica, and bury myself there, which I nevertheless did.'

Miss Webster wrote soft female poetry of the heart, and there is no reason to doubt her 'sincerity', which was perhaps the quality which attracted Monro to her work. This is an occasion, however, when we may doubt the value of sincerity as a criterion of poetic merit. Miss Webster had much to learn about economy and condensation, but she never learnt it. She needed to refine her sensibility in other ways too: to check her tendency to sentimentality. 'Summer Night' is typically banal:

> I lay alone upon the grass,
> All through a summer night,

And watched God's shining planets pass
Before my drowsy sight.

So small I felt me as I lay
Upon the dewy sod,
Yet knew myself, no less than they,
Important unto God.

Another lady whose work was given generous room in *The Chap-book* was Camilla Doyle. Her unpretentious and unremarkable observations of men and nature were expressed in conventional terms and ran to the sentimental. In 'The Six Aeroplanes' she fancied that the circling machines were doing honour to the poplar tree in her garden; in 'The Happy Ducks' she relished the delights of ducks who had a brook to swim upon.

Monro was amiably ready to see and encourage the littlest sign of talent, and the pressure of monthly publication coupled with his readers' demands for frequent issues of verse induced him to dilute the quality of the work published, so that some numbers do him little credit.

Three issues contained short dramatic pieces. F. M. Hueffer's *A House* (No. 21, March 1921) was nicely calculated to take Monro's fancy. It gives consciousness and character to man's domestic helpmates—among the characters are a farmhouse and its inmates, human, animal and inanimate. Monro's own one-acter, *One Day Awake* (No. 32, December 1922), was in prose, but its theme is a characteristic one, often handled in his verse. The habitual chattels of everyday life—The Morning Bed, The Breakfast Table, The Office Desk—are given voices and 'smoothly drawn on or off by mechanical methods'. 'A Morality without Moral', it owes a good deal to *Everyman* for its conception. John Smith, an office-worker, has 'one day awake', a day of heightened consciousness, in which he questions the habits, routines, and purposes of a lifetime, and questions his own identity, which is bound up in these things. Mr. Business, Mr. Traffic, Friends, Enemies, Amusement and Life are among the beings who come and pester him, and he narrowly escapes Death when, in the guise of a doctor, he calls at his house by mistake. The play ends with John Smith, temporarily reprieved from death, delightedly resuming his plaguey existence.

To stage it would be a fantastic jack-in-the-box feat. Yet in April 1923 we find M. Willson Disher, the dramatic critic, enquiring of Monro: 'Are you cherishing some ambitious production? Or would you be willing for a band of professional actors under an amateur organisation to do it?', and Monro replying that, though 'there are no readers for *One Day Awake* and we don't sell a copy', he was hoping to see it produced. More stageworthy was *Aria da Capo*, a brilliant little firework display, typical of one aspect of the period, by Edna St. Vincent Millay. The confection is light as air, and tends to reduce the whole of life to one level of triviality—which was, presumably, the playwright's intention.

The kind of audience to which *The Chapbook* in part appealed is hinted at in Monro's correspondence. Rejecting an essay sent in by Conrad Aiken in 1922, he said that it was 'rather too condensed and difficult for the kind of person who reads *The Chapbook* . . . your method and style assume your reader to be of rather more than average intelligence'.

The Chapbook would be better in 1923, he told Ezra Pound:

if I can get the support of contributors whom I really value. The public it appeals to is rather a difficult one, of course, being composed to a considerable extent of people who may be easily shocked and if I lose them, there will not be enough circulation to keep the things going. I shall have to take the risk however. On the whole perhaps, people rather like being shocked than otherwise.

In presenting *New American Poets* (*Chapbook* No. 36, April 1923) however, he overestimated their capacity to enjoy shock. On receiving the material from Alfred Kreymborg, the editor, Monro had reported himself 'entirely satisfied': the work was 'representative, diverse and controversial'.[1] But a proportion of the poems were

[1] This was a just comment on a selection of new and unpublished work by Robert Frost, Witter Bynner, William Carlos Williams, Babette

consciously experimental in form and not completely intelligible at a glance. *Punch* had some fun with it. It made many of Monro's readers angry and, he told Kreymborg,

> not with a useful kind of anger. Their view was that several of the poems consisted of superficial nonsense that ought never to have been printed. [Monro had] no doubt that the number, coming at the moment that it did, had a strong adverse effect on the circulation and prospects of *The Chapbook*.

The attempt to lead his public onward and outward while retaining their subscriptions was evidently a task of great delicacy.

The Chapbook's public would digest a modicum of critical discussion. Thus in February 1920, Douglas Goldring complained that criticism was dominated by a handful of individualists—Gosse, Murry, Squire, Eliot, Huxley—each working on his own principles, and he, inevitably, came to the conclusion that 'the real solution of our trouble lies in the re-discovery of a standard of values'. He had, however, no positive suggestions to offer. A similar *cri de cœur* came, in the next number, from Aldous Huxley, who thought that the 'chief need of poetry at the present time is a dose of astringent criticism of the kind once administered by the Scotch reviewers'.

In the same issue, T. S. Eliot and F. S. Flint offered partial and tentative answers to the questions: who is fitted to criticise poetry, and how should it be criticised? Eliot argued that only the poet was entitled to criticise poetry, but when he approached the problem of how it should be done, he abruptly side-stepped and, instead, drew a distinction between 'criticism' and 'reviewing' and proceeded to attack the latter.

Flint, on the other hand, sought a method of justifying his critical judgements, and made some experiments in textual analysis which anticipate the techniques of the 'new critics' of the later twenties. Before examining part of J. C. Squire's 'The Moon' and H.D.'s 'Sea Garden' he set down in a series of 'axioms' his belief that there is

---

Deutsch, Marianne Moore, Louis Untermeyer, Ridgely Torrence, Orrick Johns, John Gould Fletcher, E. E. Cummings, Jean Toomer, Wallace Stevens, Jean Starr Untermeyer, Conrad Aiken, Edna Millay, Louis Gruden and Alfred Kreymborg.

'but one art of writing, and that is the art of poetry'; that there is 'no difference in kind between prose and verse'; and that the requisites of good poetry' are 'sincerity, style and personality'. 'The test of poetry is sincerity, the test of sincerity is style; and the test of style is personality.'

Sincerity is a moral yardstick of dubious value in judging literary merit, and could be more appropriately displayed in a biographical than a textual study, however pertinacious. Nevertheless, axioms concluded, Flint proceeded to verify his impression that Squire's poem lacked 'personality, style and artistic sincerity' by inspecting the rhythm, syntax and diction of ten lines of it.

> Consider the phrases: *Asian peaks remote, dropt reflection, none but thou is tender*. The first contains an inversion of a kind which the author often uses to fit his metre or his rhyme. All inversions which are not the natural inversions of emotional stress are clumsy and inexcusable in modern poetry. The second is a contradiction in terms. Mr. Squire appears rather to pride himself upon his scientific allusions, and there is a biological reference in *The Moon* (320 *lines*); he might have applied his science here, for the light of the moon cannot in any sense be said to be dropt, still less its reflection by water. The third phrase is pedantically grammatical in one part and un-grammatical in another. . . .

and so on. The new technique of objective analysis is crude and rudimentary in its application, but is quite effective. Less effective is Flint's attempt to justify H.D.'s superiority by the same method: indeed he scarcely makes the attempt, and does little more than tell us that he knows what he likes. The original intention had been to examine the work of some ten different poets, and it is a pity that the plan was not carried out.

No. 27 (July 1922) offered the replies of twenty-seven men and women to three questions put to them by Monro, viz:

1. Do you think that poetry is a necessity to modern man?
2. What in modern life is the particular function of poetry as distinguished from other kinds of literature?

3. Do you think there is any chance of verse being eventually displaced by prose, as narrative poetry apparently is being by the novel, as ballads already have been by newspaper reports?

In an 'Introductory Apology', Monro explained that he was personally concerned to define poetry and to establish its function in contemporary society. Replies had come from about one third of the people canvassed, and Monro considered that he had approached too many writers, and not enough people in other walks of life. The authors interrogated had produced some dyspeptic rejoinders, which Monro was frank enough to quote—anonymously: 'Don't you think it's a little, shall we say, tactless of you to set such disconcerting conundrums to the producers of verse?' 'What a questionnaire for a man who is trying to forget books for a few days on Exmoor!' Others complained about the three-hundred-word limit placed on their replies, or (justly perhaps) objected to the looseness of the terms in which the questions were framed.

What most interested Monro was the diversity of opinion yielded by the questions, and he listed some of the replies to the first: whether poetry was a 'necessity' to modern man:

No—Yes, I think poetry is necessary to everybody . . . No— Yes—No art is ever a necessity. . . .—Yes— . . . always was and always will be . . .—No—Yes—No—Yes—No—Yes—a spiritual necessity . . . no longer makes an appeal . . . is a necessity to the complete man.

The general nature of the questions opened up echoing vistas of private interpretation, and each of the twenty-seven respondants took advantage of the fact. Monro was no doubt aware that this would happen, and wanted it to happen. We thus gain illuminating insight into the opinions and prejudices of, among others, Ezra Pound, T. S. Eliot, Ford Madox Hueffer, George Saintsbury, Robert Graves, Rose Macaulay, F. S. Flint, John Gould Fletcher, Holbrook Jackson, Laurence Binyon, John Freeman, Alec Waugh, Humbert Wolfe and 'a Plain Man'.

Professor Saintsbury showed academic discretion: 'Questions 1

and 2 are rather more general than such as I care to answer.'
Laura Raleigh, B.A. (Headmistress of Lilliecroft School) gave a
reassuring reply to Question 1: 'From long experience I can say confidently that those girls who are more susceptible of [*sic*] the beauties of poetry are the most docile and least likely to cause anxiety
. . .' She had also found that girls forbidden by their parents to read
the war-news, and nourished instead on 'our ancient balladry'
proved themselves 'more fitting helpmates for those whose task
has been the reconstruction of a world laid in ruins by Armaged-
don'.

Mr. Eliot's replies were laconic: '1. No. 2. Takes up less space. 3.
It is up to the poets to find something to do in verse which cannot
be done in any other form.' Pound, equally characteristically, ex-
panded his first answers, which were very brief ('1. No. Neither is
modern man a necessity. 2. What it always has been. 3. No. . . .'),
and made the occasion an excuse for a volcanic attack on 'modern
civilisation and the British literary world'.

Interesting as the replies were, they need not detain us further:
they show, as might be expected, that among literary people poetry
was still being offered reverence, as to a phenomenon beyond
human comprehension, though the contemporary interest in psychology led some writers to state their difficulty in terms of the
unconscious mind.

Two months later Harold Monro endorsed Aldington's opinion
that 'some of our poetry is "incoherent", and yet more of it "stag-
nant"; that "the poets of this generation . . . have not yet been able
to develop more than a fraction of their poetical potentialities" '.
The literary world was, it seemed, filled with the spirit of Advent,
and the publication of 'The Waste Land' in October 1922 produced
a variety of reactions among the expectant. In America, *The Dial*
awarded the author its annual prize of two hundred dollars; in
England it was treated generally with indignation and contempt.
In 'Notes for a Study of The Waste Land', Monro conducted an
imaginary interview with Eliot. Though the poet was made to
behave with insufferable arrogance throughout the interview,
Monro was plainly impressed by the poem, and rated it 'as near

Poetry as our generation is at present capable of reaching'. 'The Waste Land' was the fulfilment of lesser poets' strivings:

> Those poor little people who string together their disjointed ejaculations into prosaic semblances of verse—they pale as one reads 'The Waste Land'. They have no relation to it, yet, through it, we realise what they were trying, but have failed, to represent. Our epoch sprawls, a desert, between an unrealised past and an unimaginable future. 'The Waste Land' is one metaphor with a multiplicity of interpretations.

Monro condoned Eliot's use of literary echo, with a proviso: 'What we have to find out is whether T. S. Eliot is a sufficiently constructive or imaginative, or ingenious poet to justify this freedom that he exercises.'

Monro was still, in later years, adding a proviso to his acknowledgement of Eliot's genius. In 1929, in the Introduction to *Twentieth Century Poetry*, he conceded, with a hint of ambiguity, that 'To-day we have each our Waste Land', and, according to Conrad Aiken, believed that the poem was destined to become 'a twentieth-century "Kubla Khan" with the same sort of talismanic glitter, fragmented or fragmentary, and perhaps without final profundity in scale or idea . . . and therefore minor'.[1]

In *Chapbook* No. 4 (October 1919) F. S. Flint provided, in *Some French Poets of To-day*, a commentary on five years of French poetry concerned almost exclusively with war.[2]

To Flint war was an obscenity, and he selected his poets accordingly:

> War verse which is mere foaming at the mouth, or worse, expectoration, I do not touch. The curious will find all they may want of this in a volume called *Les Poètes de la Guerre*, which was renamed by the *Mercure de France* 'Les plus mauvais vers de la guerre'.

[1] *Ushant*, p. 258.
[2] The work of twenty-three poets was discussed and illustrated, including Jean Cocteau, Guillaume Apollinaire, Jules Romains, André Spire, Paul Claudel and the Belgians Jean de Bosschère and Emile Verhaeren.

This essay bridged the gap made when Flint's French Chronicles ceased with *Poetry and Drama* in December 1914; it was followed in November 1920 (*Chapbook* No. 17) by *The Younger French Poets*, by the same author. These essays were valuable in presenting work virtually unknown in England. Dadaism, that extreme form of verbal expressionism, was illustrated by liberal quotations from Tristan Tzara and other Dadaist poets. Flint regarded their productions partly as a hoax upon the public, and their claim to new depths of psychological abandonment as no more than 'skimming the scum off the refining cauldron and offering it as a sample of purity and sweetness'.

John Gould Fletcher's *Some Contemporary American Poets* (*Chapbook* No. 11, May 1920) gave English readers, who regarded transatlantic poetry with patronising complacency, a much-needed interpretation of ten writers, from E. A. Robinson onwards, viewing them against their national and regional background. For example E. A. Robinson, Robert Frost and Amy Lowell were treated as the diverse products of New England culture; Edgar Lee Masters, Carl Sandberg and Vachel Lindsay represented the Middle West. Ezra Pound was included, where other exiles were omitted, on the ground that he had never acquired 'the completely cosmopolitan European outlook', and remained 'actually provincial'. This survey did something to correct the illusion of the English reader (about which Fletcher had complained in a *London Mercury* article in 1920) that Vachel Lindsay was the only serious modern American poet. It was the first competent account of American poetry to appear in England for a very long time.

Thus the critical contents of *The Chapbook* conformed with its character as a light literary miscellany. The discussion of foreign work was usefully informative, the critical papers readily digested and only mildly provocative.

The Chapbook struggled with financial difficulties, for which Monro largely blamed the proliferation of periodicals. Early in 1921 Alfred Kreymborg sent him a copy of *Broom*, an 'international magazine of the arts published by Americans in Italy', and Monro replied thus:

I am always regretting that there are so many periodicals. I think the public is rather tired of them at present. . . . I do think, however, that if all writers were to collaborate more, and to contribute freely to some of the existing papers that have gone through all the effort of establishing their reputations, there would be a gain both to them and the public. As I was one of the first of the present era in the field with *The Poetry Review* in 1912 perhaps my feelings are prejudiced on the subject. Then there were not enough magazines that would accept experimental, daring or even merely interesting stuff: now I think there are too many and that strength is loss [*sic*] therethrough.

A month earlier he told another correspondent that if only a few hundred more copies of *The Chapbook* could be sold it would be a thriving affair. In the issue of June 1923 he explained the position to his readers: with a circulation of one thousand, *The Chapbook* showed a monthly deficit of twenty-five pounds. A fifty per cent increase in sales was needed to balance the accounts. An alternative solution was to stop paying contributors, for disbursements to them came to almost exactly twenty-five pounds a month—but it was impossible to get work from any but 'literary beginners' on those terms.

In sad and angry bitterness he wrote:

What a number of meretricious or wicked things exist upon the earth: false drugs; quack critics; bogus companies; Sunday newspapers; Outlines of Literature and Art! Millions of people support these, and we only need 500. Hundreds of people earn thousands of pounds through them and we are not asking to earn anything, but rather to be allowed to give something away and not for the virtue, but for the pleasure.[1]

The six numbers for the next half year would have to be amalgamated into one volume, to appear in November 1923. In fact, nothing more appeared till the annual volume in October 1924.

[1] 'Editorial', p. 3.

Some reluctance to contribute is hinted at in his reference there to 'the absence of contributions from at least half-a-dozen writers and two or three artists whose inclusion had appeared to him essential to the scheme of the number'. This number, like the succeeding one for 1925, contained graphic design of fine quality, but the tone of its written contents was displeasingly flaccid and 'pleasant'. Eliot's 'Doris's Dream Songs' and Monro's 'Midnight Lamentation' and 'The Earth for Sale' gave a note of astringency. The 1925 volume was more fully representative of the time.[1] It is a tribute to the general esteem in which Monro was held by the writers of his day that so many rallied round and put in an appearance—though not always a very creditable one—in the last issue of *The Chapbook*.

More than a twelvemonth later, in December 1926, John Gould Fletcher wrote to Monro: '. . . there is a curious integrity of purpose in you that I like and admire extremely, and I feel sure that neither *The Chapbook* nor the Poetry Bookshop ought to perish.' But the annual volume for 1925 was, in fact, to be the last, though Monro could not anticipate this, and so the series lacks a funeral oration. When Fletcher wrote to say that he believed he could raise funds in the United States for an American or Anglo-American number, Monro replied:

> . . . a year or two ago this would have been very acceptable news. Now, however, I have not the heart to revive *The Chapbook*. I had thought of bringing out one more number this spring and had kept certain manuscripts pending a final decision. These I think I shall now have to return or offer to Eliot for *The Criterion*. I think, as a matter of fact, *The Chapbook* may have had its day though I have not any doubt that I could not have resisted your offer if only I had better health and eyesight. Actually what I propose to do is to go away for a longish rest.

[1] With work by Leonard Woolf, Peter Quennell, Conrad Aiken ('Sea Holly'), H.D., Wyndham Lewis, Richard Aldington, Thomas Sturge Moore, Siegfried Sassoon, Padraic Colum, Robert Graves, Herbert Read, Osbert Sitwell, Sacheverell Sitwell, Aldous Huxley and Harold Monro among others.

Subsidised from Monro's private purse, *The Chapbook* survived longer than any other small literary magazine of the 'twenties. Towards the end of production, Monro's hope for it was merely that 'its patrons may let it lie decoratively on their tables for a few months, and that it may provide them with entertainment sufficient for the moment'.[1] It did in fact maintain a delicate balance between culture and entertainment which made it unique in its time. It set no trends in writing, nor did it seek to do so. It provided a useful outlet for verse of many kinds. The original intention, to form a survey and conspectus of the passing years, was partly fulfilled: the *Chapbooks* jointly are a mirror reflecting the uncertain lights of seven restless, anti-climactic post-war years.

3

THE FINAL PHASE

From 1926 onwards, Monro was afflicted with the eye-trouble to which he refers in the letter quoted above. As a result, his widow suspects, of his being allowed to smoke his pipe immediately after a sinus operation, nicotine poisoning led rapidly to atrophy of the optic nerve. His vision was so much reduced that he was unable to read ordinary print, or ordinary handwriting, and Mrs. Monro copied out his lecture-notes in a gigantic script. He took advice from leading Continental doctors and by the time of his death the condition of his eyes was greatly improved and he was able to read with comfort. But for a time he was wearing spectacles with heavy metal frames and lenses not much bigger than a pinhead.

His commission to compile *Twentieth Century Poetry*, in Chatto and Windus's *Phoenix Anthologies* series, was a ray of light, and he put much thought and work into its preparation. It promised to be 'rather an important book', he wrote to Edward Marsh on receiving the commission, and a little later confessed to J. C. Squire, 'I am taking this anthology tremendously seriously and spending too

[1] 'Apology', *Chapbook* No. 39 (1924), p. 6.

much time on it.' Assisted by Mrs. Monro, he read or re-read about six hundred volumes, avoiding anthology-pieces; the Introduction states, 'I have tried to find, and rejoiced when I could find, some excellent qualities in poets in whom I did not expect them.' On the other hand Herman Ould recalled 'the smile, slightly sardonic, with which he told me how difficult it had been to retain even two or three poems by poets whose work is normally regarded as impeccable. He showed me three poems by a well-known author which he had first included. On a second reading he had had to eliminate one of them; on a third reading, yet another; and in the final winnowing, even the third had to go: "It didn't *have* to be written".'[1] Towards the end, he told Richard Aldington, he found his taste 'beginning to wobble. . . . I went back to the poems that I had chosen at the beginning and found myself simply obliged to stick to the first decisions in case of having to begin all over again . . .' The volume, properly, represents only twentieth-century British poetry, but admits Hopkins, Davidson, Eliot, H.D. and Pound on other grounds. The selection from the editor's own poems was made by 'an impartial judge', Alida Klemantaski.

One would imagine that by this date the behaviour of poets could hold no more surprises for him, but he remarked to J. C. Squire on

> the extraordinary experience I went through in any case where I consulted a poet himself. . . . You yourself more or less approved my choice but then mentioned poems that you thought very much better, to which I accordingly turned, and found them without any shadow of doubt most definitely inferior to those I had selected. I must say that I consulted very few authors for the same thing happened in any case where I did.
>
> It was an excessively difficult anthology to compile, particularly with regard to fees and I was glad of your generosity.[2]
> As to the contents, you will see that you and I can be in agree-

---

[1] *Shuttle* (London, 1947), p. 310.
[2] 'You can have whatever you life for a fiver,' Squire had written. 'This is below my usual price, but I'm not going to handicap an old friend who is doing a job like this.'

ment only with regard to about half of it. Nevertheless, looking at it now from an outside point of view, I cannot help feeling that it is rather an unusual book and in that sense it seems to me legitimately to represent rather an unusual period in literature'.

Ezra Pound wrote kindly:

Good preface; and bk. worth having for Ger. Hopkins Leaden Echo and the Charlotte Mew. . . . Sorry ole Plarr not in; but recognise period. Praps you have somewhat melted off the edges of yr. image? of the age??

However, very difficult to decide. I mean what to include. And more edge wd. have made it less acceptable to the brish booblik

I spose its in plates? not sure whether dates of birth (and death if any) wdn't. be worth adding.

First effect rather that of usual god damn sugarloaf of brish poesy; but one wears through that with patience.

Oh well; considering how ready I wd. be to tell you HELL I cd. have done it much better; I daresay you can accept this tribute in the friendly spirit intended.

When you do the supplement Ill give you some unasked advice as to how to liven and leven it.

Good strong antimilitarist vein, also worth printing. Yrs. EP.

Monro sought 'to ensure that our intrinsic period might be fully portrayed', and the book runs the gamut of styles from Gerard Manley Hopkins, Ezra Pound and T. S. Eliot to John Masefield, Padraic Colum and Humbert Wolfe. The scales tip heavily against prolific traditionalists like Robert Nichols, John Freeman and Alfred Noyes, each of whom is represented by one poem. Robert Bridges, whose artistic integrity Monro respected, is well represented, while W. S. Blunt, 'Michael Field' and Anna Wickham, who were among his personal favourites, are given more space than they probably deserve. The 'good strong antimilitaristic vein' noticed by Pound helps to give the book its distinctive flavour. It is a sombre book. The visitor from Mars, searching in its pages for the character of life on this planet, would conclude that it was brooded over by conflict and frustration and the dread of death, and would head his spacecraft home again. Monro has been attracted to poems whose themes strike a sympathetic chord in his own heart. Alfred Noyes, one of his *bêtes noires*, is represented by 'Seagulls on the Serpentine', a poem about racial memory whose last stanza (except for the touch of silliness in the final phrase) embodies a favourite idea of Monro's:

> Oh, why are you so afraid? We are all of us exiles!
> Wheel back in your clamorous rings!
> We have all of us lost the sea, and we all remember.
> But you—have wings.

Eden Philpott's 'Litany to Pan' is an uncharacteristic effusion on nature's savagery and wastefulness. Adroit selection from J. C. Squire has yielded three poems, two of which are untouched by neo-Georgianism. Seven poems by Thomas Hardy set the note of sophisticated perplexity which dominates this adult and interesting collection, which has the dryness of a very dry wine.

The book was a success and, Monro told Pound in January 1930, had sold an average of a thousand copies a week since publication the previous November. This edition was reprinted four times, and was followed in 1933 by a new edition revised and enlarged by Alida Monro, of which there have again been four reprints, the final issue being in 1950.

Monro had an active connection with *The Criterion*, and some of the '*Criterion* dinners' were held at 38 Great Russell Street. Six of his poems were printed in the paper, and between 1924 and 1930 he contributed occasional book-reviews which show a sophisticated knowledge of modern poetry, and are written with care, confidence and considerable panache. *The Criterion* also accepted one of his short stories. There are drafts of short stories among Monro's early papers, most of them touched with a macabre and slightly sick fantasy. In 1919 a story of his, 'Parcel of Love', appeared in *The Little Review*. It is in a similar vein—a psychological fantasy where a man burdened with love resolves to end his pain by tying up his love with paper and string and casting it away. Running to a river-side with his parcel in his arms he hurls it in—and himself with it. The story is rapidly and economically told, and the symbolism is imaginatively exciting.

In 1930 Monro wrote to *The English Review*:

> I have been trying my hand lately at short-story writing and have finished with four or five, three or four of which have still to be revised. They have an unfortunate habit of finishing up with a death or a suicide. I did not know that little events of this kind were still objected to and I have had to have a few MSS returned from periodicals solely on the grounds of a sad ending. . . .

He enclosed a story, but *The English Review* did not print it. In 1928, however, *The Criterion* had been kinder, taking 'A True Adventure at Dawn', which is the recitation of a dream, with the hallucinatory quality of his best poetry. Walking with a female companion he encounters a friend, Basil, whom he knows to be long since dead—killed in the War. (The dream clearly relates to his friend Basil Watt, whose return he had imagined in 'Lament in 1915 (B.H.W.)'.) Basil addresses the lady, while avoiding contact with Monro. He leads them through some cottages that were

> . . . not real. Their sham fronts rattled and swayed like stage-scenery as we closed the door. Out behind were great stretches of downs, and to the right a drop over high cliffs towards the sea.

There is an extended agony of vertiginous cliff-climbing where the three characters are fixed in obscurely symbolic relationship. The nightmare ends with a cliff-fall—Monro falling, while Basil stands menacingly and invitingly on the shore below, and the woman is poised above with her hair waving in the wind. Monro's occasional ventures into fiction confirm that his bent was towards psychological inwardness.

The Bookshop's finances were an anxiety. 'It is very difficult to make two ends meet', Monro told Amy Lowell in May 1924. 'If only we had about a thousand American customers with credit accounts who would order books regularly here. . . .' A young man of twenty-two, A. S. J. Tessimond, offered two hundred to two hundred and fifty pounds to help the shop, but Monro was obliged to reject it as too small a sum to be of any use:

> . . . if someone were to suggest coming in with one thousand or two thousand pounds, such a sum would be sufficient to give the business a new lease of life. . . . It will be a struggle to get through this year, but I am fairly confident we shall get through.

In 1926 the lease on 35 Devonshire Street expired and, helped by a loan from Monro's mother, the shop was moved to new premises at 38 Great Russell Street, almost opposite the British Museum.[1] It was very soon found necessary to remove into the back part of the premises, with its entrance on Willoughby Street, and to let the front rooms to Messrs. Kegan Paul. The readings were continued in a room that already existed behind the building. The new shop had a less romantic location and less architectural charm, and the magic of the old Devonshire Street premises was never recaptured.

Some of the pioneering spirit had gone. Announcing the shop's

---

[1] *The Daily Chronicle* reported that the interior of the shop 'in vivid pinks and purples—strikes a distinctive note both in the use of primary colours and in the artistic way in which it is set out', and went on to describe 'a Futuristic shop-sign' (designed by McKnight Kauffer) showing an illuminated book and a lyre. About 13 inches by 2 inches in size, it hung from a protruding bracket, and the method of its hanging incurred the displeasure of the landlord, the Duke of Bedford, who also objected to the bright red window-frames, and demanded 'a putty-colour, to conform with the rest of the block of buildings'. One can but sympathise.

closure in a later year, Mrs. Monro wrote that whereas in 1913 modern poetry was hardly known, by 1935 there was hardly a bookseller who was 'not forced to keep more poetry on his shelves than he would have thought possible all those years ago'. Thus the Bookshop's decline was in part the measure of its achievement, though Monro's deteriorating health was certainly a contributory factor. In September 1931 Monro described the Bookshop's critical state to Lascelles Abercrombie, who had made some offer of assistance:

> I am going for eye treatment to Germany for a week or two. Meanwhile, the situation here becomes more and more alarming. We are cutting down expenses in every possible way and are in fact vacating the Reading Room on the 29th Sept. and restoring the party wall. This is a great blow as it detracts from the original character of the shop. We shall have to make arrangements to hold readings outside, but people actually expect to come to them on the premises. Also, when they have to go outside, they usually do not hang about on the premises and are even less likely to buy books.
>
> How little I want to worry you I leave you to imagine. In fact, please don't let me do so. But, as you have made a generous gesture, I feel perhaps I am not going too far in letting you know that matters are becoming rather urgent.

Less than a year later, on 16 March 1932, Monro died in a nursing-home at Broadstairs after a prolonged and distressing illness.

Mrs. Monro kept the shop going for more than three years after her husband's death, but in June 1935 informed customers in a circular letter that she was forced to close it:

> The Poetry Bookshop has been in existence for over twenty-one years and during the whole of that time it has depended for its survival on the physical and financial help that we were able to give it. For some time before he died, my husband and I frequently discussed the future of the Poetry Bookshop and had come to the conclusion that when interest in its work fell

below a certain level it must close its doors. For the past five years, I have been trying to persuade myself that the moment had not come. To-day I am unable to deny that it has arrived.

The closure of the Poetry Bookshop removed from the London literary scene a well-known and well-loved landmark. It was the product of a period of exceptional responsiveness to poetry—the years immediately preceding the First World War when, in the words of Rose Macaulay, 'there seemed a kind of poetry-intoxication going about'.[1] Once launched, the Poetry Bookshop carried on through the 'twenties, its delicate mission made more urgent as poet and public slipped further and further apart. The Bookshop, however, was the brain-child of a man nourished on Shellyean idealism and later-nineteenth-century utopianism, and the time was bound to come when the new century's spirit passed it by. Monro just escaped seeing that time come.

A remark made by William Plomer in 1955, thirty years after the shop's closure, makes an appropriate epitaph: 'I should think better of London if it still had the Poetry Bookshop.'[2]

[1] 'Coming to London—xiii', *London Magazine* IV (March 1957), p. 34-35.
[2] 'Coming to London—i', *London Magazine*, II (June 1955), p. 42.

6

Monro's Poetry—I

1

Harold Monro's reputation as a poet has chiefly depended, during his lifetime and since, on his representation in anthologies. His repeated appearances in the *Georgian* anthologies, and his association with the series as its publisher, has led to the easy assumption that he was a 'Georgian poet', and to his sharing in the critical hostility which for the last forty years that handy but imprecise term has provoked. On the strength of such pieces as 'Milk for the Cat', 'Dog' and 'Week-end' he has been dismissed as a domesticated traditionalist, writing with homely realism or sentimental whimsy of his pets and his rustic joys. Other anthologists, however, have chosen from his later work, and in such poems as 'Living', 'Midnight Lamentation' or 'Bitter Sanctuary', have revealed Monro as an unhappy human being groping nervously towards the expression of his inner life. Thus we are left with the impression of a chameleon-like poet, which a fuller study of his work partly resolves, partly confirms.

Access to his work has not been easy. Since the *Collected Poems* of 1933, there has been one selected edition, prepared by his widow —*The Silent Pool and Other Poems*, printed with war-time austerity in 1942. Messrs. Duckworth and Co., however, intend issuing a new edition, prefaced by a memoir by Mrs. Monro, and the public will have a better chance to appraise a poet whose work T. S. Eliot described in 1933 as 'more near the real right thing than any of the poetry of a somewhat older generation than mine except Mr. Yeats's'.[1]

Eliot's generous—at first sight surprisingly generous—estimate of Monro's poetry proceeds from his acceptance of it as 'one variety of the infinite number of possible expressions of tortured human consciousness'. Monro's work must be approached with this attitude of attentive and compassionate interest in the poet as an individual: perhaps not surprisingly, his work is best judged by criteria similar to his own.

Stylistically, Monro does not excel. His development was slow, and he never came to the end of a difficult apprenticeship to the craft of poetry. The apparent ease of style which he commanded in his early, derivative poems disappeared as soon as he sought a personal mode of expression. Too often he is 'all fingers and thumbs', and his work, in Paul Nash's words, 'an interesting fumble'.[2] His patient trials were rewarded in the end, however, by the partial revelation of his proper language, but before he fully mastered it—he died.

Among twentieth-century poets Monro takes a median position, with one hand held out to the Georgians, and one to the moderns, though it becomes increasingly apparent with the years that the Georgians have hold of his left hand merely. Had he survived through the thirties, his sympathies would probably have stirred him to join the new young poets in protest. Had he done so, he would have struck an isolated and rather forlorn pose, a pose fully characteristic of his career both as a poet and as a man among men. Monro's central theme, and his best claim to our attention, is his sense of personal loneliness and alienation. The theme is perennial, but it was felt with fresh poignancy in an age of anarchic standards, and by a man doomed to be in, but never quite of, the literary society around him.

In the chapters that follow I make what is in fact the first attempt to discuss Monro's poetry in any detail and at any length. The method of handling the material required some thought. There was

[1] 'Critical Note', *Collected Poems of Harold Monro*, p. xvi.
[2] Quoted by C. Aiken, *Ushant*, p. 256.

168

a temptation to base the discussion on certain significant themes in Monro's verse, and thus to produce the poet as an interesting individual, a 'tortured human consciousness'. But this seemed too partial and particular an approach for a preliminary study of this kind. It was necessary to find a framework into which a wide range of commentary could more easily be fitted. A volume-by-volume treatment of the work seemed the most appropriate. This emphasised the internal changes and developments in Monro's poetry, and at the same time made it possible and easy to view his work in relation to its day. It had, also, the lesser advantages of recognising Monro's personal selection and arrangement, and of making reference to the text a simple matter for the reader.[1] The result is a general survey and a general assessment.

2

EARLY POEMS AND 'CHILDREN OF LOVE'

Monro's first publication, the *Poems* which came out in Elkin Mathew's 'Vigo Cabinet Series' in 1906 represented, he said, 'some thirtieth part' of all he had produced since he began writing in 1896. Its remarkable mastery of technique indicates the extent of his early experiment; and its tendency to ventriloquism shows that his reading was, in certain areas, intensive.

'Clytie' is an act of homage to Keats. It is first-class apprentice-work: there is no bathos, no awkwardness, nothing to mar the vapid smoothness of the metre:

> Then on the twilight world there fell a hush,
>
> As if Eternity her hand had raised
>
> To lull the world; the brooks, the foliage lush,
>
> The birds were silent; Time stood still, as dazed

[1] The *Collected Poems* (1933) reproduces the complete contents of *Judas, Children of Love, Strange Meetings, Real Property* and *The Earth for Sale*, and includes a selection from *Before Dawn*. In addition it contains a number of poems which had previously appeared only in periodicals, and thirty never before printed.

Till those two throbbing hearts should be set free,
And come together in quick harmony.

Two more long poems on classical themes—'Ariadne in Naxos',
and 'Pausanias'—show unusual metrical facility, and are close
imitations of Keats. Two slight album-pieces, six Shakespearean
sonnets, an apostrophe to the sun and the earth ('A Song at Dawn)',
an impressionistic poem about a garden ('A Colour-Dream'), some
anapaestic stanzas on a mountain river, show, variously, the influence of Shelley, Keats, Shakespeare and Spenser. The obviously
painstaking labour that has gone into adjusting the diction and
metre proves that the author is an earnest craftsman, but nothing
in the volume suggests impatience with convention.

Next, and in marked contrast, came *Judas* (1907), an extended
poem in blank verse, prefaced with the ambiguous announcement,
'I have written this poem believing in Jesus of Nazareth'. The
pleasant inanities of the previous volume give way to unmitigated
gloom, stridency and darkness:

> . . . I touched his sleeve,
> He looked half up and murmured through his teeth,
> 'I count my shekels', then 'one, two, three, four'—
> To thirty counted. Each was stained with blood.
> Lo! as he ceased, the silence of the plain
> Suddenly like a whirlwind gathered up,
> And broke in one convulsive human shriek,
> Trembling and flashing in white agony,
> And died .   .   .   .   .
>
>   .   .   .   .   .
>
> And then athwart the still air eagerly
> Big drops fell, few at first and very large,
> Then more—but they were hot, and more again—
> But they were red;—the hissing air was red. . . .

Judas, encountered in some infernal hinterland between waking
and dream, relates his story, the story of a pushful materialist with

a quicksilver temperament who was broken in the attempt to serve a spiritual genius whom he loved but could not comprehend. Though it owes an obvious debt to James Thomson, *Judas* is a poem of some force and independence, reflecting Monro's personal gloom and his rejection of orthodox belief.

The publication of *Before Dawn* (*Poems and Impressions*) (1911), bound in stiff covers, the bulkiest book of verse Monro ever produced, solemnly affirmed his wish to be taken seriously as a poet. Agony went into its composition, anxiety into its bringing forth, and a flurry of disappointment followed upon its bad reception. The terms in which the critics condemned it were peculiarly galling: 'The general complaint', Monro told Maurice Browne, 'seems that most of it would have been better expressed in prose.' Substantiating this by quotations from Edward Thomas (a private letter) and H. G. Wells (a review in *The Morning Post*), he went on:

> What does all this mean? I am writing 'Cophetua' in prose to see. Perhaps it's chiefly true. Perhaps I'm not (metrically speaking at any rate) a poet. And yet why did all those things come to life for me as poetry, and why had I to write them down as such? Perhaps a mere habit of expression from which I shall do best to clear myself for freedom of delivery. At any rate all these devils have quite stopped me writing verse for the moment.

Monro might have expected critical censure, for a number of the poems were written in conscious defiance of convention, at least as far as their subject-matter was concerned. There were many unchallenging romantic pieces emitting the stale sweetness of *pot pourri*. Meditating above Lake Leman, joining in with a country dance in Provence, panting after the Ideal, Monro hied along in the wake of a hundred other sensitive souls. Long practice had given him a smooth competence at this kind of writing, and effectively cleared these poems of the charge that they 'would have been better expressed in prose'. That charge, it becomes clear, was levelled at

Monro's efforts to handle distasteful subjects—pain, wretchedness, evil—without making concessions to the popular preference for 'beauty' in poetry.

The book's dedication suggested the windy utopianism common at the time:

> I dedicate this book to those who, with me, are gazing in delight towards where on the horizon there shall be dawn.
> Henceforth, together, humble though fearless, we must praise, worship, and obey the beautiful Future, which alone we may call God.

But in fact, there is less of jubilant optimism in *Before Dawn* than of gloomy rumination on what is amiss with the world. The poems are the product of a morosely introspective young man, self-exiled, with a depressing record of associations that proved abortive, and with no fixed plans for the future.

That reason, will and action are good, unreason, escapism and inertia bad are notions reiterated in the book. Stylistically convention holds the poet in a Laocoön-like embrace. The titles of 'The Moon-Worshippers' and 'Strand of Oblivion' indicate their placid subservience to old formulas. Romantic manners and uses compel Monro to inflated and prolonged utterance, and the ratio of thought to words is depressingly low. But still there are hints of the poet whose interest was centred in 'the spectres and the "bad dreams" which live inside the skull'.[1] The amorphous monsters of 'Two Visions' have a hideous vitality in spite of the *terza rima:*

> Two visions came to me. At drear midnight,
>   When first I laid my weary head adown,
> The chamber filled with chasms on my sight,
>
> And the wide darkness gathered in a frown;
>   And I, who had dreamed wonders through the long
> Sweet daylight of that last enduring crown

[1] T. S. Eliot, 'Critical Note', *Collected Poems of Harold Monro*, p. xv.

Humanity, the subtle and the strong,
  Should wear as in fulfilment on his brow,
Was haunted by the phantoms that belong

To deepest living Hell. From high to low
  The sultry room was gradually filled
As with vague matter, that began to flow

Into some form, irresolutely willed,
  And palpitating while it gathered shape,
Floated, then sank and groaned; rose, chattered
                    and trilled;

Broke in stark faces, mouths and eyes agape;
  Then shrank again and indolently slept;
Then sprang with guttural noises of the ape

And so on for twenty-eight stanzas.

Here and elsewhere one sees the influence of James Thomson. Monro set considerable store by 'The Swamp', a repulsive poem set in a Breughel-like hell-scene, which shows no squeamishness in handling distasteful imagery. There are other small signs of an unequal struggle between convention and individuality. Mrs. Grundy was defied a little: 'Don Juan in Hell' was a 'very scandalous poem', which the Poetry Recital Society would certainly veto, he told Browne; and again: ' "The Virgin" has caused quite an excitement among those who have seen it so far. Women usually rage against it.'[1]

Faith in the future was off-set by disgust with the present. There was a harsh anti-clerical, sceptical vein of thought, and bitter strictures on contemporary types who to Monro represented social evil. Among the twenty-three 'impressions' which occupy the second part of the volume, is a series of lampoons on the callous plutocrat, the flinty-hearted factory-owner, the vapid young man of good breeding, the idle glutton, the hypocritical philanthropist,

[1] (8 March 1910; 24 July 1911) Maurice Browne Collection, University of Michigan.

the heartless seducer. The potency of the satire is reduced by the bitter, almost hysterical tone of attack; and one tires of the monotonous quatrains. But the poems represent a new departure, an attempt at social comment very unlike the romantic languors of the 1906 volume.

Behind this book was the wish to bring poetry face to face with 'life'—the impulse which, in the same year, brought 'The Everlasting Mercy' and Brooke's *Poems* (some of them 'unpleasant') before a shocked but stimulated public. Life in its nastier aspects offered to the poet who was in reaction against 'poetic' themes an abundance of material.

Infinite leisure and solitariness had encouraged the verbosity, the idealism and the bitterness of *Before Dawn*. But in 1911 Monro's life entered a new phase. His ideals were finding some fulfilment in the foundation and running of *The Poetry Review, Poetry and Drama* and the Poetry Bookshop, and he was in stimulating contact with every kind of poet. All this is reflected in his next volume, *Children of Love* (1914). A small collection of sixteen poems—his output during the preceding three years had been limited by the pressure of his other activities and perhaps by a more rigorous self-criticism—its most striking feature is its diversity. There is no homogeneity of style, little of idea, unless it is the vein of radicalism, though this is less pronounced than in *Before Dawn*.

The diversity can be very clearly seen in the divergence between the pieces which open and close the book. The title-poem, 'Children of Love', is an allegorical tableau: the child Jesus meets the child Cupid in a landscape borrowed from a quattrocento Florentine painting:

> The holy boy
> Went from his mother out in the cool of the day
> Over the sun-parched fields
> And in among the olives shining green and shining grey.

· · · · ·

> Suddenly came
> Running along to him naked, with curly hair,
> That rogue of the lovely world,
> That other beautiful child whom the virgin Venus bare.

The meeting is a pretty fancy; but the conduct of these Botticellian babes is heavy with moral implications which are made explicit—a vice of Monro's—in a parenthesis:

> (Will you not play?
> Jesus, run to him, run to him, swift for our joy.
> Is he not holy, like you?
> Are you afraid of his arrows, O beautiful dreaming boy?)

Jesus cannot see any fun in this sort of thing and, dropping 'for the sadness of life' a compassionate tear upon Cupid's cheek, withdraws.

Nowhere else in Monro do we meet the blend of mawkishness and rhetoric found in the following stanza, with its knowing apostrophe to humankind, and its affected use of the definite article and of the perfect tense to give a suggestion of timeless significance to the scene:

> Cupid at last
> Draws his bow and softly lets fly a dart.
> Smile for a moment, sad world!—
> It has grazed the white skin and drawn blood from the
>   sorrowful heart.

Almost defiantly out of touch with new trends in verse, 'Children of Love' is given the place of honour in the book. With its suave imagery and carefully managed rhythms, it was a piece of craftsmanship which Monro felt confidence in presenting.

The poem which closes the book, 'The Strange Companion (A Fragment)', also describes an encounter, and again it is an 'unreal' one; but this time the colloquy takes place inside the skull and bears the marks of painful experience. Fragmentary and imperfect as the poem is, in terms of Monro's poetic evolution it is the most important in the book, for he discovers here an effective symbolism in which to represent internal happenings. The furtive, shambling little man who attaches himself to the poet anticipates the half-discovered presences in Monro's later poems of introspection.

The 'strange companion', half liked and half loathed, is the inherent weakness that betrays him into booze. ' "I have known this long, long while, all there is to know of you",' says the little man, catching his victim at a moment of lowered vitality.

> That strange companion came on shuffling feet,
> Passed me, then turned, and touched my arm.
> He said (and he was melancholy,
> And both of us looked fretfully,
> And slowly we advanced together)
> He said: 'I bring you your inheritance'.
>
> I watched his eyes; they were dim,
> I doubted him, watched him, doubted him. . . .
> But, in a ceremonious way,
> He said: 'You are too grey:
> Come, you must be merry for a day'.
>
> And I, because my heart was dumb,
> Because the life in me was numb,
> Cried: 'I will come. I *will* come'.

Off they go on a jogging course:

> So, without another word,
> We two jaunted on the street.
> I had heard, often heard,
> The shuffling of those feet of his,
> The shuffle of his feet.
>
> And he muttered in my ear
> Such a wheezy jest
> As a man may often hear—
> Not the worst, not the best
> That a man may hear.

176

Their miserable cohabitation is punctured by the victim's forlorn attempts at self-justification:

> We lived together long, long.
> We were always alone, he and I.
> We never smiled with each other;
> We were like brother and brother,
> Dimly accustomed.
>   Can a man know
> Why he must live, or whether he should go?

> He brought me that joke or two,
> And we roared with laughter, for want of a smile,
> As every man in the world might do.
> He who lies all night in bed
> Is a fool, and midnight will crush his head.

The adventure hurries on down in stunted, unco-ordinated rhythms to bellicosity, maudlin sentiment and moral incapacity:

> When he threw a glass of wine in my face
> One night, I hit him, and we parted;
> But in a short space
> We came back to each other melancholy hearted,
> Told our pain,
> Swore we would not part again.

> One night we turned a table over
> The body of some slain fool to cover,
> And all the company clapped their hands;
> So we spat in their faces,
> And travelled away to other lands.

The poem ends with the perverse wish that every man might find

> A strange companion so
> Completely to his mind
> With whom he everywhere may go.

A manuscript version, however, adds another stanza, ridding the

poem of any obscurity, and pointing out what might be overlooked
—its kinship with earlier attempts ('The Swamp', 'Moon-Worshippers') to show the fearful dangers of will-lessness and mindless-
ness. Speaking of these 'strange companions', Monro went on:

> There must be one for every man
> If he but try
> To search before he die
> If he will pass, before he pine
> Along the ways that lead to wine
> But if he any time begin
> To strive for virtue—or for sin
> Though he may try with all his will
> I think he shall not ever find
> A strange companion to his mind.

It is tempting (though entirely hypothetical) to suppose that
Ezra Pound may have influenced Monro to delete this stanza,
which made the poem's moral needlessly explicit. We know that
he worked over the opening passages of the poem, suggesting
alterations which made for greater flexibility in rhyme and rhythm,
and for a more dramatic presentation. (Pound pencilled his emendations on a typescript version of the first sixteen lines. Not all his
emendations were incorporated in the final version—in particular
there was resistance to Pound's obstinate deletion of rhymes—but
the document is interesting proof that Monro was willing to some
extent to respect Pound's advice.)

'The Strange Companion' owes much to the poet's new freedom to
be 'unpoetic' and to the verbal economies practised by Pound and the
Imagists. Shabby and ignominious words fit a shabby ignominious
theme. The awkward, graceless, jerky rhythms are an immense
advance on what Monro was doing in, for example, 'Two Visions'.
But the poem is very far from being a piece of imitation—it is essentially original, for the interior world with which it deals is private to
Monro.

The volume contains two other poems which are in fact patently
'experiments' in the new fashion, impressionistic mood-poems, dab-

bling in free-verse rhythms. These poems, 'Great City' and 'London Interior', were sent, with a third poem, 'The Leaves', to Harriet Monroe for inclusion in *Poetry*, but before she could use them, Monro had printed the first two in *The Poetry Review* for December 1912. In sending them, Monro enclosed a letter:

> I shall be glad if you find you can use them though I am not quite sure they would be any credit to me. This you will know better than I can. Perhaps they appear very artless, though, as a matter of fact, if they are failures, it is probably due rather to overartfulness; for, as you may gather, I have been working on very definite principles. I have taken a great deal of trouble with them. This free verse however is a curious medium that nearly as often completely fails as succeeds. . . . I find the result of seeing so much bad poetry is that I become fretful and diffident about producing any myself.[1]

Monro's work is a compromise between free verse and metrical verse, retaining rhyme and near-rhyme in all but one poem, 'Great City'. That poem opens with a paragraph handled with a fine sense of verbal music:

> When I returned at sunset,
> The serving-maid was singing softly
> Under the dark stairs, and in the house
> Twilight had entered like a moonray.
>
> Time was so dead I could not understand
> The meaning of midday or of midnight,
> But like falling waters, falling, hissing, falling,
> Silence seemed an everlasting sound.

But the poem degenerates into forlorn nostalgia for the country-side, which drives the poet restlessly out of doors:

> I passed into the streetways, and I watched,
> Wakeful, almost happy,
> And half the night I wandered in the street.

[1] (12 Oct. 1912), University of Chicago Library.

179

Edward Thomas wrote to say that this was his favourite poem in the book, 'but I am going to risk asking you if the last line strictly records a fact'. Thomas's doubt shows his discernment, but evidently provoked from Monro a firm statement that his nocturnal wandering was fact, for Thomas wrote a second time:

> My letter was crude and yours a tender response. I ought not to have thought it just possible the wandering on the street— or the *extent* of it—an exaggeration for emphasis. But I know so well that one discovers slowly that one must not do such things.[1]

'London Interior' observes more strictly the rules for Imagism as set out by Pound—it is more objective, and employs brief, clear, concrete images:

> It is sad in London when the gloom
> Thickens, like wool,
> In the corners of the room;
> The sky is shot with steel,
> Shot with blue.
>
> The bells ring the slow time;
> The chairs creak, the hours climb;
> The sunlight lays a streak upon the floor.

'The Leaves' (which was not included in *Children of Love*, nor in *The Poetry Review*) shows how delicately Monro could imitate the refinements of free impressionistic poetry:

> London is ripe
> To drop its fainting leaves,
> And the tall lights
> Shine in the evening above red trees.
> Dark mist glides
> Rolling low along dark roads,
> While above, in transparent night,

[1] (11 Nov. 1914; 15 Dec. 1914) Lockwood Memorial Library, University of Buffalo.

The white clouds trail and pass.
London faints and grieves.
Voices are soft in the street;
Shadows roam and meet.
Listen, the crisp leaves fall.
It is the time when wanderers with cold eyes,
With fainting eyes, call.
It is the time
When we remember all, strive to forget all.
Listen, the leaves fall.

Nothing by Monro appeared in Pound's *Des Imagistes* (1914), but neither 'The Strange Companion' nor any of these three poems would have been out of place there.

The two poems by which Monro is best remembered are in *Children of Love*—they have been repeatedly included in children's anthologies. In 'Milk for the Cat' Monro shows himself suddenly and impressively in perfect control, the master of at least a minor part of his trade. If greatness were measured by success in achieving one's object, 'Milk for the Cat' would have a claim to greatness. As it is, it remains—as the author recognised—a very *good* poem. William Plomer recalls a 'mixed gathering' in London, where

'That's Harold Monro,' said one of his contemporaries, and then called out to him in a teasing voice, 'Monro! *Miaow, miaow!*'

Monro turned, looked displeased, and said in a serious tone: 'That's a *good* poem, Z. That's a good poem.'[1]

Pinknose, a black female animal belonging to Monro and Miss Klemantaski, is subjected to a scrutiny not entirely kind, while she satisfies her 'creeping lust for milk', and then curls her satiate body in the great armchair. The poem succeeds because of its limitations. A narrowly domestic setting is established in the opening lines, and the cat appears no more than the decorative inmate of the drawing-

[1] 'Coming to London—i', *London Magazine*, II (June 1955), 42; reprinted in *Coming to London*, ed. J. Lehmann (London, 1957).

room, fascinating if you think about it, but otherwise part of the
furniture. Set her beside D. H. Lawrence's snake, and she stands
bare of symbolic overtones, and unlike the fish of Rupert Brooke
she induces no comparison between her life and that of humans.
This is a cat looked at with an attentive eye but an unreflecting
mind.

Monro's knack of lighting on lively and appropriate descriptive
words is seen to advantage in this purely descriptive piece, and by
sheer cumulative effect achieves a measure of felicity:

> And presently her agate eyes
> Take a soft large milky haze,
> And her independent casual glance
> Becomes a stiff hard gaze.
>
> Then she stamps her claws or lifts her ears
> Or twists her tail and begins to stir,
> Till suddenly all her lithe body becomes
> One breathing trembling purr.
>
> . . . . .
>
> The white saucer like some full moon descends
> At last from the clouds of the table above;
> She sighs and dreams and thrills and glows,
> Transfigured with love.

The regular and decorous stanzaic pattern is made interesting
by cunning variations of stress and tempo, and, all in all, the poem
shows, as T. S. Eliot said, an 'extraordinary cleverness'[1] which
saves it from insipidity. But it is cleverness of a kind that cannot
interest the mind of an adult for long. According to William
Plomer, Monro was in the habit of mentioning that the poem had
earned him 'a then surprising sum of money in anthology fees',[2] and
Richard Church, writing in 1933, names over one hundred pounds
as the figure.[3]

---

[1] *Egoist*, IV (Sept. 1917), p. 119.
[2] 'Coming to London—i', p. 42.
[3] *New Statesman and Nation*, V (3 June 1933), p. 738.

'Milk for the Cat' bears the hallmarks of early Georgian poetry—
it is freshly observant of life, and employs common language, but,
metrically, it is traditional and owes nothing to foreign influences.
One—not entirely fortunate—aspect of its success was that it
helped to establish Monro's reputation as a domestic poet.

The poem curiously entitled 'Overheard on a Saltmarsh' is
another school-book classic, which countless pairs of small children
have rendered 'in front of the class'. It is an isolated freak of fancy
—a verbal tug-of-war between a fretfully acquisitive goblin and an
unyielding nymph who refuses to give away her green glass beads.
Fairy poetry was not Monro's vein, and the example of Stephens
and De la Mare seems the likeliest explanation for this single
attempt. It was careless of him to mix nymphs with goblins and to
place a lagoon in the proximity of a saltmarsh; his care went into
polishing the clever contrapuntal rhythm of the lines, and into
paring down the dialogue to a brief minimum:

> Nymph, nymph, what are your beads?
> Green glass, goblin. Why do you stare at them?
> Give them me.
>   No.
> Give them me. Give them me.
>   No.

The remarkable diversity of style presented by *Children of Love*
is the only justification, but I think an adequate one, for making a
catalogue of most of its contents. 'Hearthstone', for instance (whose
title smacks of Wilfrid Gibson), is a simple poem written in rhymed
couplets, with the monolithic structure that Monro achieved on the
rare occasions when he was able to control his parenthetic thoughts.

Like 'Milk for the Cat' this is a 'good' poem. Like that poem, it
gives a factual description of a domestic scene, but this is a scene
of rural domesticity, a 'week-end' scene. Monro's sensuous delight
in plain country living is concentrated in an imagined picture of a
fire-lit cottage room, with two drowsy occupants, human and
animal, waiting for bed:

I want nothing but your fireside now.
Friend, you are sitting there alone I know,
And the quiet flames are licking up the soot,
Or crackling out of some enormous root:
All the logs on your hearth are four feet long.
Everything in your room is wide and strong
According to the breed of your hard thought.
Now you are leaning forward; you have caught
That great dog by his paw and are holding it,
And he looks sidelong at you, stretching a bit,
Drowsing with open eyes, huge, warm and wide,
The full hearth-length on his slow-breathing side.

This passage is unified by an emphasis on bigness and strength, which extends to the mental qualities of his 'friend', and leads one to suppose that the friend is male. Another poem of about this time —unpublished—called 'Love of Comrades', openly airs Monro's views on 'friendship' between the sexes, making Mrs. Monro's testimony that she is the subject of 'Hearthstone' easier of acceptance.

'Suburb' perpetuates the vein of social satire that was strong in *Before Dawn*, using the same compressed iambic line with its implication of epigrammatic brevity. But the treatment is more sophisticated, and the anti-romantic attitude, the sour and distasteful imagery, the posture of scorn, have parallels in the early work of Eliot, Sassoon or Osbert Sitwell. Our judgement of the poem is likely to be swayed by memories of Eliot's far more cosmopolitan range of reference and more condensed style.

The poem seems to owe no direct debt to a French original, and the choice of words is certainly typical of Monro. His flair for the *mot juste*, though it operated only in the area of sensory description, was perhaps his greatest verbal asset. The two opening lines of 'Suburb' are an instance of this, with their neat telescoping of sound, sight and 'atmosphere'. The concentration of 'colour' into the verbs is another characteristic trait.

Dull and hard the low wind creaks
Among the rustling pampas plumes.
Drearily the year consumes
Its fifty-two insipid weeks.

Most of the grey-green meadow land
Was sold in parsimonious lots;
The dingy houses stand
Pressed by some stout contractor's hand
Tightly together in their plots.

Through builded banks the sullen river
Gropes, where its houses crouch and shiver.
Over the bridge the tyrant train
Shrieks, and emerges on the plain.

The writer's point of view is the peculiarly detached one of a person looking down from a fast-moving train: summerhouses conceal scenes of tense sexual encounter described in faintly lubricious terms, which anticipate the tone of the Tiresias episode in 'The Waste Land':

Sometimes in the background may be seen
A private summer-house in white or green.
Here on warm nights the daughter brings
Her vacillating clerk,
To talk of small exciting things
And touch his fingers through the dark.

He, in the uncomfortable breach
Between her trilling laughters,
Promises, in halting speech,
Hopeless immense Hereafters.

She trembles like the pampas plumes.
Her strained lips haggle. He assumes
The serious quest . . .

The outbreak of war in August 1914 produced a quick response from Monro. Five poems on the subject were included in *Children of Love*, which came out in November. They remained aloof from the surge of patriotism, idealism and relief that swept the country in the early stages. Far from joining in the popular hymn, in 'The Poets are Waiting', Monro doubted whether a God existed to whom battle-songs might be raised. This incoherent poem seems to spring from a real sense of spiritual inadequacy. Jehovah, the ancient lord of hosts, had lost his potency, and there was no substitute deity to invoke against the dragonish Prussian war-machine:

> Hefty barbarians,
> Roaring for war,
> Are breaking upon us;
> Clouds of their cavalry,
> Waves of their infantry,
> Mountains of guns,
> Winged they are coming,
> Plated and mailed,
> Snorting their jargon.
>
> . . . . .
>
> To what God
> Shall we chant
> Our songs of battle?

The outbreak of war had indeed failed to inspire the poets in Monro's circle, Georgians and modernists alike. In commenting on the situation, however, Monro reserved his sarcasm for the types of poet whom he particularly disliked:

> The professional poets
> Are measuring their thoughts
> For felicitous sonnets;
> They try them and fit them
> Like honest tailors

186

Cutting materials
For fashion-plate suits.

The unprofessional
Little singers,
Most intellectual,
Merry with gossip,
Heavy with cunning,
Whose tedious brains are draped
In sultry palls of hair,
Reclining as usual
On armchairs and sofas,
Are grinning and gossiping,
Cake at their elbows—
They will not write us verses for the time;
Their storms are brewed in teacups and their wars
Are fought in sneers or little blots of ink.

The poem is an uneasy mixture of satire and prophecy, thrown up at a moment when the petty rancours of every day faced the threat of national disaster. It comes from the shock of this encounter, and its elements are, inevitably, imperfectly blended. It is, because of this, interesting, whatever it lacks in finesse.

'Youth in Arms', the sequence of four poems which follows, is again not well written, but it is valuable in giving the point of view of a man who resisted the tide of popular emotion. It is interesting, too, in that it expresses attitudes which we associate with later phases of the war, and with men who had been in the trenches.

Rupert Brooke, in the sonnet-sequence '1914', identified himself with his generation, exclaiming:

Now, God be thanked Who has matched us with His hour,
And caught our youth, and wakened us from sleeping,
With hand made sure, clear eye, and sharpened power,
To turn, as swimmers into cleanness leaping. . . .

Monro took a detached look at the newly enlisted soldier and discerned a bellicose young puppy:

> Happy boy, happy boy,
> David the immortal willed,
> Youth a thousand thousand times
> Slain, but not once killed,
> Swaggering again to-day
> In the old contemptuous way;
>
> . . . . .
>
> Leaning backward from your thigh
> Up against the tinselled bar—
> Dust and ashes! is it you?
> Laughing, boasting, there you are!

According to Monro, it was not God who had matched these innocents with their hour:

> Greybeards plotted. They were sad.
> Death was in their wrinkled eyes.
> At their tables, with their maps
> Plans and calculations, wise
> They all seemed; for well they knew
> How ungrudgingly Youth dies.

'Soldier' dwells longer on the happy thoughtlessness of the boy, puts him again in the jolly atmosphere of a bar in order to contrast this evening with the time when he will be found dead in a ditch. Hamlet-like, Monro professes admiration for the man who can act without thought, but he was himself too much of an intellectual to sound convincing. An undercurrent of contempt for the soldier runs through the poem, becoming very obvious towards the end:

> *We* dream of War. *Your* closing eyelids keep
> Quiet watch upon your heavy dreamless sleep.
> You do not wonder if you shall, nor why,
> If you must, by whom, for whom, you will die.

This, one infers, is to be sub-human. Monro's soldier may be a hero, but he is pudden-headed and a bit of a braggart, thinking war a great adventure.

The last two poems of the sequence are about events in the field and are therefore based on hearsay. But they anticipate the tone of later war-poets who were actually there, and they achieve some measure of grim realism. At this date Brooke, who had been badly shaken by his first taste of war on the Antwerp expedition, was still writing with passionate idealism; Monro's 'Retreat' is crude and jejune, but tries to catch, in a direct way, the thoughts, words and snatches of song ejaculated by a wounded, nervously exhausted soldier:

> Damn the jingle. My brain
> Is scragged and banged—
>
> > *Fellows, these are happy times;*
> > *Tramp and tramp with open eyes.*
> > *Yet, try however much you will,*
> > *You cannot see a tree, a hill,*
> > *Moon, stars, or even skies.*
>
> I won't be quiet. Sing too, you fool.
> I had a dog I used to beat.
> Don't try it on me. Say that again.
> Who said it? *Halt!* Why? Who can halt?
> We're marching now. Who fired? Well. Well.
> I'll lie down too. I'm tired enough.

The last line anticipates the ironies of the trench-poets, and some of their pity is suggested when Monro addresses the dead man in the final stanza of 'Carrion':

> Hush, I hear the guns. Are you still asleep?
> Surely I saw you a little heave to reply.
> I can hardly think you will not turn over and creep
> Along the furrows trenchward as if to die.

189

Instead of the nobility of sacrifice, Monro speaks of the disposition of a corpse, substituting 'carrion' for Brooke's 'rich dead'; where Brooke imagined for the fallen a nebulous but glorious future as 'pulses in the eternal mind', Monro's thought is that their bodies will be 'fuel for a coming spring'.

A convinced anti-militarist, Monro had made his point, and thenceforward wisely left battle-poetry to the poets who were in the field.

Monro's poetry was outwardly transformed by the influences funnelled to him through the Poetry Bookshop and his two periodicals. Romantic attitudes and vocabulary have disappeared. Crude insult has matured into the far more complex and oblique satire of 'Suburb'. The incredible phantasms of 'Two Visions' have given place to the jaunty and credible tempter of 'The Strange Companion'. The trend of the times towards accuracy of statement, precision and informality of language carried Monro with it, with some temporary loss of personality. *Children of Love* is a hopeful and ingenious book, but it has no dominant themes, no settled character —a reader not primed in advance might think that its sixteen poems were the work of half-a-dozen pens. It is a set of experimental pieces by a man uncertain of his style, but amiably unattached, and ready to learn from anyone whom he thought might have something to teach him.

His eclecticism won for Monro the privilege (accorded to no other poet) of contributing both to *Georgian Poetry 1913–15* and to Pound's *Catholic Anthology*. 'Milk for the Cat', a poem that possesses 'style' and yet is remarkably style-less, attracted both editors. Marsh, who admired polish and had a taste for pretty fancies, selected in addition 'Children of Love' and 'Overheard on a Saltmarsh'; Pound, sensing where the germs of life were, took 'The Strange Companion', 'Hearthstone' and 'Suburb'—he avoided the modern but derivative poems 'Great City 'and 'London Interior'.

The book marks a distinct stage in Monro's growth as a poet. It is not entirely fanciful to extend the metaphor and to say that *Poems* was infantile, that the rebelliousness of *Judas* and *Before Dawn* was adolescent, and that in *Children of Love* Monro was a youth acquiring self-knowledge partly through aping his contemporaries. An unusual flair for satisfyingly concrete description, and an emergent faculty for candid introspection are the hopeful and oddly divergent signs of originality.

7

Monro's Poetry—II

'TREES' AND 'STRANGE MEETINGS'

Trees (1916) and *Strange Meetings* (1917) expand the scope of Monro's verse in a direction for which nothing in *Children of Love* prepares us. Like the two later volumes, *Real Property* (1922) and *The Earth for Sale* (1928), they incorporate a body of semi-philosophic speculation, and the four volumes together offer a changing, but consistent view of life that is distinguishably Monro's own.

In opening the discussion of Monro's poetry, I suggested that its best claim to our attention was that it expressed an uncommon man's experience of life. The point should be made again here: it is on the personal and semi-philosophic poems in the last four books that, I think, Monro's standing as a poet should be assessed—rather than on the small quantity of skilful but shallow work by which he was, for the most part, represented in the *Georgian* anthologies. Such pieces as 'Milk for the Cat' and 'Overheard on a Saltmarsh' from *Children of Love*, and 'Dog', 'Thistledown' or 'The Nightingale near the House' from *Real Property* argue a power of detached, extraverted observation which, unfortunately for his peace of mind, was not typical of Monro.

Before discussing *Trees* and *Strange Meetings*, we should briefly consider the tendency of Monro's thought during the first decade of this century, which roughly coincided with his twenties. His prose writings, his verse writings and the events of his life show him following the general current of 'advanced' thinking on social and religious questions. He joined the Fabian Society, and remained socialist in sympathy to the end of his days; though when one finds him, in the Samurai Press phase, temporarily adhering to the Nietzschean and quite unsocialistic principles of *A Modern Utopia*, one suspects that at this time he was attracted by iconoclastic and utopian ideas *per se*. Experiments in simple co-operative living on lines marked out by Ruskin, Morris or Tolstoy attracted him until hard experience disillusioned him; and there was a time, when he and his wife were about to leave rural Ireland, when they discussed moving to 'the Garden City' of Letchworth. He belonged, in short, to the band of earnest radicals who sought to reform society from within, and who thought they found, in the simplicity of co-operative work in natural surroundings, an answer to the evils of industrial capitalism.

This gentle creed was founded on a belief in the goodness of man, allied to a belief in the goodness of the earth. The concept of 'the Earth' was central to Monro's philosophy of life. In notes for a talk on 'The Youngest Poets', given before the First World War, 'a new instinct is awakening', he declared, 'a feeling for the earth. Earth no longer as a torture place, cruel and dreadful, but rather as raw material for a paradise of the future.' Along with the rejection of earth as 'torture place' went the rejection of the religion in which he had been educated. In the early prose writings and in *Before Dawn* the rumblings of rebellion against orthodox religion were heard when he criticised institutional Christianity. He advanced to overt iconoclasm in the projected epic poem 'Jehovah',[1] begun in about 1909, which was to expose to ignominy the paternalist conception of the deity.

Jehovah was 'an ignorant and boorish ogre indeed to place before a modern world', he wrote in notes for a lecture on 'The God Myth in Modern Poetry' delivered in 1915; and in support of his views attested that 'Shelley believed that the supreme good of earth would be brought about by the overthrow of the idea of God.' Man, Monro thought, was at last 'laying claim to the possession of the earth'.

The belief that modern man was divided from nature in a harmful way had very general currency among the Victorians, to look no

[1] See Appendix.

further back, and was an important theme in the work of many of Monro's contemporaries, among them D. H. Lawrence and E. M. Forster. But Monro's formulation of the idea most closely resembles that of Edward Carpenter (1844–1929), the English apostle of Walt Whitman and a leading advocate of the simple life, with whom he had had 'frequent hear-to-heart conferences'[1] in Italy. They probably canvassed Carpenter's theory, as set forth in *Love's Coming-of-Age* (1896), that marriage should be a free association of equals; and also his plea, expounded in *The Intermediate Sex* (1908), for the recognition and acceptance of 'Uranian' (homosexual) men and women. Both subjects touched Monro's personal problems.

But it is Carpenter's view of mankind's spiritual situation, and of his relation to the earth, that is echoed most clearly in Monro's thought. Carpenter came under the influence of Whitman at Cambridge in 1868, when he first encountered his poetry. It acted like a solvent on the mind of a bewildered undergraduate with repressed homosexual tendencies. Furthermore, the heady pantheism of *Leaves of Grass* stimulated his mystical sense. His adulation of Whitman was unbounded, and he travelled to America to see him. Then in 1881 the *Bhagavad Gita* fell into his hands, and all at once he found himself 'in touch with a mood of exaltation and inspiration —a kind of super-consciousness—which passed all I had experienced before'.[2] Out of this mystical afflatus he produced his Whitmanesque prose-poem *Towards Democracy* (1883), which is the kernel of his later prose works. Among these is *Civilization: its Cause and Cure* (1889), in which he fitted his experiences of heightened consciousness into a system analogous to the Christian scheme of the Fall and Redemption. Civilisation, he said, was the result of a 'loss of unity' within man's nature, from which arose 'self-consciousness', a distressing but necessary phase from which he would rise to a higher state of consciousness:

> To the early man the notion of his having a separate individuality could only with difficulty occur; hence he troubled himself not with the suicidal questionings concerning the whence and

---

[1] Arundel del Re, 'Georgian Reminiscences—i', p. 328.
[2] *My Days and Dreams* (London, 1916), p. 106.

the whither which now vex the modern mind. For what causes
these questions to be asked is simply the wretched feeling of
isolation, actual or prospective, which man necessarily has
when he contemplates himself as a separate atom in this immense universe. . . . But when he feels once more that he, that
he himself, is absolutely, indivisibly and indestructibly a part
of this great whole—why then there is no gulf into which he
can possibly fall . . .[1]

In notes for a lecture entitled 'Can any Religion meet the Condition of Modern Society?', delivered after the war, Monro voiced
a strikingly similar view of civilised man:

. . . self-consciousness takes him out of the fresh air into that
dark tunnel through which he is now at present passing. While
he is fumbling about in that darkness muttering or shouting
like a madman innumerable questions, nothing can help him—
he must work his way through.

What precisely it is, to which man must 'work his way through',
Monro's notes do not reveal, but his poems give some answer to the
question, an answer close to the spirit of Carpenter, who, in the
same book, writes that

. . . when the Civilization-period has passed away, the old
Nature-religion—perhaps greatly grown—will come back. . . .
Man will once more *feel* his unity with his fellows, he will feel
his unity with the animals, with the mountains and the
streams, with the earth itself and the slow lapse of the con-
stellations, not as an abstract dogma of Science or Theology,
but as a living and ever-present fact.[2]

A simple autochthonous religion made an appeal to men and
women who had a general knowledge of Darwin and Frazer, who
had discovered their 'subconscious' minds, and who were thus
accustomed to contemplating their primordial roots. In as far as
Monro had a religion it was of this kind. Having cast threatening

[1] p. 46.   [2] p. 45.

Jehovah out of the sky, he turned back to 'the Earth', including in this concept a varied collection of sustaining powers. He was attracted to this faith by his temperamental needs: painfully aware of his isolation and insecurity as an individual, he saw the truest hope of peace in a connection with sources of vitality which underlay consciousness, and which held him and all creatures in a common embrace.

But this was a faith with no established iconography, and in much of his work from 1914 onward, Monro was looking for symbols that would convey his intuitions intelligibly to a modern audience. In the post-war period he gave a lecture on 'This Century', and quoted Emerson: 'The experience of each age requires a new confession.' A little lower down a laconic note runs: 'God?—Fortunate dog with visible God.' The poet who had to represent invisible forces was not so fortunate.

His first attempt to do so was in 'Trees'[1] which is fundamentally a visionary poem, isolated and foreign in its period. Here Monro tries, among other things, to blend mysticism with the everyday simplicities of Georgian verse. Its opening passages record an authentic effort to achieve mystical union with the non-self, with 'treeness'. Though in the event Monro does not achieve union, he is in no doubt here of the reality of a Something behind appearances with which human beings can have fructifying contact.

Robin Skelton, in *The Poetic Pattern*,[2] sees the poem as concerned specifically with 'the perception of, and the creation of, poetic symbol'. This, I think, is a case of special pleading. Skelton's book is concerned with the functioning of poetic imagination, and without too much straining of the poem he has arrived at the view that it, likewise, deals with the 'process of devising secondary or tertiary images from primary ones'. Admittedly a poem which hinges on

[1] Before its inclusion in *Strange Meetings*, 'Trees' had appeared in *The English Review* (Nov. 1915), and in a choice limited edition of 400 copies, printed on hand-made paper and illustrated by James Guthrie at the Pear Tree Press (1916).

[2] (London, 1956) pp. 122–8.

the intercourse between the known and the unknown allows of a rich variety of interpretations, the validity of which it is equally hard to prove or to disprove—the 'unknown' quantity is readily converted into what we will. I myself, for example, would urge that 'Trees' is in part a fragment of self-analysis, Monro's first confession of what he felt to be a serious psychological difficulty—an inability to subdue 'Mind' to the influence of 'the Unseen'. But Skelton's interpretation seems to me unnecessarily to narrow the poem's scope, and to present other difficulties which it would be tedious to go into here.

The opening sections (I and II) I take on their face value—as an account of an experiment in meditation, following a formula made familiar by the handbooks of practical mysticism. Mysticism was enjoying a vogue in the early years of the present century. The Theosophical Society, founded in 1881, had animated mystical ideas and increased interest in eastern occultism. In 1910 Evelyn Underhill's *Mysticism: a Study in the Nature and Development of Man's Spiritual Consciousness* appeared, and went into its sixth edition in 1916. This was a comprehensive and rather formidable book, and for those who could not digest it she produced, in 1914, *Practical Mysticism, a Little Book for Normal People.* These and similar works offered welcome draughts to those whose souls were a-dry in the wastes of scientific materialism. The cult had its less desirable side—Evelyn Underhill speaks of 'the pseudo-mysticism which is industriously preached at the present time'.[1] It seems likely that Monro had attended lectures on the subject or, more likely, studied some of the literature.

His choice of trees as an object of concentration is orthodox: trees are well established in mystical tradition as effective prompters of ontological perceptions. He may perhaps have read Richard Jefferies' *The Story of my Heart* (1883) where trees are frequently associated with the author's deepest communings with nature. Edward Carpenter regarded the state of union with non-self at which Monro aimed as an intimation of cosmic consciousness, and in *The Art of Creation* (1904) he quoted Plotinus, Schopenhauer, the

[1] *Mysticism,* p. 3.

197

Upanishads, Eckhardt, Whitman and Tennyson in support of his
view that such a state was possible. He did, in fact, specifically mention the union of 'the self' with that of a tree, and Monro may have
taken the hint from there. Or from a variety of other sources.

The opening section of 'Trees' reads like an account of an un-
practised experiment in meditation, and is couched in language of
surprising informality. The metaphysical theme leads one to expect
a vatic tone of voice, the 'cosmic' manner so much disliked by
Monro and his contemporaries when they encountered it in Victorian verse. As if determined to avoid this, Monro opens in a voice
of businesslike instruction, nudging his reader with the insistent
and chummy second person:

> One summer afternoon, you find
> Some lonely trees. Persuade your mind
> To drowse. Then, as your eyelids close,
> And you still hover into those
> Three stages of a darkening doze,
> This side the barrier of sleep,
> Pause. In that last clear moment open quick
> Your sight toward where the green is bright and thick.
> Be sure that everything you keep
> To dream with is made out of trees.
> Grip hard, become a root; so drive
> Your muscles through the ground alive
> That you'll be breaking from above your knees
> Out into branches . . .
>
> .   .   .   .   .
>
> Pull, (so trees live). Thrust! Drive your way!
> The agony of One Idea will twist
> Your branches. (Can you feel the dew?)
> The wind will cuff you with his fist.
> The birds will build their nests in you.
> Your circulating blood will go
> Flowing five-hundred times more slow.

A thousand veils will darkly press
About your muffled consciousness:
So you will grow.
You will not know,
Nor wonder, why you grow. . . .

Monro is nearing the second stage of the way, where 'recollection' opens into the loss of consciousness of self. Tone and diction alter. The imagery seems to be released from a level of imagination to which he rarely penetrated, and is a sample perhaps of what would have emerged had he 'muffled his consciousness' more often and for longer. There is a rhapsodic passage, an exultant and spontaneous vision of liquid green. In its opening lines, glorified Tree is still tree-like, but, as the powerful jet of words begins to fail, trees lose distinction, dissolve to water, and end as a residual green stain:

> The trees throw up their singing leaves, and climb
> Spray over spray. They break through Time.
> Their roots lash through the clay. They lave
> The earth, and wash along the ground;
> They burst in green wave over wave,
> Fly in a blossom of light foam;
> Rank following windy rank they come:
> They flood the plain,
> Swill through the valley, top the mound,
> Flow over the low hill,
> Curl round
> The bases of the mountains, fill
> Their crevices, and stain
> Their ridges green. . . .

But the poem is the record of a failure. Monro cannot lose himself in communion. 'Unworthy sloth', 'too much mortality', his 'wavering conscience', expose him to the onset of distractions, and the indignant trees expel him from their paradise. His expulsion forms the brief second section of the poem.

In the two final sections (III and IV), the straining after paranormal experience is over. Calmly Monro reviews his failure and what he has learned from it:

> Tree-growth is but a corridor between
> The Seen and the Unseen.
> Trees are like sentinels that keep
> The passage of a gate
> From this sleep to that other sleep:
> Between two worlds they wait.
> If they discover you, you cannot hide.
> Run backward. They are stern.
> You may be driven out that other side,
> And not return.

For the few initiates, movement between the 'two worlds' is safe and easy. The description of these abundant beings has a quasi-devotional air which makes them seem less men than spirits:

> There are some men, of course, some men, I know,
> Who, when they pass,
> Seem like trees walking, and to grow
> From earth, and, native in the grass,
> (So taut their muscles) move on gliding roots.
> They blossom every day: their fruits
> Are always new and cover the happy ground.
> Wherever they may stand
> You hear inevitable sound
> Of birds and branches, harvest and all delights
> Of pastured and wooded land.
> For them it is not dangerous to go
> Each side that barrier moving and fro:
> They without trepidation undertake
> Excursions into sleep, and safely come awake.

It may be worth noticing, in connection with Skelton's interpretation, that there is no hint that these fortunate individuals are poets exclusively, or artists of any sort. Monro is pointing to a dichotomy which affects mankind in general. If he had intended a particular reference it would have been most unlike him not to give plain notice of the fact.

The poem might have ended with its paean to the *illuminati*. In fact it enters on a new phase, where trees are seen in a different light: they are natural vegetables once more, but yet they are endued with a mysterious attractive power. Expressed in highly spiced erotic terms, Monro's dread sounds like an affectation borrowed from the nineties:

> So if they tempt you, as a woman might,
> Make of their love an Immorality,
> And if they haunt you, regulate your sight
> That tree love may seem like Adultery;
> And never visit them at all by night.

Expressed in homely language brushed with animism, the same sentiment affords one of the best passages in the poem:

> And when we see,
> Clustered together, two or three,
> We are almost afraid to pass them near.
> How beautifully they grow,
> Above their stiles and lanes and watery places,
> With branches dipping low.
> To smile toward us or to stroke our faces
> Crowding the brink of silence everywhere,
> They drown us in their summer and swirl round,
> Leaving us faint: so nobody is free,
> But always some surrounding ground
> Is swamped and washed and covered in by tree

Again, aesthetic tact might end the poem here. In fact, it drags its length along in an extended catalogue of the uses to which man puts wood. Though this has some good lines, it seems a contrived exercise of fancy. On the symbolic level, however, the poem had not yet run its full course: it was necessary to show how average sensual man treated the archetypal sentinels. On the whole, rather well—the tables and chairs, the ships, the violins, the railway sleepers in the catalogue are made of endearing stuff, and in the end we cannot harm the Unseen Tree.

'Trees' is a meditation on a single theme, modulating from one imaginative level and back again, and thus posing difficult problems of design and diction which Monro has only partly solved. Writing to Edward Marsh (6 May 1917) and speaking of 'Journey', Monro discussed 'the kind of thing I am aiming at and experimenting in . . . a rhythm that may change as often as necessary as, for instance, Wordsworth's great ode'. 'Trees', too, is made up of loosely related paragraphs which vary in pace, rhythm, syntax and diction, giving the poem the fluid cascading form of an *Art Nouveau* design, which suits the discursive nature of the thought. It is loosely held together by a simple grammatical device: shifts from one grammatical person to another mark the transitions between paragraphs, and impose an almost dramatic pattern on Monro's rambling ruminations. 'You' is used to suggest a familiarity between poet and reader; 'I' indicates the lonely soul of the poet; 'he' is used scornfully of the common man, while 'they' has two meanings—it signifies trees in their mysterious otherness, and the men who have access to their secret wisdom. 'We' denotes the average uninitiated man and woman. 'It', which occurs very rarely, and almost always in impersonal constructions, comes into its own once only: at the end, when trees find their apotheosis as Tree, which

> Lingers immovably where it has stood,
> Living its tranquil immortality
> Impassive to the death of wood.

Diction and rhythm are caught up in the strained tension between rapture and the matter-of-fact which affects the whole poem. If the poem leaves a final doubt of its 'sincerity' the cause is here. Monro has been at too great pains to elaborate an essentially simple intuition. The point of departure is naïve wonderment: a commonplace class of objects, seen by the innocent eye, has taken on a fresh and extraordinary appearance. Trees are no longer trees, but strange enigmatic presences. In 'Strange Meetings' (which was published in the following year) he found an appropriately direct and simple way of making a basically similar statement.

Meanwhile, we need only compare 'Trees' with much of the verse in the *Georgian* volumes on the theme of Nature to appreciate its basic integrity.

In an unkind and, on Mrs. Monro's testimony, by no means accurate anecdote about Monro's drinking, Richard Aldington describes how Monro

> kept embracing tree trunks, and telling me how much he loved trees. Of course, I know all Georgian poets love trees, but I thought he should not have been so ostentatious about it.[1]

That all Georgian poets loved trees is more justified than many generalisations. 'It's a very arboreal book',[2] Robert Nichols remarked of *Georgian Poetry 1918–19*, and it was the later Georgians' specious devotion for woods, and the speciously poetic way in which they expressed it that gave the anthology what T. S. Eliot called its 'minor-Keatsian'[3] tone. 'Trees' (which was never included in the *Georgian* Volumes) had an integrity of purpose, and demanded an exertion of mental muscle in the making, which set it clearly apart from the flabby reveries of Robert Nichols, Francis Brett Young, John Freeman, W. J. Turner or Edward Shanks.

An interesting comparison may be drawn between 'Trees' and Edmund Beale Sargent's 'The Cuckoo Wood', which occupies nine pages of *Georgian Poetry 1911–12*, and was certainly familiar to Monro before he started 'Trees'. The Cuckoo Wood is a 'mystic place' with 'magic paths' and 'wizard' flowers, where cuckoos' cries, seven times repeated, beguile a man's senses and steal his soul . . . and on a sudden lo! he is metamorphosed into a beech tree. Pan dwells in the wood with a full complement of naiads, dryads, satyrs

---

[1] *Life for Life's Sake*, p. 262.

[2] Quoted in a letter from Robert Graves to Edward Marsh in C. Hassall, *Edward Marsh*, p. 473.

[3] *Egoist*, V (March 1918), p. 43.

and nymphs and, to cut a long story short, the mortal incurs the god's wrath and escapes being 'touched' only by inches. One example will suffice to give an idea of the quality of the verse:

> Noxious things of earth and air,
> Get you hence, for I prepare
> To flaunt my beauty in the sun
> When all beside me are undone.
> Cuckoo! Cuckoo! Pan shall see
> The surge of my virginity
> Overtop the sobered glade.
> Luminous and unafraid
> Near his sacred oak I'll spread
> Lures to tempt him from his bed:
> His couch, his lair, his form shall be
> By none but the fair beech-tree.

The spectacle of myth so devalued and so meretriciously applied was a warning to Monro to effect his transformation of man into tree in fresher terms. The mystical paraphernalia of 'Trees' must have had a sharper edge in 1916 than it has to-day, and if it loads the poem with esoteric pretensions, it shows Monro's resolute striving after independence of expression. 'Trees' is at least a courageous poem.

I

> If suddenly a clod of earth should rise,
> And walk about, and breathe, and speak, and love,
> How one would tremble, and in what surprise
> Gasp: 'Can *you* move?'

> I see men walking, and I always feel:
> 'Earth! How have you done this? What can you be?'
> I can't learn how to know men, or conceal
> How strange they are to me.

Most of us experience occasional twitchings of the sense of wonder, when phenomena staled by familiarity suddenly take on an
extraordinary appearance. Acquaintance with this intimate region
enables us to follow Monro's musings in the title-piece 'Strange
Meetings', a series of twenty-one short poems.

Monro is seized with surprise at the existence of biological life,
at its proliferation, at the multiplicity and variety of conscious
creatures on the earth. The cycle of human birth and death is
expressed in the fragment of a myth: man is the sport of casual and
indifferent forces, and his individuality is submerged in the life of
the species:

II

The dark space underneath is full of bones,
The surface filled with bodies—roving men,
And floating above the surface a foam of eyes:
Over that is Heaven. All the Gods
Walk with cool feet, paddle among the eyes;
Scatter them like foam-flakes on the wind
Over the human world.

III

Rising toward the surface, we are men
A moment, till we dive again, and then
We take our ease of breathing: we are sent
Unconscious to our former element,
There being perfect, living without pain
Till we emerge like men, and meet again.

Eyes, the tenderest and most discerning organ of sense, symbolise
human consciousness. But an accumulation of floating eyes gives
an idea of rudimentary and casual life—fishes' spawn—and the
combined suggestion is of a condition at once exposed, sensitive
and of no consequence.

The existence of 'other minds' is an insoluble problem, though
in a psychological rather than a philosophic sense. Underlying

Monro's piteous complaint at the puzzles and difficulties that beset relationships is the belief that all living things, being descended from a common Mother Earth, are brothers:

IX

A flower is looking through the ground,
Blinking at the April weather;
Now a child has seen the flower:
Now they go and play together.

Now it seems the flower will speak,
And will call the child its brother—
But, oh strange forgetfulness!—
They don't recognise each other.

Eyes are used repeatedly in 'Strange Meetings' to suggest a vivid, slightly repellent, contact that is necessarily remote. Eyes stare uncomprehendingly, self-absorbed. The looks that pass between bird and human convey no sympathy, only fascination:

X

Yesterday I heard a thrush;
He held me with his eyes:
I waited on my yard of earth,
He watched me from his skies.

My whole day was penetrated
By his wild and windy cries,
And the glitter of his eyes.

Encounters between human beings, too, are reminders of their separateness, the separateness which, as Carpenter taught, was a condition of civilised man. The bleakness of man's isolation is succinctly defined in lines of apparent simplicity, whose effect, however, depends on adroit management—'haunt', 'endure' and 'foreign', applied in unexpected ways, are made to yield the necessary nuances:

IV

You live there; I live here:
Other people everywhere
Haunt their houses, and endure
Days and deeds and furniture,
Circumstances, families,
And the stare of foreign eyes.

One of the poems in 'Strange Meetings' consists of an enigmatic series of images of which the last is

A tall man rubbing his eyes in the dusk,
Muttering 'Yes'; murmuring 'No'.

It might well be Harold Monro. The advice which he gives mankind is to seize and reverence what it has—the earth:

You may not ever go to heaven;
You had better love the earth:
You'll achieve, for all your pain,
(What you cannot understand)
Privilege to drive a flower
Through an inch of land.
All the world is in your brain:
Worship it, in human power,
With your body and your hand.

In 'Strange Meetings' Monro attempted to convey matter of serious import, even of tragic implication, in consciously ingenuous terms. Sometimes—generally when he is speaking of human relationships—he succeeds; elsewhere the discrepancy between subject and treatment is noticeable enough to be a blemish, to convince the reader that he is being talked down to, and to make him wonder why.

One need not return as far as Blake or Wordsworth for examples of this kind of simplicity: several Georgians adopted innocent voices as part of the general reaction against rhetoric. Monro could find plenty of precedents in the work of W. H. Davies and Ralph Hodgson (both of whom he admired), and in James Stephens. But though these men sprinkled their lyrics with homespun wisdom, they did not, like Monro, try to combine ingenuousness of style with a semi-philosophic theme.

It was not merely the traditions of mysticism that had made Monro seek enlightenment under a tree. Powerful voices joined to urge his generation out of the city. A long tradition of romanticism extolled the spiritual benefits of communion with nature; among the latter-day romantics, Ruskin and Morris advocated honest toil in rural surroundings, while Whitman and Stevenson praised the joy of the open road.

Many of the younger pre-war poets were convinced that the country was a source of regeneration for the tired urbanite. Arundel del Re writes of the early Georgians:

> It was this common love for the country and what it stands for—clean, fresh, healthy living—that formed what perhaps was the strongest bond between these men of such different character and upbringing ... they brought into the grim hustle of congested Bloomsbury a sense of open spaces, a whiff of the keen, scented air of the downs in Spring, and the friendly, natural atmosphere of a tap-room in some old-fashioned wayside 'pub' specially true [*sic*] of Davies and Hodgson about whose clothing there always seemed to hang an indefinable smell of 'shag', heather and dip....[1]

Wilfrid Gibson, Edward Thomas, Robert Frost, Lascelles Abercrombie and their wives (with John Drinkwater in frequent residence) set up their informal poets' colony in Gloucestershire, but Monro was free to seek the comfort of green fields only at weekends. Murky, jostling and noisy, the neighbourhood of Holborn, the Gray's Inn Road and Chancery Lane was intolerable without some

---

[1] 'Georgian Reminiscences—i', p. 328.

weekly break. The week-end habit was established in good society early in the twentieth century, and for the less well-off a country cottage was a cheap and easy means of escape to the still-unspoiled home counties. Very soon after his return to London, Monro had found himself a rural retreat.

His earliest cottage was near Bishop's Stortford in Hertfordshire. Mrs. Monro remembers visiting it once in a motor-cycle and side-car, before they were married. This was followed by a cottage at Rayleigh in Essex, and visits to this place form the subject of 'Every Thing', 'Week-end', and 'Journey'. Mrs. Monro's friendship with Maurice Hewlett's daughter, who lived in West Wittering, suggested the flat coastal region of Hampshire, leading to Selsey Bill, as their next destination. In 1924 they took Challens, a house a few miles outside Chichester, and later moved to Castlefield Cottage on Sidlesham Common. The death of Monro's mother and of Mrs. Monro's mother found them with quantities of furniture on their hands, and they removed to a larger house, Crablands House, near Selsey, which could accommodate it.

Monro's enjoyment of country pleasures seems not to have changed with the years—in the late 'Country Rhymes' he is saying essentially the same things as he said in 'Hearthstone' in 1914—and Mrs. Monro has told me that he spoke of retiring to the country. Nowhere does he praise a citylife—his attitude is fairly indicated in 'Invitation to a Sea Holiday':

> From hopeless London we can find a way,
> Surely, to daylight and the biting spray?
> Trains there will be that go
> We know
> Rasping along their rails at gorgeous rate.
> Come then, my comrade, O delightful mate,
> And let us find
> That cliff where rough invigorating wind
> Shall blow salt air into our London faces,
> For there are many places.

> What then? We shall be like two specks of dust
> Brushed out of London. Soon our tarnished eyes
> Shaking away their rust
> Will take the lively light of clean surprise.

From the poems alone we should not conclude, as Mr. Eliot has done from his personal knowledge of the man, that he was held to the city 'as much by the bondage of temperament and habit as by that of external necessity'.[1] The poems, however, make it abundantly clear that he was in no meaningful sense a 'nature poet'. The praises of nature in the early volumes are too derivative to be of any account, and when he began to find his own voice he wrote as an excursionist, wrapped up in rural domesticity, and fully aware that he was in *terra incognita*:

> Here, in this other world, they come and go
> With easy dream-like movements to and fro,
> They stare through lovely eyes, yet do not seek
> An answering gaze, or that a man should speak.

'Unknown Country', from which these lines are taken, examines with melancholy resignation his failure to communicate with the local inhabitants. For all his patient tact in the pub, the 'city-soiled' visitor cannot win their confidence, or wrest from them their 'secret':

> There is a riddle here. Though I'm more wise
> Than you, I cannot read your simple eyes.
> I find the meaning of their gentle look
> More difficult than any learned book.

And he is left asking

> Must I always stand
> Lonely, a stranger from an unknown land?

'They took a little trip for a little week-end to a little cottage where they wrote a little poem on a little theme',[2] wrote Richard Aldington of the Georgians in general—but the cap fits Monro best:

[1] 'Critical Note', *Collected Poems of Harold Monro*, p. xv.
[2] *Life for Life's Sake*, p. 110.

he alone lived a life that oscillated regularly between London and
the country, and he alone thought of making verse out of the exchange. It was the title of his sonnet-sequence 'Week-end' (included
in *Georgian Poetry 1916–17*) that was used by critics hostile to the
Georgians in the phrase 'week-end poetry'. Unkinder than 'Sunday
painting', it suggests not only amateurishness but affectation and
triviality.

It may seem odd, then, that I include the sequence, and a handful of related pieces, with Monro's personal and semi-philosophic
poems. However, the poet's perfect frankness about his status as a
spare-time countryman clears him of the charge of affectation on
that score; and Mr. Eliot defends him against the charge of triviality by urging that the week-ender's is 'not only a state of mind
important enough to deserve recording in poetry, but it also becomes, in some of Monro's poems, representative of something
larger and less easily apprehensible, a *poésie des brefs départs . . .*'[1]
And I would suggest that the whimsical animism that pervades
the poems under discussion, sentimental though it is, is nevertheless a genuine expression of the habit of mind which produced
'Trees' and 'Strange Meetings'.

Monro's attitude to the external world was coloured by an
obsessive craving for relationship. This drew him to the comforting pantheism of Edward Carpenter, who taught that all life was
one and was experienced as one by the child and the primitive, and
by souls advanced to cosmic consciousness. 'Trees' wistfully yearns
for the experience; 'Strange Meetings' dwells upon the lack of it;
'Week-end', 'Every Thing' and 'Journey' play at 'let's pretend we
have it'. The pretence is a childish make-believe, but nonetheless
gives Monro obvious delight.

Accordingly, trains become 'dear gentle monsters' that 'ramble
through the countryside'. Pots and pans are 'half-inanimate domestic things' with pushful little lives of their own:

> Since man has been articulate,
> Mechanical, improvidently wise,

---

[1] 'Critical Note', *Collected Poems of Harold Monro*, p. xv.

(Servant of Fate),
He has not understood the little cries
And foreign conversations of the small
Delightful creatures that have followed him
Not far behind;
Has failed to hear the sympathetic call
Of Crockery and Cutlery, those kind
Reposeful Teraphim.
Of his domestic happiness; the Stool
He sat on, or the Door he entered through.

The fantasy has the quaintness of the brothers Grimm when

    the old Copper Basin suddenly
  Rattled and tumbled from the shelf,
     . . . . .
  Twisted itself convulsively about,
  Rested upon the floor, and, while I stare,
  It stares and grins at me.

'Week-end', ten sonnets long, is a celebration of animistic joys.
Monro and his companion had to cram their pleasures into a very
short space of time. Tremulous expectation, joyous recognition,
poignant farewell followed each other in rapid succession, and
emotion spilled over to make the house and its chattels partakers
in their delight:

The train! The twelve o'clock for paradise.
Hurry, or it will try to creep away.
Out in the country everyone is wise:
We can be only wise on Saturday.
There you are waiting, little friendly house:
Those are your chimney-stacks with you between,
Surrounded by old trees and strolling cows,
Staring through all your windows at the green.
Your homely floor in creaking for our tread;

The smiling teapot with content spout
Thinks of the boiling water, and the bread
Longs for the butter. All their hands are out
To greet us, and the gentle blankets seem
Purring and crooning: 'Lie in us, and dream.'

Cosy anthropomorphism is extended to the trees outside the window:

The oak is talkative to-night; he tells
The little bushes crowding at his knees
The formidable, hard, voluminous
History of growth from acorn into age.
They titter like school-children; they arouse
Their comrades, who exclaim: 'He is very sage.'

The 'sulky kettle' has a name, Murry (it was named after one of Monro's clerks). The comestibles are adjured:

Coffee, be fragrant. Porridge in my plate,
Increase the vigour to fulfil my fate.

Last thing at night, the ghosts of former tenants join the happy company:

Let us be going: as we climb the stairs,
They'll sit down in our warm half-empty chairs.

On Sunday morning Monro and the partner of his idyll press their hearts against the ground to hear 'each through the other, every natural sound'. As they depart, how reluctantly, for London, they wave good-bye to the house, to the tree:

Good-bye, ecstatic tree,
Floating, bursting, and breathing on the air.
The lonely farm is wondering that we
Can leave. How every window seems to stare!

The situation is full of opportunities for bathos of which Monro seems innocently unconscious. But altogether, 'Week-end' is a

213

literary disaster, and the choice of the sonnet form was only the first of the author's blunders.

By 1917 Monro had experienced considerable success in his career, and his personal life was founded on his maturing relationship with Alida Klemantaski. *Strange Meetings* is Monro's happiest book, and in spite of all its irritating and gauche ineptitudes (indeed, because of them) it represents, as a whole, a great advance on his previous work. Whatever was idiosyncratic in his apprehension of life had now taken its place as the dominant theme of his poetry. Moreover, he had thrown aside his facile competence in imitating other men's styles, and was casting about for an idiosyncratic manner of expression. This was admirable, though the result, both then and afterwards, too often turned out to be an 'interesting fumble'.

8

Monro's Poetry—III

'REAL PROPERTY' AND 'THE EARTH FOR SALE'

The contents of Monro's next volume, *Real Property*, were divided into two to mark his sense of a division in his work that needed some explanatory gloss. Part I was dedicated to 'any careful and thoughtful reader whose mind may move in harmony with my own', and a prefatory note ran:

> About six years ago I discovered that certain poems I was then writing, or carrying, unwritten, in my mind fell naturally together into a group or sequence, for which the title that presented itself to me was 'Real Property'.
>
> Having become conscious of this, I drew up the scheme for a sequence; but the imagination preferred to remain independent, and most of the poems, thus artificially planned, remained unwritten. The fragments of my sequence now, after much hesitation, are published in the first part of this book. Anybody who may so desire will be able easily to recognise both the relation of the different poems each to each, and the central idea which holds them all loosely together.

If we include 'Prayer to Memory' which is placed, an invocation to a goddess, as a preliminary to the whole of the book, a total of twelve poems survives the collapse of his scheme. Though Monro did not give to this group of fragments the title 'Real Property' which the completed series would have borne, for the sake of convenience and to bring out their community of theme, I shall use the name here.[1]

---

[1] The title of the book is in italic (*Real Property*), and the title of the poem placed in inverted commas ('Real Property').

The completion of a large-scale work on a serious theme was a satisfaction that Monro craved but never enjoyed. His epic 'Jehovah' at which he persevered with nagging persistence over many years, would have been abandoned early on if he had had clearer insight into his imaginative and constructive limitations. Mrs. Monro has spoken to me of the demands that the bookshop and his other activities made on his time and of his consequent harassment and frustration as a poet; but this is only a partial explanation of his failure to produce work on a grand scale.

It seems, from the fragments that survive, that 'Real Property' would have followed the pattern of 'Strange Meetings', and consisted of a series of short poems loosely related to a central theme—a device suited to Monro's discursive tendency but open to the suspicion that it is less a deliberately planned 'form' than something accidentally arrived at when his architectonic powers gave out. As the poems now stand—the imagination having 'preferred to remain independent'—they could not possibly be tucked into any scheme, however loose. But the 'central idea', an immense idea, still emerges from these twelve poems, distinguishing Monro from his contemporaries, who in 1916 and thereabouts were occupied with war-poetry, with Georgian pastoral verse, or, in the case of the *Wheels* coterie, with letting off verbal fire-crackers.

'Real Property' considers the individual consciousness in relation to powers which predetermine, support, delimit and control it, speaking in a confusion of terms loosely derived from evolutionary and psychological theory, from physics, from the Bible, and sometimes from Monro's own invention. Monro's original intention, apparently, was to present a comprehensive secular view of the human condition against the background of current scientific and pseudo-scientific thought. There was nothing in English poetry to parallel the scope of 'Real Property' until, in 1921, T. S. Eliot wrote a series of poems which, pruned and edited by Ezra Pound, was published as 'The Waste Land'. Eliot and Monro were alike concerned with man's image of himself, which after the battering of centuries was threatened with final disintegration by the war, and with finding a vital root beneath the surface chaos through which life might be renewed. The comparison must not be pressed. Eliot's thinking had a historical and mythological bias, and he related the dilemma of modern man to the decline of a cultural tradition. Monro, seeing civilisation as an evil, did not trouble even to discuss the wasteland. He waved history aside and reverted to the conjectural prehistory of the biologist and the anthropologist thinking that balance was to be sought in a new acceptance of dim primeval forces in the hinterland of modern consciousness. Our real property lay underground.

The theme set Monro an extraordinarily difficult task in the selection of symbols and in the establishment of their relation each to each. Where Eliot, with Pound's assistance, succeeded in co-ordinating a series of very diverse poems into a complex web of ironic cross-reference, Monro abandoned the struggle. His personal anxieties about the relationship of unconsciousness and conscious-ness, of 'heart' and 'mind', carried within themselves the necessity of failure: only those, like the fortunate ones of 'Trees', whose 'fruits are always new and cover the happy ground', could succeed. The complaint is made again here, in 'The Silent Pool':

> Those quarrellings between my brain and heart
> (In which I'd take no part)
> Pursue their violent course
> Corrupting my most vital force
> So that my natural property is spent
> In fees to keep alive their argument.

And 'Prayer to Memory', the introductory piece, is at once an invocation to the Muse and a petition to a goddess who is veiled, inaccessible, and guards the knowledge that might yield harmony between man's mind and the Earth. A half-conscious archaeologis-ing tendency may have guided the unco-ordinated rhythms, which read rather like a literal translation from an antique votive tablet. The contours of the goddess are vague, but she is more than merely the personification of racial memory. She is omnipotent and omnis-cient—the sum of all the powers beyond human ken, and the closest we ever come, perhaps, to Monro's God.

But the mysterious female figure looms only briefly. 'Earthliness' has to do with mankind's racial inheritance which is active in the psyche, demanding recognition. Contact with primitive urges, vestiges of evolution, may be made by anxious meditation down the passages of time, to the point where a subliminal 'Voice' is heard, recognised and accepted with a Whitman-like and not entirely convincing gusto:

Soul, oh my soul,
Here is your master,
God and begetter, yes hundredfold father. He lives

Deep in your flesh,
Soul of my body, O Soul:
You must be faithful to him. He is God unto you.

If he is wild
Is he not you?
If he is wanton, not you? If rebellious, not you?

In the young world,
Out of the sea,
Slowly he crept with you, feeling his way to the sun;

And in the light,
High on the beach,
Laid down your body, and moulded the shape of
                                             your soul.

The matter of this poem was already familiar to the reader of 1922, who had no doubt about biological evolution, and had learnt from Freud of the dark power of instinct. The times demanded a far more subtle and informed application of the theme.

'One Moment Only' has a comparable message—it strenuously proclaims the wisdom of the blood, in terms reminiscent of some of D. H. Lawrence's rawer moments. But the blood-bath endures for 'one moment only':

Brain, could you not have dreamed a little longer?

On the other hand, 'The Silent Pool' presents the unconscious in a different aspect—as quiet, tranquillising and easy of access:

> Look downward in the silent pool:
> The weeds cling to the ground they love;
> They live so quietly, are so cool;
> They do not need to think, or move.
>
> Look down in the unconscious mind:
> There everything is quiet too
> And deep and cool, and you will find
> Calm growth and nothing hard to do,
> And nothing that need trouble you.

So far, only those poems which urge communion with 'the unconscious' have been discussed, and they are all, in greater or lesser degree, unconvincing pieces of exhortation, employing obvious images which would inevitably enter even the flattest prose discussion of this topic. Since 'Real Property' was written, forty-five years of such discussion have intervened, and this we must allow for. Even so, the fact remains that Monro has left these images rudimentary, unexplored—partly, perhaps, to render them lucid, but certainly through a want of imaginative afflatus.

In one form or another, this paucity of imagination, this matter-of-factness in the use of words—amounting at times to insensitivity—is characteristic of 'Real Property'. Coupled with it is an uncertain handling of cadence and metre. Unwilling to commit himself either to rhyme and metre or to free verse, he writes clumsily in both media, sometimes combining the two in one poem.

Probably the least successful of his efforts to establish a pantheon of secular gods was 'Gravity', where Newton's law was deified, and offered devout praise:

> Fit for perpetual worship is the power
> That holds our bodies safely to the earth.
>
> When people talk of their domestic gods,
> Then privately I think of You.

In his development of the theme, which has the absurdity of some similar eighteenth-century attempts to animate scientific forces, abstract and concrete meet in laughable incongruity:

> We ride through space upon your shoulders
> Conveniently and lightly set,
> And, so accustomed, we relax our hold,
> Forget the gentle motion of your body—
> But You do not forget.
>
> Sometimes you breathe a little faster,
> Or move a muscle:
> Then we remember you, O Master.

Gravity, with strange illogicality, is credited with the ability to act in defiance of itself:

> While people meet in reverent groups
> And sing to their domestic God,
> You, all that time, dear tyrant (How I laugh!)
> Could, without effort, place your hand among them,
> And sprinkle them.

Traces of this falsely childish voice—for wonder at human littleness in relation to natural law deserves more dignified expression—occur elsewhere in 'Real Property', half-obliterating Monro's personal, adult commentary on existence.

Meanwhile, other voices intervene, and are disturbing in other ways. 'Underworld' harks back for its symbolism to passages in early drafts of 'Jehovah' and to parts of *Before Dawn*. Using cumbrous anapaestic rhythms and long lumbering lines, it presents a picture of the necropolis beneath our feet. The repulsive description of the worm-like dead groping in their subterranean caverns for rebirth is worth noting, for the accumulation of rudimentary life was an image of which Monro had a rooted horror. He made notes for a work (never written) which would view a man's life in six relations—as 'I', 'thou', 'he', 'we', 'you' and 'they'; and the personal, impromptu statement expresses wonder and repulsion far better than the poem:

> Heap of small wallowing crayfish on a barrow (at Lyon I think) being sold by auction (also those in Theobalds Road, when the salesman asked me what the Devil I wanted, staring). That sense of horror each time: same in battle pictures or scenes in Hell (Versailles? Wiertz, Doré) when writhing human bodies are thrown in a heap. Supposing the whole world of human flesh were thus piled into a mountain who then would be missed, or who found? And in that mass what value would there be? Nevertheless it would be a mountain shrieking *We*.

The notion of the paradise-garden was, again, firmly rooted in Monro's imagination. As he himself expressed it in an undated fragment preserved among his papers:

> That old clear imagery I was taught in my youth
> Haunts my brain ever
> The image of that old garden
> Where Adam and Eve wandered among their thoughts
> Unafraid, unfrightened.

It appears in diverse forms throughout his writing career—from the early 'Paradise', a wry, freethinking comment on Eden, where Adam and Eve see no difference between God and the Serpent, to the late 'Blurred Etching'. 'Seed-time outside Eden' and 'Outside Eden' intervene, each playing on the polarity of action and repose, thought and sensation, male and female. 'The Garden', which like the last-mentioned poem is in *Real Property*, is more interesting— an odd hybrid, combining the magic garden of myth with the commonplace at its commonest. Mrs. Monro has told me that the story is true: Monro did in fact meet a man who told him he could show him a wondrous estate—and when they arrived it was not there. If this was so, the experience ran true to the vein of Monro's thinking, and in the poem has largely been transformed into allegory.

The man who directs Monro is an anonymous, ambiguous figure, second cousin to the Strange Companion, whose office was also to escort others. Similarly, the poem begins abruptly, off-handedly; and similarly the man is given to convivial drinking—which puts their comradely fantasy in an ironic light:

> He told me he had seen a ruined garden
> Outside the town.
> 'Where? Where?'
> I asked him quickly.
> H said it lay toward the southern country;
> He knew the road well: he would take me there.
>
> Then he sat down and talked
> About that garden.
> He was so grandly proud and sure of it,
> I listened all the evening to his talk.
>
> And our glasses were emptied,
> Talking of it.
> We filled them and filled them again,
> Talking of it.
>
> He told me of the trailing flowers
> Hung on the ruined walls;
> The rivers and their waterfalls;
> The hidden woods; the lawns, the bowers.
>
> Small cool plantations; palm and vine,
> With fig-tree growing by their side,
> And violet and maidenhair
> And
>
> II
>
> we were late in conversation
> Talking of that most wonderful garden,

And filled our glasses again and again
Talking about that beautiful garden. . . .

(The caesura between 'and' and 'we', indicating a belch, a hic-
cough, or just a mental cul-de-sac, is a hopeful sign of technical
sophistication.)

Searching all day, they found what seemed to be the place—but
no. After the man had 'cooked the coffee we had brought', he found
he was mistaken. It began to dawn on the narrator that the garden
might be an illusion:

And so I watched him move about.
Indeed, it was the garden he had meant;
But not the one he had described.

Yet in a moment of communion he shared the vision:

. . . suddenly from out his conversation
I saw it in the light of his own thought:
A phantom Eden shining
Among his dreams.

Profuse excuses for not entering the garden outside which they
were seated poured from the man's lips. They parted. When they
met again by chance the man tried hard to avoid a confrontation.
But at the mention of the garden, the vision of rapture seized them
both. They rushed to the gate, where the angel-janitor stood weep-
ing, with dropped sword, permitting entry:

. . . . but we
Feared, and turned back to our own world.

The poem has obvious affinities with 'Trees', but the role of the
guide, and his relationship to the narrator, gives 'The Garden' a
psychological complexity which saves it from being just one more
statement of how hard it is to penetrate 'unconsciousness'.

The poem is agreeably free of those intrusive little flags pointing
to the meaning with which 'Real Property' is sprinkled. As a result
it is not entirely easy to interpret. It can be understood in terms of

Carpenter's 'three stages of consciousness'. The two men are thus victims of civilisation, fallen from natural innocence, but as yet incapable of cosmic consciousness. It was probably in a way somewhat similar to this that Monro intended the poem to be interpreted. But the fact remains that it is the half-confiding, half-distrustful relationship between the men—an element that is kept in the background—that is the vital principle of the poem, giving it an emotive power lacking in the poems that we have thus far discussed. The central problem of relationship, as Stephen Spender has plausibly pointed out, Monro 'declines to face': '. . . so the inevitable glasses are brought out and the two friends evoke this vision of the relationship they desire'.[1] Monro's urgent, perennial problem of loneliness has disturbed the pattern of borrowed symbolism.

I shall discuss finally two poems from *Real Property* where the imagery has not been borrowed with conscious contrivance from science or mythology, but which grows and develops from roots in Monro's psyche.

Houses and parts of houses occur many times in his work, rarely as scenes of happy domesticity. In 'The Silent Pool' he had compared the individual to a fragile house resting on the solid earth, the 'real property' which gives the sequence its name:

> I am so glad that underneath our talk
> Our minds together walk.
>
> . . . . .
>
> We have our houses, but we understand
> That our real property is common land.

In 'Fate', a man is a lonely prisoner in a single room, ignorant of why he is there, and of who put him there, but tormented by ceaseless, unanswerable questions. The other inhabitants of the house ignore his existence. This nightmarish analogy was alive and mean-

---

[1] *Criterion*, XII (July 1933), p. 680.

ingful to Monro. His vocabulary has become spartan, his rhythms
tense and inhibited. The analogy unfolds slowly and organically,
and the pathos of loneliness, which is implicit in it, only emerges
towards the end:

> I have so often
> Examined all this well-known room
> That I inhabit.
>
> There is the open window;
> There the locked door, the door I cannot open,
> The only doorway.
>
> When at the keyhole often, often
> I bend and listen, I can always hear
> A muffled conversation.
>
> An argument:
> An angry restless argument of people
> Who live behind;
>
> Some loudly talking,
> Some dimly into separate conflict moving,
> Behind the door.
>
> . . . . .
>
> Meanwhile from out the distance
> Sounds reach me as of building other houses:
> Men building houses.
>
> And if they ever
> Should open up a doorway in the wall,
> And I pass onward,
> What should I take them
> Beyond those doorways, in the other rooms?
> What shall I bring them,
> That they may love me?

Fatal question!
For all the jangling voices rise together:
'What should he take them?'

'What should he take them?'
Through that locked door there is no final answer.
They are debating, endlessly debating. . . .

Elsewhere in this poem Monro has jeopardised the life of the image by offering to interpret it (the voices are Fate, and Fate equals the sum of the forces that predetermine individual destiny); but in 'Introspection', the poem to be discussed next, the image is presented without explanatory gloss. It is essentially the same, but now the place of confinement is viewed from the outside. Consciousness is 'that house across the road', a shut, unventilated house peopled by restless, aimless, unsatisfied ghosts. The poem is a small self-contained hell, and is, I would guess, a direct account of a bad dream. It has undergone little polishing and retains its original uncouth force.

The people in the house, like the couple in 'A Game of Chess' from 'The Waste Land' spend their time in perpetual expectation of 'a knock upon the door', and there are other marked correspondences between the poems, which seem to justify discussion. 'Introspection' was copied into a manuscript book dated 1918–19; it was printed in *Poetry* in March 1920, and included in *Real Property* (published in March 1922). 'The Waste Land' was not published until October 1922, and so, if either poet is the other's debtor, it would seem to be Eliot.

There is perhaps no more than a coincidence of feeling, a common response to a post-war mood, in the similarity between parts of 'A Game of Chess' and 'Introspection'. Yet it is tempting to suppose that one among the varied literary memories woven into 'A Game of Chess' was Monro's evocation of futility, set in the confinement of a house, a poem which has, in fact, a remarkably haunting fascination.

Into Eliot's masterly treatment of the theme enter both the voluptuous but unsavoury boudoir and the jolly but wretched pub.

It is in the intervening section that the parallelism with Monro's less culturally sophisticated piece occurs. Sources for this dramatic sequence have been found in multiple references to Shakespeare, in a reference to Ezekiel and to Virgil;[1] and Eliot himself, in his notes, acknowledges sources in Webster and Middleton. However we care to interpret Eliot's use of literary echoes, it seems clear that any echo of a living and far from celebrated author like Monro will be of a different kind. It seems possible that Eliot, attracted by the situation of people trapped in restless ennui inside a house, unconsciously adapted it in his mind, developing the dramatic possibilities latent in the scene. Thus the series of frenetic questions, which in Monro's poem is addressed to the void by no one in particular, becomes an expression of the neurosis of the trapped woman.

It may be argued that the boot is on the other foot, that these effects were already in Eliot's repertoire, and that 'Instropection' is itself little more than an amalgam of echoes from 'Prufrock' and 'Gerontion'. Was not Gerontion housebound, and tormented by 'Tenants of the house,/Thoughts of a dry brain in a dry season'? Moreover, 'Introspection' bears in manuscript the alternative title 'Procrastination', and was not Prufrock the arch-procrastinator? All this is true, and both this poem and 'Fate' have something of the atmosphere of early Eliot: influence undoubtedly ran from Eliot to Monro. Yet it is not easy to explain in these terms a parallelism so close and so extended. It is very probable that Eliot had seen 'Introspection' before he wrote the passage in question, and it is more reasonable to suppose that the striking parallelism in mood, setting and language derives from his memory of it, than that Monro's muse, haunted by Eliot-like thoughts, turned out a poem uncannily akin to a poem of Eliot's which was as yet unwritten.

For good measure, I quote Monro's poem in its entirety. The relevant section from 'A Game of Chess' is appended in a footnote.

That house across the road is full of ghosts;
The windows, all inquisitive, look inward:

[1] See Glover Smith: *T. S. Eliot's Poetry and Plays* (Chicago, 1956), pp. 81–82.

All are shut.
I've never seen a body in the house;
Have you? Have you?
Yet feet go sounding in the corridors,
And up and down, and up and down the stairs,
All day, all night, all day.

When will the show begin?
When will the host be in?
What is the preparation for?
When will he open the bolted door?
When will the minutes move slowly along in their hours?
Time, answer!

The air must be hot: how hot inside.
If only somebody could go
And snap the windows open wide,
And keep them so!

All the back rooms are very large, and there
(So it is said)
They sit before their open books and stare;
While some will move untiringly about
Through all the rooms, for ever in and out,
Or up and down the stair;

Or gaze into the small back-garden
And talk about the rain,
Then drift back from the window to the table,
Folding long hands, to sit and think again.

They do never meet like homely people
Round a fireside
After daily work . . .
Always busy with procrastination,
Backward and forward they move in the house,

228

Full of their questions
No one can answer.
Nothing will happen. . . . Nothing will happen. . . .

Monro would have been wise, for the sake of his reputation as a
literary artist, to have omitted some of the fragments of 'Real
Property' which, 'after much hesitation', he published; others show
him undeniably a poet. But he was slow to discover the nature of
his talent and its precise dimensions. In attempting a panoramic
view of the human situation he was exceeding its limit. His deployment of 'scientific' reference was, in one aspect, an attempt to

---

'My nerves are bad to-night. Yes, bad. Stay with me.
Speak to me. Why do you never speak? Speak.
What are you thinking of? What thinking? What?
I never know what you are thinking. Think'.

I think we are in rats' alley
Where the dead men lost their bones.

'What is that noise?'
                    The wind under the door.
'What is that noise now? What is the wind doing?'
                              Nothing again nothing.
                                        'Do
You know nothing? Do you see nothing? Do you remember
Nothing?'
          I remember
These are pearls that were his eyes.
'Are you alive, or not? Is there nothing in your head?'
                                        But
O O O O that Shakespeherean Rag—

It's so elegant
So intelligent
'What shall I do now? What shall I do?
I shall rush out as I am, and walk the street
With my hair down, so. What shall we do tomorrow?
What shall we ever do?'

                    The hot water at ten.
And if it rains, a closed car at four.
And we shall play a game of chess,
Pressing lidless eyes and waiting for a knock upon the door.

bolster up his private intuitions with a body of 'objective' fact, and thus to go against his nature. This being so, it is not surprising that the experiment goes awry, and his scientific paraphernalia by its shallowness and banality makes him ridiculous. He had to find a more personal language in which to project an essentially personal and unique attitude to life.

Part II of *Real Property* was dedicated to 'the Zoo and its Owner', and a prefatory note stated that the contents were

> ... chiefly fugitive poems written at various periods during the last ten years. Their subjects are natural; they have no metaphysical background, nor, as those in the First Part, do they form a group. Some of them are tainted with slight *Georgian* affectations, which no amount of polishing could successfully remove.

The poems in the second Part clearly took second place in Monro's esteem. The reference to *Georgian Poetry* (his italics make it clear that he has Marsh's series in mind) is a sufficient hint of his determination to dissociate himself from the latter-day Georgians' abuses of style. These abuses had been summed up by T. S. Eliot, reviewing *Georgian Poetry 1916–17* in *The Egoist* under his pseudonym 'Apteryx', as 'pleasantness' of two kinds: 'the insidiously didactic, or Wordsworthian (a rainbow and a cuckoo's song)' kind; and 'the decorous, playful or solemn, minor-Keatsian, too happy, happy brook, or lucent sirops' kind.[1] In discussing *Strange Meetings* a few months earlier, the same critic had recognised Monro's divergence from the group:

> He is one of those (for he is to be associated with the Georgians) who has the most consistently pursued one direction. He is less literary, often more natural, he is also less a little-Englander, and deserves a public not purely insular.[2]

[1] *Egoist*, V (March 1918), p. 43.
[2] 'Reflections on Contemporary Poetry', *Egoist*, IV (Sept. 1917), p. 118.

But in his 'Critical Note' to the *Collected Poems* Eliot puts the opposite case:

> Now Monro, with his amiable, but uncritical capacity for admiring other people's verse, gives me the impression of having tried, in some of his earlier work, but probably unconsciously, to be more like other writers than he really was.[1]

Monro's rather shamefaced acknowledgement of 'slight *Georgian* affectations' suggests that by 1922 he had consciously perceived this trait in his work. The dedication is puzzling: only three of the nine poems in the second Part touch on the animal kingdom in a manner even remotely zoological, and one is tempted to wonder if by 'the Zoo and its Owner' Monro was making a covert reference to Edward Marsh and his *protégés*!

His position as publisher of the series never prevented him from giving frank public expression to his views on its demerits. In *Some Contemporary Poets (1920)* he noted that the movement was becoming inbred; a tendency towards a *Georgian* manner was noticeable:

> Some of the writers are imitating each other in choice of subject or treatment, or style. This volume [*GP 1917–19*], unlike the first, could not be taken for a haphazard selection from the poetry of the period. It is too like the compilation of a *Group*.[2]

The history of his own representation in the series is worth noting. Two poems from *Before Dawn* in the first volume; three from *Children of Love* in the second, chosen, as we noticed earlier, for technical polish rather than originality. When the third volume was under preparation, Monro wrote to Marsh soliciting a more generous spread than he had yet enjoyed, and was accordingly lavishly represented by work from *Strange Meetings*. But the work chosen emphasised the mawkish strain— the whole of 'Week-end', 'Every Thing' and only brief extracts from 'Strange Meetings' itself. Monro's prominent contribution to this volume, the first of the series to come in for intensive derision from the critics, hardly suggested discontent with the now-emergent late-*Georgian* ethos.

[1] p. xiv. [2] pp. 24–25.

In fact, Monro seemed set on taking to extreme and perverse limits the laudable intention of early Georgians to relate poetry to everyday life by talking of 'little', commonplace themes. If we care to name names, which Mr. Eliot refrains from doing in the extract quoted above, we see that Monro has been hearkening too admiringly to the note of simplicity in Davies, Hodgson, Stephens and De la Mare.

Coming now to the last two volumes of *Georgian Poetry*, in which mutual imitation, vapid nature-worship and 'poetic' posturings have replaced the rugged integrity of the first two volumes of the series, we find Monro still a contributor, represented by eight poems, six of which were reprinted, with some alteration, in the second Part of *Real Property*. It is among these poems that the 'slight *Georgian* affectations' to which he confessed are found. 'Dog' is a case in point. Whereas 'Milk for the Cat' was a piece of precise, objective observation we now have:

O little friend, your nose is ready; you sniff,
Asking for that expected walk,
(Your nostrils full of the happy rabbit-whiff)
And almost talk.

And so the moment becomes a moving force;
Coats glide down from their pegs in the humble dark;
You scamper the stairs,
Your body informed with the scent and the track and the
          mark
Of stoats and weasels. moles and badgers and hares.

Monro's gift for concrete description is here overlaid with sentimental 'pleasantness'. Much the same might be said of 'Thistledown'. Had he been content merely to describe the plant as his acute eye saw it, Monro would have produced something entirely inoffensive. The admixture of sentimental fancy spoils it:

They grip their withered edge of stalk
In brief excitement for the wind;
They hold a breathless final talk,

And when their filmy cables part
One almost hears a little cry.

While all of the poems in this condemned second part of the book
have characteristic undertones, roots in Monro's brooding ruminatory cast of thought, the overlay of Georgianism is apparent, and
the alterations which Monro made in these pieces before he allowed
them to appear in *Real Property* were less extensive or far-reaching
than he himself suggests. Brooke's influence is readily seen in
'Goldfish', though it lacks the panache of his 'Fish'.

'The Nightingale near the House' is a late, last bow to the old
romantic languors of his earliest volumes, a dexterously executed
piece produced by cross-pollination from the lyrics of W. J. Turner,
John Freeman, Robert Nichols, the masters of the neo-Georgian
style:

That star-enchanted song falls through the air
From lawn to lawn down terraces of sound,
Darts in white arrows on the shadowed ground;
    While all the night you sing.

My dreams are flowers to which you are a bee,
As all night long I listen. . . .

From the date of his public repudiation of Georgianism, 'pleasantness' of every kind is notably absent from Monro's published
work. Increasingly, he faces up to reality. But even *Real Property*,
affected as it is by the saccharine influence of late-Georgianism,
impresses one, as a whole, as the work of a man whose interest is
centred, as Mr. Eliot wrote, 'never in the visible world at all, but
in the spectres and the bad dreams that live inside the skull, in the
ceaseless question and answer of the tortured mind, or the un-
spoken question and answer between two human beings'.[1]

There is a quickening of imaginative power in the verse of Monro's
last eight or so years, which contrasts ironically with his ill-health,

[1] 'Critical Note', *Collected Poems of Harold Monro*, p. xv.

with the failing fortunes of the Bookshop, and with the collapse of *The Chapbook*. Misfortune may have increased his self-knowledge, and in turn given rise to the greater intimacy of self-revelation that we find in these poems. Certainly his final years were full of dismay and despair. How far the duality of his sexual nature affected his earlier years we are unlikely ever to know, but towards the end it was more overt, involving him in a mesh of gossip and distress, driving him back to the comfort of alcohol.

Conrad Aiken remembered:

> . . . that final dinner in London, over the bookshop, where, after meeting the Tsetse at the door—who was just coming out, and who warned him that Arnault was 'not altogether himself' —he found the unhappy man seated at the table, his head in his hands, all but speechless, or his speech reduced to four-letter words of imprecation, imprecation from the last depths of loathing and despair. Incapable of serving the cold collation which had been laid out on the side-board, he rolled his head in his hands (while D. served himself) and cursed his existence, cursed everything, cursed everyone, but above all cursed the utterly meaningless caprices and bad jokes and filthy con-niving of a destiny that would compel one to fall in love, for instance, with a dishonest little tailor's assistant, who was utterly incapable of fidelity; and thus to destroy all that one had believed in, or been faithful to, in one's life, all that was good. What was it for? What? And the muttered imprecations would begin again, round and round and over and over, in an ecstasy of self-loathing.[1]

Richard Church wrote of Monro's last years, when the restraints of Georgianism were broken and

> . . . fear and intangible shames broke out from those darker regions, and he had to face them. Towards the end they were leaping at him like wolves, and to one onlooker at least the impression is that a life which had not been lived on a large

[1] *Ushant*, p. 259.

scale, went down with heroic grandeur and a burst of poignant music that made most of the poet's earlier work negligible. Hitherto he had pushed away the emotional responsibilities, though crying out against himself for doing so. He was thus ill-equipped for the bleaker stages in life's journey . . .[1]

The later poetry shows a variety of new tendencies. There is a new lyrical tenderness, and contrasting with it a new exposure of horror on a world scale. There is also, occasionally, an interpenetration of language and feeling that transcends the imaginative limitations of earlier years and lends colour to the belief that Monro was on the eve of writing his finest poetry when he died.

'Too Near the Sea' was written in January 1915 and revised in January 1926. It is a tissue of metaphors leading to an image that outdoes the rest in imaginative abandon:

> Yesterday and to-morrow will be waves
> Breaking in calm succession on to-day.
> Earth-life pales down to sea-foam. Flesh behaves
> Like sifted ashes.
> Cold slow ocean washes
> All round, and then it washes me away.

The connection between the succession of waves and the passage of time had been made by Shakespeare and many others. The thought that biological life is foam on the surface of time is Monro's. In 'pales down' he has invented a phrase which combines the suggestions of pallor and death with the notion of a dwindling—the notion, troublesome to him, of the diminished importance of life when seen in the mass. From this the transition to the image of the washing of the waters round the ashy, worthless deposits of dead bodies was easily made—'pale as ashes' is a commonplace. And these ashes recall not only the residue of human cremation. They are 'sifted' ashes—the powdery remains of a fire that has died. The sense that death is an inexorable chemical process is reinforced

---

[1] 'The Work of Harold Monro', *New Statesman and Nation*, V (3 June 1933), p. 738.

by the verb—'behaves' is a cliché of detached scientific writing.
'Cold', in the next line, thus combines two meanings—physical
coldness and emotional coldness. The cold inevitability of death is
conveyed in the slow, tranquil movement of the line, and by posi-
tioning 'all round' as he has done, on the next line, Monro delays
the reader, makes him 'turn', and thus imitate the advance and
withdrawal of the waters which obliterates the refuse on the shore.
The omnipotence of water has been taken to throw up the pathos
of human impotence, but the symbol has been handled with a freedom that leaves the crude, unworked metaphorical approximations
of 'Real Property' far behind.

This new imaginative and verbal relaxation was never fully
exploited. 'Bitter Sanctuary' remains its most impressive monu-
ment, but in 'Elm Angel' we find Monro yielding his imagination to
a simple sensory stimulus, and producing a poem unlike anything
he had written before. It was published by Faber and Faber as an
'Ariel Poem' in 1930, decorated with wood-engravings by Eric
Ravilious. A series of pictures passes effortlessly before Monro's
mind as, seated in a public garden in Wiesbaden, he listens to the
sound of a dove. The pictures are beautiful and romantic, and each
one is set down in a single line, giving an effect as charmingly reposeful as the gentle murmurations of the bird:

> Wrecks trembled deep in their perpetual tomb;
> A quiet dropped upon the summer room.
> Now a blue hooded honeysuckle lane.
> A garden built of roses on the wane,
> Sahara buried under naked sand,
> A boy with large eyes from an eastern land,
> Muffled islands with hushed seas between
> And one white temple glowing through the green.

At a cursory glance, noticing that the poem begins and ends with
a question, we expect the customary search after unattainable
answers. But the final '—Where?' is only a dreamy speculation
about the whereabouts of the dove among the trees; and the open-

ing 'O, why?—' with the rejoinder 'Only a dove can venture that reply', seems to be mocking at metaphysical probings. Doves, Monro suggests, do not concern themselves with ratiocination; better to be non-rational for a while. The flow of association which forms the main body of the poem is the result, and Monro gives himself to it with an almost Keatsean abandon. Indeed, the influence of several romantic poets, but especially of Keats, is seen in the conception and imagery of the poem, and when the stream of images is exhausted and the poet returns to earth, he finds it suffused with a romantic unreality:

> . . . coming back, no place but only sound,
> No elm that grew from any earthly ground,
> But, heavenly throughout the atmosphere,
> One ring dove cooing, crooning, cooing—Where?

'Elm Angel' is an agglomeration of unworked images, and as such its value is limited. One does not want too many such pieces— but to find Monro in the condition of passive surrender to fancy that makes such poetry possible is remarkable.

It would be grossly misleading to imply that the signs of fresh power were more than fitful, uneven, incomplete. Monro was still well aware of the tension between 'questioning intellect' and the fullness of life that ate at the heart of his creative work. The moment of waking was still the moment when self-consciousness pounced like a vulture:

> Slow bleak awakening from the morning dream
> Brings me in contact with the sudden day.
> I am alive—this I.
> I let my fingers move along my body.
> Realisation warns them, and my nerves
> Prepare their rapid messages and signals.
> While Memory begins recording, coding,
> Repeating; all the time Imagination
> Mutters: You'll only die.

> I am alive—this I.
> And in a moment Habit, like a crane,
> Will bow its neck and dip its pulleyed cable,
> And swing me forth, oblivious of my question,
> Into the daylight—why?

Monro's distaste for machines had emerged in earlier poems—in 'Clock', and 'Crossing a Bridge', for example—and it reappears with renewed force in the later work. In their impersonal, unreasoning, unconscious operation they symbolised what he feared was the nature of the universe. In a literal sense, too, they seemed to him to jeopardise the chance of happiness, for they separated people more and more from the healing touch of nature. Each of these connotations is involved here, where Monro cringes before life itself, and before life as man has organised it.

By contrast, a flood of natural images greets a sudden, spontaneous moment of psychic harmony, between faculties that resemble Jung's four 'functions of consciousness':

> . . . suddenly, as if without a reason,
> Heart, Brain and Body, and Imagination
> All gather in tumultuous joy together,
> Running like children down the path of morning
> To fields where they can play without a quarrel:
> A country I'd forgotten, but remember,
> And welcome with a cry.
>
> O cool glad pasture; living tree, tall corn,
> Great cliff, or languid sloping sand, cold sea,
> Waves, rivers curving: you, eternal flowers,
> Give me content, while I can think of you:
> Give me your living breath!
> Back to your rampart, Death.

This poem, 'Living', gives the fullest, most explicit analysis of Monro's private *angst*, as far as he consciously understood it. It is not a late poem (the typescript is dated September 1924) and is conceived in Monro's schematic, expository vein.

Another poem of this period, though its manner is bizarre and extravagant, is recognisably the product of similar preoccupations. In fact, 'Dream Exhibition of a Final World' can be read as a passionate warning of the fate which threatened the world through over-mechanisation, and, at the same time, be understood in terms of Monro's psychic condition. For, his note tells us, it derived its subject-matter from 'a series of actual dreams and nightmares, some on the same or successive nights, others at intervals of several months'.

The dread of machines was widely felt in the 'twenties. Robert Nichols's novel *Golgotha and Co.* (1923) was a fantasy of the future in which a capitalist oligarchy 'launched' Christianity once again on the world in order to distract its restless serfs from dreams of liberty. The means used were modern methods of communication— the press, radio, the film. In Richard Aldington's *A Fool i' the Forest* (1925) the malign power of capital and the threat of the machine were attacked again. The 'Vision of Hell', being a vision, was licensed (like Monro's poem) to contain enormities on a vast and improbable scale:

> Out of ten thousand towering chimneys
> Gushed black and greasy smoke
> That whitened to a cloud of banknotes.
> On the cloud sat God the Tradesman
> Playing at the pianola
> 'Onward, onward, Christian soldiers'.

Monro was close to Aldington in his brash use of ugliness for its own sake, but his love of the earth combined with his dislike of capitalism and mechanisation to give his poem a further extension of meaning.

The term 'Final' in the title was used 'to designate that condition of ultimate stupidity which, it appears, will inevitably precede the awakening of man to a recognition of his own intelligence, and to the meaning and object of human life'. When the poem was first published, in *The Chapbook* for 1925, no comment was needed upon the word 'Exhibition': the public was well aware of the British Empire Exhibition, 'the eighth wonder of the world', held at Wembley during the summers of 1924 and 1925. Monro's poem was not meant as a satire on the Exhibition, but his dreaming mind found in its marvels an abundance of matter with which to build his nightmares.

The British Empire Exhibition was an ostentatious attempt to reassert the values of imperialism. The great Palaces of Engineering and of Industry displayed British mechanical skills; the halls put up by dominion and colonial governments gave glimpses of exotic products and ways of life. An Amusement Park caused *The Times* to forsake its customary tone of approval for the Exhibition: it was 'a truly astonishing forty acres, distracting, terrifying, marvellous in its very abomination'. A railway conveyed pleasure-seekers around the Park, and music spoke softly to them from loud-speakers and microphones. They might descend into a mock coal-mine and examine its quarter-of-a-mile of underground workings. They might visit the Palaces of Beauty and of Neptune, fitted out by Pears and MacFisheries. The interior of the Palace of Beauty dazzled the eye with its luminous plaster. Ten recesses in its walls contained ten young ladies, their costumes and activities represent-ing such celebrated beauties as Helen of Troy, Nell Gwynne, Mrs. Siddons and 'Miss 1924'. The walls of the Palace of Neptune dis-played huge tanks of fish, and in the centre of the building was a tank where diving feats were performed, and natives plunged for pearls. Elsewhere there was boating on the lake, dancing on three dance-floors, and one could eat in any of fifty-four Lyons' restaur-ants, from the 'Lucullus' where royal visitors were fed, to cheap cafés for the working man.

The Empire Stadium was proclaimed the largest theatre in the world. Here, on St. George's Day, 1924, George V opened the Exhibition with tremendous military pomp. The successful trans-mission of his speech was a landmark for 'listeners-in'. On Empire Day, just over a month later, there was held a service of thanks-giving for God's hand in the Empire. The Cup Final was the

Stadium's most notable sporting event, but the Pageant of Empire, in three parts and occupying three evenings, attracted great crowds in spite of the persistently wet weather of 1924. A cast of fifteen thousand men, women and children, with three hundred horses, fifty donkeys, seventy-two monkeys, besides llamas, camels, elephants, doves and falcons, portrayed the spread of Empire 'Westward Ho!', 'Eastward Ho!' and 'Southward Ho!'.

There was a 'Torchlight and Searchlight Tattoo'. It was rare, said *The Times*, to find 'two consecutive hours so closely packed with thrills' as in this 'extraordinarily realistic representation'. There was a mock air-raid on London, in which 'enemy' aircraft got through anti-aircraft batteries and interweaving searchlights to drop incendiaries, starting fires that were promptly put out by the Fire Brigade. There was a realistic representation of Balaclava, 'in which the spectator gets all the thrills and some of the terrors of battle without ever actually seeing the conflict itself'.

Unwholesomeness lurked in these artificially produced thrills. The entire Exhibition was bound to be only a simulacrum of life, made up of objects subtly falsified by being torn from their proper environment. The exhibits had lost their right function, and were solely objects of gaze. The degradation of a world where everyone is either a *voyeur* or the willing object of a *voyeur's* curiosity is the subject of Monro's nightmare. Technology replaces nature, dawn is mechanically simulated:

The murky curtains roll apart. A gigantic Proscenium.
Dawn.
The purple lips of the Siren begin to twitch.
Eastward, a giant arc-light reflects through my dream
Glaringly, into a forest of chimneys.
Heavy upon my chest the large gorilla squats,
Holding, loosely, my throat.

. . . . .

Within the electric proscenium
There shall be dawn every day, imitated;
Whatever the season, beautiful, artificial,

241

Such as the Worker loves, bright like a picture postcard.
The exhibition was planned to endure through final humanity.

The last specimens of earth's fauna are on show in a sumptuous
zoo, among them the final example of a human type:

. . . in a cage on wheels, lined with satin and moss,
To be moved at his mood, and filled with mechanical birds,
There lives, walking up and down, in tweed, with a stick of
 rarest ash-plant,
Murmuring, making a note, or sipping beer from a tankard,
(Gloated upon by the crowd),
Rarer than lion, or granite, the last, last, Nature Poet.

Regiments of charabancs, their hooters roaring, wait ready to
tour the preserved specimens of natural scenery:

Here are the old cascades,
Warranted still in their ancient courses,
Guaranteed to be haunted yet by the spirit of beauty,
Mumbling mysteriously far within their barb-wire enclosures.

Religious freedom is protected in 'one gigantic cold enclosure' full
of churches, mosques and synagogues made of corrugated iron:

For nobody fights any more about any religion.
Nobody troubles the clock-work heart of the God,
Lest cog, chain, piston, crank of the great machine
Should waver to hear or argue, or break, like a heart.

Round a huge arena, a mob gathers to enjoy a vicarious thrill:

Tank! Bomb! Tank! Bonb! Every Terminus ending here!
Beautiful hail of blood. Millions killed in a minute.
War final, War! Never a shortage of bodies.
Watch the game, heroes! Hurrying clouds of corpses!
(Only a Magnate need gnash his teeth at Another.)
'Card of the War, sir? No seats left.
One in the upper circle. Only a thousand guineas'.

It is a mechanical world in which 'Aeroplanes flood the sky writing the news, and heaven/Films to the world, and winks'. The phantasm who presides over it is a morbid mechanical construct:

> . . . Two battleships for feet,
> Two Eiffel Towers for legs, for your thin arms,
> Two cranes that, either, lift ten thousand tons;
> Your ribs long spans of bridges, your cold heart
> Big Ben . . .

Inevitably, the contrasting vision is of good fellowship in the natural paradise:

> . . . where the long sand is hot,
> And the slow tide rises and falls.
> Breezes play lightly through meadows in long, dwindling,
>   sunsets.
> You bathe your limbs, you talk slowly; birds are all Friendly.

But as the piece is in one sense **a propaganda** poem, it had to finish with a topical reminder of what was happening to the English countryside in the 'twenties:

> Oh, the Charabanc,
> Real; and there's the new, tall, factory chimney,
> Real: and there, his cart-load real with bricks
> The saw-dust jerry-builder trolleys along the road,
> Real.

'Dream Exhibition of a Final World' fails to give satisfaction, largely because its terms of reference are ambiguous, and we are left uncertain of whether its subject is private neurosis or public calamity.

Some of the later poems make personal disclosures of a new sort, in that they touch on particular personal relationships, and show Monro agitated by particular loves, fears and frustrations. Up to this time he had almost entirely avoided the autobiographical or anecdotal reference, fixing his statements about emotions in the sphere of generalities. Significantly, the two most obvious exceptions to this rule are 'Lament in 1915 (B.H.W.)', which is about the death of his friend Basil Watt, and 'Officers' Mess (1916)', which is about loneliness, and a trivial failure in communication, seen in the context of a greater one—the War. This last is by far the best of his war-poems, the unpretentiousness of the language matching the candour of the sentiment:

> I search the room with all my mind,
> Peering among those eyes;
> For I am feverish to find
> A brain with which my brain may talk,
> Not that I think myself too wise,
> But that I'm lonely, and I walk
> Round the large place and wonder—No:
> There's nobody, I fear,
> Lonely as I, and here.

Finding at last a few men who want to discuss serious things, he tries to make contact:

> They asked me my philosophy: I brought
> Bits of it forth and laid them on the floor.
> They laughed, and so I kicked the bits about,
> Then put them in my pocket one by one,
> I, sorry I had brought them out,
> They, grateful for the fun.

> And when these words had thus been sent
> Jerking about, like beetles round a wall,
> Then one by one to dismal sleep we went:
> There was no happiness at all
> In that short hopeless argument
> Through yawns and on the way to bed
> Among men waiting to be dead.

Like these two poems, the later ones concern relationship. In each case relationship has gone awry, or it is threatened; and in every case it is fraught with anxiety and pain.

'The One, Faithful . . .' a poem published by Monro's widow after his death, sadly analyses the progress and decay of an attempt to establish a friendship without 'the initial toll / Of comradeship through necessary wine'; and the sad corollary when he turns to his wife for consolation:

> So shall I turn to you my only friend
> And going to you find you always there?
> (I thought that) I return to you. I bend
> My lips towards your eyes for what I miss
> But just as we are sloping toward our kiss
> I feel them moistened by your lonely tear.

In 'Romantic Fool' he is abashed and dumb in the presence of the person he loves, terrified of expressing his feeling lest he destroy what relationship they have. The circumstances behind 'Journey to Reclaim a Ghost' are dark. In it, Monro is drawn to visit the mean street in which the loved one has lived, and may yet be living. But only the mother and sisters are there, and an interview of paralysing awkwardness is followed by a whirl of subtle and tormented introspection:

> What journey it has been to find your street!
> Outside your street again, what shall I do?
> Who are you really I have longed to meet?
> What atmosphere have I disturbed?
> Where may I wait,
> Where watch the consequence
> Of this adventurous trail of fate,
> Or passionate chance?
> What do?
> Where journey hence
> Away from you?

Herman Ould has written of Monro that 'he craved friendship more avidly than anybody I ever met',[1] and goes on to speak of the 'recurrent element of fear in his mental make-up—the fear of being repulsed or misunderstood—which set up a forbidding barrier between him and the world. At times this was very acute and he would imagine that some of his oldest friends were deliberately avoiding him. Once, in a letter to me, he wrote 'Don't pass me by in the street'; and at another time, because I had had to put off a meeting: 'Fully understood. And I'm very glad that I needn't have any manias or complexes of the persecution order. I'm gradually discovering that when one's friends neglect one, there is nearly always a good reason".'[2]

It may be interesting here to consider the impression Monro made on some other contemporaries. That he was haunted by a sense of alienation which handicapped his day-to-day relationships with them is apparent from their comments. Dr. Monk Gibbon in a letter to the author describes Monro as 'a tall, dark, gentle individual who was not actually shy but who had a distinct touch of reserve as though deliberately holding back from all unnecessary clatter of tongues'. John Gould Fletcher spoke of his 'iron gruffness and lack of cordiality'.[3] Clifford Bax found him 'humourless and saturnine'.[4] 'Was he not a really rather reserved man'? Iris Barry wrote to me, 'Or was I awkward and shy?' Eric Gillett, broadcasting fifty years after the event, recalls how 'disconcerted' Monro had seemed when the young man arrived to take up his lodging over the shop in 1912. He mumbled something and vanished into his room to get the key; 'dour and hard to understand' was Gillett's judgement.[5] '. . . he was most of the time a saturnine and forbidding person', wrote Herman Ould, 'and many poetry-lovers have hesitated to visit his shop because they could not face the atmosphere of oppressive gloom which Harold's heavy and dour personality unwittingly created . . .' 'Tributes to his quiet solicitude in hand-

---

[1] *Shuttle*, p. 306.   [2] Ibid., p. 308.
[3] *Life is My Song* (New York, 1937), p. 50.
[4] *Some I Knew Well* (London, 1951), p. 174.
[5] B.B.C. talk, 28 Sept. 1962.   [6] *Shuttle*, p. 306.

ling customers in the Bookshop, and his reputation as a good host counterbalance these impressions to some extent. And the remark made by Frank Morley in a letter to the author that he was 'loved of all but his real courage known only by few' seems to be a revealing generalisation.

His wife was, clearly, a source of comfort, warmth and reassurance for Monro in a lonely and frightening world. 'Where She Lives' give his acutely nervous reaction to a transient quirk of perception, when suddenly everything seemed unreal, and she—remote and strange:

> We love the room; and it is ours;
> But when I came to you to-day,
> You were possessed by other powers:
> You spoke, but you were far away.
>
> I saw you pale against the wall,
> Half hidden in a shaft of light.
> I thought I heard a petal fall,
> Yet disbelieved both sound and sight.
>
> The traffic on the street roared by:
> I tembled in the room alone.
> I heard you move, then heard you sigh;
> Yet wondered: Is she here, or gone?
>
> Your lips were moved, yet, one by one,
> Your words like dropping petals fell.
> I whispered: surely, she is gone;
> Cried inwardly: I cannot tell.
>
> Room, come to life! Shine phantom wall!
> Light, light, become you calm, and keen!
> The shadows tremble, and are tall,
> And everything is dimly seen.

247

Put your cold hands, and may they fall,
Loose, gently, on my tortured mind.
Room, come to life; shine phantom wall.

The greatest and the ultimate loneliness for Monro, ending communication for ever, was death. A posthumously published poem,
'Safe Passage', puts this with moving directness:

I would so like Life to die, if only
One did not think too much of being lonely,
And of the large and angry forms that rise
All night in dreams and fill their hopeless skies.

Mrs. Monro spoke of his 'rigid belief that this life is all, and there
is no future beyond the grave'.[1] Writing to Sturge Moore shortly
after his death she confided that her husband had feared death
above all things. The thought of death marks the nadir of sadness
in a group of tenderly sad lyrics, written to his wife during the
late 'twenties and early 'thirties. 'Great Distance' and 'Silence
Between' are howls of pain, released when separation became un-
bearable. But 'Midnight Lamentation' is the finest of these poems,
turning on the defeat of love in death. Here, the fumbling hesitations
and uncertainties of Monro's style are adventitious aids:

When you and I go down
Breathless and cold,
Our faces both worn back
To earthly mould,
How lonely we shall be!
What shall we do,
You without me,
I without you?

I cannot bear the thought
You, first, may die,

[1] B.B.C. talk, 21 Feb. 1955.

Nor of how you will weep,
Should I.
We are too much alone;
What can we do
To make our bodies one:
You, me; I, you?

. . . . .

Is then nothing safe?
Can we not find
Some everlasting life
In our one mind?
I feel it like disgrace
Only to understand
Your spirit through your word,
Or by your hand.

I cannot find a way
Through love and through;
I cannot reach beyond
Body, to you.
When you or I must go
Down evermore,
There'll be no more to say
—But a locked door.

'Bitter Sanctuary' won the distinction of publication in *The Criterion* in October 1931. It was at once obvious that Monro's achievement was fortified to an unusual degree by this single work. In writing of it, critics used superlatives: T. S. Eliot, while admitting that no single poem, and no few poems, gave the essence of Monro, allowed that 'the nearest approach, and the direst excruciation, is his last "Bitter Sanctuary" '[1] Ezra Pound called it 'his last

[1] 'Critical Note', *Collected Poems of Harold Monro*, p. xvi.

and probably "best" poem',[1] and believed that here Monro's inward 'content' attained 'unencumbered objectivity'.

According to Mrs. Monro, the poem's action was based on an experience in hospital. Rough notes for the poem were, she says, dictated to her by her husband when he recovered consciousness after a mastoid operation. The 'white attendants' are thus theatre-nurses, dimly perceived under the influence of an anaesthetic. She maintains that its significance is limited to this particular event, and that it has 'nothing to do with his view of life'. In the light of the poem's depth and variety of suggestion, however, it is hardly possible to uphold so restricted a view of its meaning. A medical experience may have provided the outline of the symbolism, but the resultant work incorporates much more. The fact that in a manuscript draft Monro has struck out the title 'Bitter Sanctuary' and replaced it with 'The Alcoholics' is itself an indication of this. The cross-currents of attraction and repulsion which meet in the poem suggest the state of mind of the neurotic who is seeking escape, whether through alcohol or by some other means—who is, as Conrad Aiken wrote of Monro in his last years, 'obsessed with his need of death'.[2]

The ambiguity comes out at once, in the title. The woman who guards the entrance of the bitter sanctuary is repellent. Her 'varnished thin magenta lips' are cruel in their thinness, and in their colour and texture they are meretricious—possibly in the original sense of the word.[3] With a cold callousness she relieves or rejects

---

[1] *Criterion*, XI (July 1932), p. 592.   [2] *Ushant*, p. 239.

[3] Though 'Bitter Sanctuary' has no sexual connotation, it has obvious features in common with the *belle dame sans merci* theme. It is worth noticing Monro's solitary earlier treatment of the theme in 'Coronilla'. This poem, which is heavily redolent of the 'nineties, made its incongruous appearance in *Strange Meetings* (1917). The symbolism is prurient and perverse: the 'heavy yellow tepid flower' which beguiles the man is inextricably confused with the evil woman with 'the stare above the little mouth', who seduces and then kills him. Several points of resemblance suggest that 'Bitter Sanctuary' is partly a remote echo of the earlier poem:

> Now all the sappy little leaves
> Are clinging to his frozen lips;

the wretches suing for admission, and vulgarly picks her teeth in the intervals. In her shuttered room the photos of former 'clients' lie abandoned among the dirty nicotined plush. The tawdry sophistication suggests the entrance to a shady drinking-club, possibly a brothel. The sounds coming from it are devitalised; the man who works there is a 'lackey'; everything emphasises the moral decrepitude of the place. The prevailing sense of lassitude is reflected in the excessive, unnatural heat that has 'locked the heavy earth'. It has 'given strength to every sound' and it thus an image also of the abnormal perceptions of the partly anaesthetised man.[1]

The house, while he is still groping for it, is felt as corrupt. As soon as his knuckles rap on the door the emotional climate alters. With the logic of nightmare, an insubstantial hearse—the threat of a hearse, as it were—passes by on the other side of the road and disappears. Simultaneously the character of the house changes. It is morbidly gloomy now, but no longer corrupt. The woman has changed: her diction and manner have a sacerdotal air:

> He: 'Is there room inside?'
> She: 'Are you past the bounds of pain?'
> He: 'May my body lie in vain
> Among the dreams I cannot keep!'
> She: 'Let him drink the cup of sleep.'

It is an interview with a sphinx, whose question can only be understood in the light of the man's reply, which seems to satisfy her. It would be narrow-sighted to hope that one could finally disentangle the 'meaning' of this condensed exchange. The man's

> And she has drawn the shutter back,
> And drawn him with her finger-tips.
>
> . . . . .
>
> Yellow, yellow is the flower;
> Fatal is the bloom;
> And no one any time returned
> Who slept inside the shuttered room.

[1] The draft version made him 'drowsy with morphia', and the reference to a drug commonly used to alleviate pain during sickness tells us more about his condition than the more general 'in anaesthesia' of the final version.

words do, however, suggest that the qualification for entry is a despair so deep, a defeat so total, that all that is sought is an end of consciousness. This is borne out by the emendation which Monro has made from the draft version's 'among the dreams I long to keep' to the final 'among the dreams I cannot keep'. The longing to retain dreams has been replaced by the recognition that to retain even the comfort of dreams is impossible. The man is brought nearer to a condition where pain and pleasure are matters of indifference, a condition 'past the bounds of pain'. The sense that a formal initiation into despair is taking place is confirmed as the poem proceeds. The 'white attendants' who 'fill the cup' are as much acolytes administering a sacrament as nurses giving an anaesthetic.[1]

But before he drinks the man has time to observe, with his fuddled senses, other presences in the place:

> Thin arms and ghostly hands; faint sky-blue eyes;
> Long drooping lashes, lids like full-blown moons,
> Clinging to any brink of floating skies.

These spectres are forlorn rather than frightening, pathetic female wraiths with a delicate beauty. The stress on arms, hands and downward-looking eyes may originate in a memory of nurses, seen by the eyes of a patient lying supine on a bed. Their state of mind (which will soon be his own) is desolate:

> What hope is there? What fear?—Unless to wake and see
> Lingering flesh, or cold eternity.[2]

One of these beings, herself not quite surrendered, seeks to restrain him from drinking the cup:

[1] The charismatic overtone was more obvious in the draft version where the suppliant 'touches the golden cup and swallows moonlight'.

[2] That these lines refer to the state of mind of the sanctuary's inmates is clearer in the draft, which reads:

> They have no hope. What fear?—unless to waken and see
> Either stark flesh or else ruthless eternity.

O yet some face, half-living, brings
Far gaze to him, and croons:
She: 'You're white. You are alone.
    Can you not approach my sphere?'
He: I'm changing into stone'.
She: 'Would I were! Would *I* were!'

Images of cold and death and of the cold dead moon mingle and
blend in these and the preceding lines with an openness to the
vagaries of imagination rare in Monro. The distant woman who
sees with sympathy that he is 'white' and 'alone', and invites him
to approach her 'sphere', speaks with a spiritual authority which,
combined with her other attributes, gives her the character of a
moon-deity or moon-spirit. If a recollection of the lunar heaven of
Dante's 'Paradiso' is embedded here, as seems possible, that vision
of blessed spirits has been touched with the acid of bitterness.
Dante too gazed with indistinct vision on a throng of pallid ghostly
faces, the faces of women who had broken vows during their earthly
life and were condemned to the lowest sphere of heaven. But these
spirits were blissfully contented with their lot. In the words of their
spokeswoman:

> Frate, la nostra volonta quieta
> virtu di carita, che fa volerne
> sol quel ch'avemo, e d'altro non ci esseta.[1]

Monro's moon-woman is discontented; and though at one
moment she bids him come and share her order of existence, at the
next she urgently wishes that like him she were 'changing into
stone'. She thus embodies the contradictory impulses, towards life
and towards death, that make this place at once bitter and a
sanctuary.

[1]   Brother, our love has laid our wills to rest,
    Making us long for what is ours,
    And by no other thing to be possessed.
Divina Commedia, 'Il Paradiso', III, ll. 70–72 (Dorothy Sayer's translation).

The sequence of five lines that comes next is in startling contrast to what precedes and follows it. The regularity of its jogging rhythm would be enough to set it apart, and in describing what is in some sense the 'real world', the external world of action and event, it is utterly remote from the internal drama that is the main theme of the poem. A little reflection, however, discloses that a very odd picture of reality is provided:

> In the morning through the world,
> Watch the flunkeys bring the coffee;
> Watch the shepherds on the downs,
> Lords and ladies at their toilet,
> Farmers, merchants, frothing towns.

This is the eighteenth-century Never-Never-land depicted in Claud Lovat Fraser's drawings, where quaintly costumed figures decorate the pretty scenes, eternally vacuous and eternally content as they go about their pre-Industrial Revolution occupations. For an accurate interpretation of this fantasy and its bearing on the rest of the poem, it would be necessary to understand how far Monro himself saw it as absurd, and how far it represented for him, in some sense, an ideal. We may plausibly, I think, take it as being one of the 'dreams' that he had been unable to keep—a childlike, innocent, hopeful view of life that had turned out to be at odds with the facts. One of its merits is that it is a primly ordered world, where everyone knows what his function is and knows how to perform it. By contrast, the inner experience of the man in sanctuary is chaotic, and his confusion is expressed in lines that are made to appear metrically out of control:

> But look how he, unfortunate, now fumbles
> Through unknown chambers, unheedful stumbles.

In the final section, which acts as an *envoi*, Monro stands back and comments as from a distance on the consequences of entering 'sanctuary'. Up to this point he has, one feels, been writing from personal experience, but now he speaks with less assurance, on hearsay:

How do they leave who once are in those rooms?[1]
Some may be found, they say, deeply asleep
In ruined tombs.
Some in white beds, with faces round them. Some
Wander the world, and never find a home.

The tranquillity of these lines springs from a deep, settled pessimism that accepts doom as part of the natural order of things. The poem ebbs away with a movement, and in a mood, that recalls the end of 'Too Near the Sea', which ran:

> Cold slow ocean washes
> All round, and then it washes me away.

But in 'Bitter Sanctuary' it is not the simple and involuntary process of extinction that is figured. 'Lingering death' is a possible alternative to 'cold eternity'; and the calm stoicism of the earlier poem is softened here by pity for creatures who are involved in a chain of events which they have, to some extent, chosen. The victim who is long since dead reposes in a neglected tomb; newly dead, his corpse lies incongruously in the decorous sickroom. (Or perhaps in this tableau the patient is still alive, and lies in the special isolation of the sick man among his 'visitors'). The third and last picture shows him, psychologically broken, seeking in vain for a way out of insecurity, loneliness, the sense of alienation.

'Bitter Sanctuary' has the power to stimulate the imagination

[1] This is strongly reminiscent of a line in James Thomson's 'The City of Dreadful Night'. The whole of that poem, which is itself an exploration of the abodes of gloom and despair, suggests itself as an influence on 'Bitter Sanctuary'. The line mentioned above, and the whole of the stanza to which it belongs, are worth quoting to illustrate the correspondence of theme and mood:

> What men are they who haunt these fatal glooms,
> And fill their living mouths with dust of death,
> And make their habitations in the tombs,
> And breathe eternal sighs with mortal breath,
> And pierce life's pleasant veil of various error
> To reach that void of darkness and old terror
> Wherein expire the lamps of hope and faith?

and to hold it in a state of excitement that survives prolonged re-reading and study. Pound, in saying that here Monro's 'own content . . . attains unencumbered objectivity',[1] has found the source of the poem's distinction. Monro's habitual restraints have at last gone—under the relaxing influence of the anaesthetic perhaps—and he has yielded a poem that faithfully sets forth an inner 'meaning' through a tissue of living images. A degree of obscurity is inherent in the nature of so personal and subjective a theme, and Monro has been content to let the obscurities be, leaving the poem to some extent enigmatic and thereby the richer. 'Bitter Sanctuary' suggests that the way was finally opening for Monro to a new freedom of utterance—but in less than six months after its publication he was dead. There was

> . . . no more to say
> —But a locked door.

[1] *Criterion*, XI (July 1932), p. 592.

Conclusion

In considering Monro's poetry as a whole, one is struck by the intrinsic interest of his themes which, while they are intensely personal, are yet explicable and communicable to other people; and simultaneously one is overtaken by disappointment that he did not evolve in time an adequate means of self-expression. His difficulty was not that he was over-dependent on other men's styles. He emerged from the customary phase of total dependence on past masters during the cradle years of modern poetry, experimented gingerly with the new techniques and, when he found they did not suit his need, dropped them. Mr. Eliot considers that if Monro had been a poet who 'could have worked out his own method in isolation, and ignored the attempts of his contemporaries, he might earlier have found a more personal idiom'.[1] This suggestion must not be followed too far. The affectation of simplicity which characterises some of Monro's contributions to *Georgian Poetry* was partly the result of too uncritical an admiration for W. H. Davies and James Stephens, but Monro undoubtedly gained more from the new freedoms won by his contemporaries that he lost in imitating them. The few instances of direct imitation are very candid—'London Interior' and 'Great City' openly copy Imagist work, for example—and for the most part Monro is making an independent search for the means of expression. The love of animals and of country pleasures was deeply engrained in his character and was a legitimate subject for his verse. It is significant that when he realised that late-Georgian 'affectations' had entered his poems on these themes he at once revised them, and did not repeat his

[1] 'Critical Note', *Collected Poems of Harold Monro*, p. xiv.

mistake. Eliot, by demonstrating how adequately symbols, un-assisted by comments and explanations, could define complex psychological and spiritual states, assisted Monro towards self-expression in such poems as 'Introspection' and 'Bitter Sanctuary'; his example in no way hampered him.

Occasional traces occur of the styles of poets of earlier centuries. 'Strange Meetings' continually recalls Blake; Herrick and Marvell are models for a few lines in 'Midnight Lamentation' and 'Trees':

> How frail the body is,
> And we are made
> Only as in decay
> To lean and fade.
>
> . . . . . .
>
> Your circulating blood will go
> Flowing five hundred times more slow.
> A thousand veils will darkly press
> About your muffled consciousness.

Influences such as these are light and superficial. In the examples quoted they are so naked that Monro seems to have taken licence from Eliot to indulge in literary echo.

The obstacles that stood in his way were not external influences but internal disabilities—a none-too-acute ear, a none-too-acute sense of the ridiculous as far as his own work was concerned, and, more important, an impediment to the free flow of imagination, which gave an impoverished, cerebral quality to some of his most seriously intended poems.

Broadly speaking, Monro's technical mistakes fall into two classes—there are mistakes in the choice of form, and mistakes in the detailed deployment of words and sounds. Mistakes in the choice of form can be exceedingly perilous, causing a poet to miss his way for a lifetime. Fortunately, Monro's innate good sense prevented him from devoting himself exclusively to projects like 'Jehovah' and 'Real Property' which over-taxed his powers. Small errors of judgement, like the unsuccessful attempt in 'Trees' to graft together the high and the low in manner and matter, or the use of the sonnet-sequence as a vehicle for sentimental narrative in 'Week-end', can be accepted as the inevitable toll paid by a poet restlessly in pursuit of his own voice. In 'Strange Meetings', a casual grouping of short reflective pieces with no pretence to an over-all plan, he was moving in the right direction. To us, wise after the event, it seems that he was most at home in short, intense poems where imagery and action strictly subserve private emotion or vision; and that he found greatest freedom when the symbolism was taken from dream.

Among the poems necessarily ignored in this general survey, there are a number which attempt this kind of introspection, and help to establish in the reader a respect for Monro's underlying poetic gift. Or, to state the case differently, they force us to acknowledge Monro as a poet when his apparent carelessness, his rank insensitivity to words, had begun to make us doubtful whether the term could be applied to him in any useful sense. Frequently one good stanza, a few expressive words, reveal the sensitivity of the emotion, the idiosyncratic flavour of the reflection that has moved him to write, while the rest of the poem drifts towards irrelevancy, or tastelessness, on a current of slack writing. His manuscripts give ample evidence that he did not rush into print—'Gravity', for example, one of the most infelicitous of his poems, was 'written July 1918; copied August 16 1918' and emended again for publication in *Real Property*. 'The Earth for Sale' to which Monro drew attention by making it the title-piece of his next volume, was 'drafted 1922, corrected and finished 1924'. Nevertheless, from the opening to the concluding stanza, it has the appearance of a casual first draft:

> How perilous life will become on earth
> When the great breed of man has covered all.
> The world, that was too large, will be too small.
> Deserts and mountains will have been explored,
> Valleys swarmed through; and our prolific breed,
> Exceeding death ten million times by birth,

Will halt (bewildered, bored),
And then may droop and dwindle like an autumn weed.

. . . . .

I had been thinking of that final Earth.
Then I remembered she herself would lick
Her own lithe body clean, and from her girth
Wipe any vermin that might cling too thick.

Damned! Damned! Apparent conqueror to-day—
Oh, evanescent sway!
O drunken lust!
O swarming dust!

Man makes himself believe he has a claim
To plant bright flags on every hill he swarms;
But in the end, and in his own wild name,
And for the better prospect of his fame,
Whether it be a person or a race,
Earth, with a smiling face,
Will hold and smother him in her large arms.

The entire poem is on the brink of bathos. The two opening lines are portentous but reserved, as if holding back momentarily before a grand development of their thesis; what follows is the anti-climactic third line, which is comically inadequate in its verbal humdrumness—not in its idea—to fulfil its role. The next four lines are an ill-co-ordinated jumble of staccato phrases, remarkably condensed in meaning, but inexact and fortuitous in their wording. Why should valleys, one wonders, follow deserts and mountains in the catalogue of desecration? They do not extend the list of intact, inaccessible places, nor do they suggest a significant contrast. A more judicious poet would have avoided using a passive future perfect in line 4, and paused to reflect on the impression which the casual mathematics in line 6 was likely to make. The epithets in parenthesis—'bewildered, bored'—have the air of words temporarily 'standing in' until the writer has hit upon the right ones. The last line of this stanza offers a facile and flavourless comparison.

The poem proceeds to its misanthropic end, forecasting the final destruction of the human race when, through excessive reproduction, it finds that there is nothing left to eat. Each line offers its peculiar gaucheries: the clumsily extended verb in the opening line, the use of 'that' in the same line, which is not quite idiomatic, the dull prosaic quality of the first two lines together, the crudely expressed metaphor that ends the quatrain. The fit of misanthropy which underlies the next four lines becomes absurd when it is digested into frenzied phrases, called forth, one senses, at random at the dictates of rhyme. The unhappiest feature of the finale is its awkward broken rhythm. Syntax has been left to ramble uncontrolled—into such an absurdity as the otiose line 'Whether it be a person or a race'.

It is not, I am convinced, mere pedagogic carping that directs particular attention to this aspect of Monro's work. Infelicities occur too often, and damage the work too much, to be casually overlooked. They become the more puzzling when one recalls the polish and good craftsmanship of *Poems* (1906) and of some of the work in *Children of Love*. It is impossible to avoid the conclusion that, once he had begun actively to seek his own style, he viewed his work with special indulgence—with, in fact, a blunted sensibility. This unconscious leniency went hand in hand, I think, with a conscious poetic. Monro's verse was a homespun fabric, with a naturally rough texture. He aimed at a plain diction, at speech-rhythms, at a direct, near-colloquial tone which reflected his preference for the unpretentious, a preference which had been fostered by admiration, at a formative period, for the work of such early-Georgians as Brooke, Masefield, Davies and Hodgson. It led him into the childishness found in 'Trees', 'Strange Meetings' and 'Week-end', into frequent bathos, into ragged and uncouth versification. From time to time, however, it enabled him to achieve the effect of immediacy, as though the poet were so wrought up by nervous concern that he had spared no thought to polishing his numbers:

How did you enter that body? Why are you here?
At once, when I had seen your eyes appear

Over the brim of earth, they were looking for me.
How suddenly, how silently
We rose into this long-appointed place.
From what sleep have you arrived . . .

Bathos resulted only when the subject, as in 'Gravity' or 'The Earth for Sale', demanded more distinguished treatment. In such a poem as 'The Strange Companion' Monro's unpolished poetic manners become his greatest asset. In a poem of the same period, 'The Hopeless Argument', a powerful effect of irony is achieved by giving youthful idealism a high-toned voice and treating the disillusion of old age in language deliberately degraded:

I saw two old men sitting by a stove,
Repeating loud illustrious stories
Of blood, and half-forgotten glories.

I said: 'You seem discursive. What of love?'
One said: 'It is a most distressing thing.'
The other, without teeth, began to sing.

So to those old men sitting by that fire,
Trying to warm their hopeless shaking fists,
Dibbing and cuffing their unhappy wrists,

I said: 'Oh, what then of our great desire?'
One cried: 'Desire is certainly no matter.'
The other's crumbling jaws began to chatter.

Then I stared down on them with bitter eyes,
For I was young, and so they wished me dead;
This being wrong, contemptuously I said:

'You are too old for love, but not for lies'.
Shivering, one put on his tattered hat;
The other leant across the fire and spat.

In 'The Garden' a rather similar contrast in diction is used to point up the difference between the ordinary world and the world of vision.

It should be remembered, too, that poetry for Monro was something *heard*. Irregularities which offend the metronome that we carry inside our reading heads can be assimilated agreeably into the pattern of the metre when the work is spoken out loud. Even so, Monro abused the licence which he gave himself to leave his work in a roughly finished state, and many an interesting poem disappoints for this reason.

The inhibition which prevented him from reaching down to the sources of his undoubtedly vital imaginative life was, however, a far graver handicap, and one which began to undergo modification only in his last years. He spoke of this psychic costiveness in his published work, and among his unpublished papers it is stated again:

> So with myself do I retire
> And on my inward stage
> Burn with a slow ungrateful fire
> That simmers, but can't rage.

It remains to recapitulate the themes which were threaded through Monro's work and reveal to us the quality of his response to life: the obsessive loneliness; the longing for relationship, and the fragile subtlety of a relationship once it has been achieved; the yearning to be released from self-consciousness; the never-satisfied pursuit of an acceptable idea of God; a lasting pleasure in the countryside and in domesticity. Among his papers are a number of fragments which express these themes yet again, and it seems to me that they are worth quoting by way of conclusion. Though, even by Monro's standard, they are unfinished, each has some shade of meaning to add to what has already been said. One is aware in these fragments, as in so much of Monro's work, of complex states of mind, perhaps only half-understood by Monro himself, and beyond his skill to verbalise fully.

1. (no date)

> Still still
> The individual
> Still I hope
> And hunt among them all
> To meet, to find
> A kindred mind
> —There is no hope at all.
> I wander everywhere
> To seek my friend. . . .

2. (*c.* 1923)

> I am loving/mowing [Monro's alternative]
> And you are like the April grasses growing
> I cut you off and baulk
> Your talk
>
> I am waiting
> I need not pause for you come quickly fating
> But give me all I want—
> Yet can't
>
> You are going
> With all our difference all too plainly showing
> You ask me to be true—
> To you?
>
> I am living
> I'm hard and lively grateful and forgiving
> You seem to me like stone
> I'm alone.

3. (no date)

> Everything with foolish brain
> In the intellectual mood
> Querying the cause of pain

264

Urges to be understood.
Let us if we can attain
To a second innocence
Steeping the excess of brain
In the happy flood of sense.

4. (*c.* 1921)

... I definitely know
That this quaint product (man) at uncouth rate
Will (I am sentimental) slowly go
Down to the obvious end Fate makes of fate.

And we, though we shall often reappear,
Are doomed by nature of our hopeless dim
Half-guessed tired thought to dwindle out in fear
Of God (who is He?) never having Him.

5. (9 March 1924)

I found some friends, and fewer, fewer still
I found them chiefly in my dogs and books,
Or water, or great mountains, or the swill
Of water in the evening flight of rooks.
I hated talking though I loved the lips
That spoke the words. I hated all my kind
Unless from brain-top down to finger-tips
It gave me produce of the active mind.

6. (*c.* 1923)

Out of those mingled passions I come back
Into this place which seems to me like home.
To this one presence of acquainted life
I difficultly bring myself and come
To the near touch with peace I had before
And that I feel again when I do claim
My household door
And know and understand that it is all the gentle same.

I love each little object I may touch;
My carpet, chair, desk, curtain
They are the intimate hard friend [*sic*] and such
Clear proof and certain
That I before have known this happy place
And do belong to my own time and race.

Monro's role as literary entrepreneur was modified and clarified by the fact that he himself wrote poetry and considered it as a vital part of his activities. He could in no sense be seen as the detached patron of independent means, on the model of Edward Marsh; he was a poet doing practical field-work for his art and for his fellow-poets. In England, where trade is felt to be socially degrading, it was a generous mark of his dedication to set up shop and sell the commodity. The whole emphasis of his mission was upon the practical involvement of poetry with life. 'Poetry is not a lofty, exotic, ultra-mundane product', he told a post-war audience, 'but it is about *life*, as we know it, and as lived by us.' In his lectures he said very little about 'art' or about 'poetry', and many of them were earnest efforts to explain what the poets of his own time were doing. Towards these men he felt a special responsibility, and if the audiences before whom he produced them at poetry-readings were partly made up of devotees who came for the wrong reasons, his fellow-writers understood that Monro himself valued poetry for the right ones.

In *Some Contemporary Poets* (*1920*) he made it clear that he distrusted professionalism in literature: it led a poet into writing what he knew his public would buy, and a critic into telling lies for a fee. He himself was in the happy position of not depending on his literary enterprises for his bread-and-butter and so, in spite of his position as a tradesman, he retained the virtues and privileges of the amateur. He did not pose as a pundit, admitting in *Some Contemporary Poets* that he might well have overlooked, that very poet whom the future will recognise as the true genius of our time'.

A talk given in the early 'twenties shows how he viewed his position:

> I keep an establishment called the Poetry Bookshop and in that capacity I am a kind of intermediary of a practical kind between poetry and the public. It happens in the course of my occupation that I have to direct the attention of those with whom I come into contact towards that which appears to me the most delightful or entertaining in the poetry of our time. But that does not mean that I claim to know the best poetry from the worst, or to be a good judge or in any sense an expert.

But a jealously guarded individualism, not a weak distrust of his own opinions, underlay these modest disclaimers. He 'liked' or 'disliked' a poet's work, and it was idle to argue with him. 'He cared passionately, though not always discriminately, about poetry', Eliot has written with characteristic diplomacy, '. . . and anyone whose poetry he liked was sure of his support.'[1] His tragedy was not that he liked what was bad, but that he failed to respond sufficiently quickly to what was good. In this way the chance of publishing Thomas and Eliot was lost. 'He would take five years to learn', wrote Ezra Pound, adding that 'his more-esteemed contemporaries have gone on for twenty years in unconsciousness and will ultimately die in their darkness'.[2]

Monro's years of opportunity were from 1912 to 1914, when poetry was in a state of flux; 1913 and 1914 were his years of maximum influence, when the Poetry Bookshop was a living centre—out of it issued *Poetry and Drama*, the only paper of its kind in England, with a steadily growing reputation; into it the poets—especially the younger ones—came to enjoy Monro's hospitality, to meet Monro and each other, to lodge in his upstairs rooms; and into it the public, moved by a sudden renewal of interest in poetry, came to buy books and to hear the poets read. The war interrupted

---

[1] In a letter to Marvin Magalaner (21 Jan. 1947). Quoted by him in 'Harold Monro—Literary Midwife', *Arizona Quarterly*, V (Winter 1949), p. 328.

[2] *Criterion*, XI (July 1932), p. 582.

Monro's progress, but it is wrong to suppose that but for it he would have become a dynamic leader among writers, with the ability to direct the course of writing or criticism. With a disposition that yearned to see differences reconciled, he was incapable of that vigour of preference that the brilliant editor or publisher needs. After the war, Eliot and Squire, men of very decided preferences, emerged to carry on a critical tug-of-war in which Monro played little part.

His work as editor and publisher was useful, but modern poetry would have developed no differently had he not been there. His real *métier*, which he fashioned for himself, was to be a channel of communication between poets, and between poets and the public. It was in this role, where he found relief for his bitter sense of isolation, that he made his unique contribution to the social history of modern poetry.

Appendix

The real action of the spirit of Man is to break the fetters of
Good and Evil and smash the idea of absolute Godhead.

This conviction, set down in an undated manuscript note,
inspired Monro's efforts to write an epic poem about the god
Jehovah—efforts sustained over a period of at least fourteen years.

Another note (undated but probably made in 1916) records that

> It is now seven years since I first conceived the idea of writing,
> in the form of a poem, the plain account of the birth, life and
> death of the God Jehovah with the object of fixing his place in
> mythology. The three or four definite attempts I have made
> were one after the other reluctantly abandoned. Almost every
> year I have made a fresh beginning, and still I find myself
> inadequate to the task.

Eleven years later he was to make a final attempt to compose his
thoughts on this towering theme.

The first mention of Jehovah is in a letter of 6 June 1909, where,
in reply to Maurice Browne's strictures on some poems he had sent
him, Monro admits that, under the influence of Nietzsche and
Victor Hugo, he has tried 'a very dangerous experiment'. Browne
thought the poems attacked what was already dead: the vengeful
deity of the Old Testament—but no,

> Jehovahanism is still a mighty and moving power which has
> more than two centuries of life in it. Besides, my whole tilt . . .
> is not against the worship of J., but against the spirit of that

269

worship which permeates society and is the backbone of the Imperialistic instinct—or rather notion—which still has five centuries of life before it. The majority of us still find ourselves inadvertently thinking of God as the enormous figure we learnt to picture in our childhood. I have brought him into being as a type of anthropomorphism and tried to make him speak in the ridiculous way that such an abstraction would be bound to speak.

These poems have not survived, but they seem to have put an old cat among contemporary pigeons. Monro had, he said:

> . . . tried to make people in the first part behave exactly as they would behave and moreover do like to picture that they would behave. Far from wishing to flatter any middle class I rather imagined myself, if anything, irritating it to fury by the sequel.

This experiment stands apart from all subsequent ones, which have a family resemblance. The *disjecta membra* of up to a dozen false starts can be examined among Monro's papers, and stylistic evidence, content and the occasional date make it possible to arrange them in roughly chronological order.

The three earliest fragments are largely in blank verse, with a strong Miltonic or Keatsean flavour, and take the history of Jehovah no further than his evocation from the 'House of Dust', his appearance to Moses, and his ascendancy over the other Hebrew gods. At this stage, Jehovah seems on the whole to be a Good Thing; one fragment shows the Listener (imagination) striving to discover Jehovah, and in conflict with the Keeper (motherhood), who seeks to keep him in ignorant thrall. In another version Jehovah arises from the House of Dust with the splendour of a Satan or a Hyperion. The third and longest version, which bears the dates '13/9/10', '8/11/10', and then 'Begun again July 1915', followed by 'Fresh sketch Oct. 1916 (Manchester)', borrows its ideas from comparative anthropology, and traces the emergence of monotheism from the worship of rocks, of ancestors and of a multiplicity of gods. It was probably of this version, in its earliest phase, that he wrote to Browne from Ascona, Switzerland, in September 1910: 'after nearly torturing myself to death over that Jehovah poem, suddenly, after midnight, I saw the whole thing on a totally different plane . . .'

From this stage onward, Monro made very little headway with actual composition, but his ambition to write the epic remained a constant irritant and challenge. Time after time he drew up skeletal plans for the work, developing his idea of Jehovah as 'a type of anthropomorphism', a being evoked by man from his own unconscious mind. While he is confined in the Ark, the Deity is in close contact with his people, but gradually he frees himself and escapes to 'heaven', whence he communicates with the Jews through the prophets—and, grown to be a jealous, tyrannical and childish old god, he is annoyed that the prophets are finer beings than himself. (A note remarks, 'When a God becomes objective is free in himself [*sic*] apart from the people who made him he declines'; and another scrap declares that Jehovah 'invents good and particularly *immortality* as a kind of sport during his leisure time to serve him by acting mechanically on earth and save him future trouble'.) Under such a king, heaven is in a state of progressive decline, and Jehovah feels the need to seek another kingdom on earth. Jesus is seen by Monro as a notable force for good, and he has various ways of fitting him into his mythological framework. At all events, Jehovah becomes incensed with him for spreading notions of universal brotherhood (Jehovah is 'The direct opponent of the "World Republic"— he is the god of "nationalism", and each state for itself'.), and so perverts his teaching, rendering it useless by setting up the Roman Catholic Church as a mouthpiece for his own authoritarianism. He happily basks in the incense rising from Roman altars, but is irritated at being confused with Jesus. Senility is overtaking him, and the later drafts predict his downfall, which occurs in various ways.

In one version the last three books of the epic run thus:

5. *On Earth.* Man tries to make his voice really reach Heaven and find out whether God is there. He tries every way including the Salvation Army, etc.

6. *In Heaven.* Man gets into Heaven and floods the whole place. All the sects are there, but the throne is tottering.

7. *On Earth.* Ruin of heaven, Paradise, and all. The return to earth. Great War. The Future. Make sure of the earth.

But one headed 'Now or never version', and dated 29/9/23, has a more pessimistic conclusion. In books VII–X, the senile Jehovah deserts his empty heaven, and in the guise of a tall, rich and silent Semite, visits the United States and Europe whence, despairing of establishing a new covenant with mankind, he retreats to heaven, only to find it in ruins. In a fit of temper he destroys heaven and tumbles through space, ending up as a little ragged Jew on a Whitechapel doorstep. To establish his final covenant he gets control of the armaments of the world: man shall burn himself to death, and from his ashes a new mankind will rise.

One more attempt to plan the epic followed this 'Now or never version'—on 15 April 1923, he drew up a brief prose outline on two foolscap pages, 'after reading "The Longest Journey"'.

But the epic was never to be written. Monro lacked the sustained imaginative power and the constructive ability needed for a work of this immensity, and there were probably factors inherent in the conception which undermined it: it was essentially destructive, the product of moods of angry defiance, a dumping-ground for frustrations and aggressions that could not be freely expressed in living. The attacks on Jehovah in the later versions, and the conception of his ignominious old age seem to be directed by a personal malice. Monro's persistent need to denigrate Jehovah, the representative of tyrannical authority, is obviously bound up with his own psychic condition—which (fortunately) it is not my task to analyse.

Though he may, in the last resort, have looked in his heart and written, his treatment of the problem of Jehovah was very plainly influenced by his reading. In a memorandum jotted down at a date not earlier than 1918 he adjures himself

To read: Bible Golden Bough Gibbon Idea of God Renan Folklore of the Old Testament.

How systematically Monro followed this strenuous course of reading one cannot tell, but with the exception of the first volume of Herbert Spencer's *Principles of Sociology*, it lists the most prominent works of the day on the origin of religion, more particularly the origin of Christianity. These books provide a commentary on the Bible, which was Monro's basic text. Gibbon was about that time enjoying, at the hands of the rationalists, a resurrection as 'a pioneer of humanism', and Monro was of course seeking, in *The Decline and Fall of the Roman Empire*, Gibbon's humanist interpretation of the rise of the Christian religion. Renan's *Life of Jesus* again treated Christianity as an episode in secular history, stressing the democratic tendency of its idea of the brotherhood of mankind. *The Golden Bough* of J. G. Frazer, which traced the origin of the idea of God to primitive animism, and drew disturbing parallels between Christian and pagan mythology, came out in 1890, and immediately acquired a mighty reputation. His *Folklore of the Old Testament* (1918) applies the techniques of comparative anthropology once more, this time producing myths of the creation, the fall, the flood, and many other anologues to the biblical narrative, from the folklore of the 'backward races'. Grant Allen's *Evolution of the Idea of God* (1897) was unlucky enough to appear seven years after *The Golden Bough*, but fortunate nevertheless in establishing itself as a standard work. Grant Allen, who was indebted to Herbert Spencer for most of his ideas, rejected Frazer's animist theory in favour of what he called the 'humanist' theory: his gods almost invariably took their origin in the spirits of departed human beings.

In the books on his reading list, Monro found a mine of material which could be used to iconoclastic purpose in his anti-epic. And the list is, in a more general sense, interesting for the light it sheds on the sources of Monro's scientific and rationalist ideas.

We have not quite reached the end of the story, for in *The Earth for Sale*, the depository of Monro's most melancholy conceptions, Jehovah at last achieved the dignity of print. Sixty-three lines of verse, a microcosm of the epic, remain from Monro's long hours of creative agony. The poem, undated, is copied in a manuscript book and, following after poems written in 1927 and 1928, was no doubt

also composed at about that time. 'God of the World' is its
title.

It is in two parts. The first part harks back to the ancient rivalry
of the gods as they jostled for dominion:

> In the beginning there were raging voices,
> Fierce cries of all the gods in tumultuous rivalry,
> Pitting and girding the nations; limited though
> And trimmed, and only a portion of the earth
> Was bitten by the cruel fire of rival godhead.
>
> . . . . .
>
> For, each to each, 'Here is my chosen people'
> Thundered, and every little horde of humanity,
> Having created its god, blinked and obeyed him.

The poem proceeds immediately to the twentieth century, and
discovers that the gods, senile and decayed, have lost most of their
potency:

> . . . they slumber
> Deep in house of dust, or there are some who doze
> In their own homesteads by their ancient fires

> If they were to stir themselves to activity

> . . . wheezy they would sound and pale would be their
> voices:
> They would not quarrel like gods; their lightning
> would crackle damply.

The gods are quiescent—with one exception, Jehovah, who is
out and about in the world. The second part sketches in a few lines
what occupied whole books in the epic—the character and history
of Jehovah—and is alive with mockery and distaste. Monro sneers
at Jehovah:

> It pleased you that your prophets should moan for you
> On earth; your kings and judges and popes should rule

Vicariously, while you reclined in heaven.
O ancient Covenanter, bargain maker,
You will not claim to be the father of Jesus?

The poem next enquires into Jehovah's present doings on earth, with a note of vituperation that must have some of its roots in anti-semitism: Jehovah is where the money-bags are, and has his hands on the instruments of war—or, yet again, he may be some insignificant wretch, as contemptible but less powerful:

> ... Are you now on earth
>
> . . . . .
>
> A bearded Semite heavily bejewelled,
> Bemotored and beyachted and bemansioned?
> It may be that you travel from continent
> To continent, promoting your great wars,
> On your little world,
> Your revolutions and your market movements
>
> . . . . .
>
> Or do you only hairdress; organgrind; beg?

The poem ends with a glimpse of a vacant heaven, abandoned by both god and man, where

> ... all the wings are furled,
> And one by one sweet angels, unemployed,
> Have innocently fallen fast asleep.

Finis

Bibliography

1 HAROLD MONRO'S PUBLISHED WORKS

1 *Books and Pamphlets*

Poems, Elkin Mathews, London, Vigo Cabinet Series, No. 37, 1906.
Proposals for a Voluntary Nobility, (with Maurice Browne) Samurai Press, Ranworth Hall, Norwich, Jan. 1907; 2nd ed. Feb. 1907.
The Evolution of the Soul, Samurai Press, Ranworth Hall, Norwich, April 1907.
Judas, Samurai Press, Cranleigh, Surrey, Nov. 1907; Sampson Low, Marston, London, 1912.
The Chronicle of a Pilgrimage: Paris to Milan on Foot, Sampson Low, Marston, London, 1909.
Before Dawn (Poems and Impressions), Constable, London, 1911.
Children of Love, The Poetry Bookshop, London, 1914.
Trees, The Poetry Bookshop, London, 1916. (Edition of 400 copies, printed by hand and illustrated with six woodcut designs by A. K. Sabin at the Temple Sheen Press, East Sheen, Surrey.)
Strange Meetings, The Poetry Bookshop, London, 1917.
Some Contemporary Poets (1920), Leonard Parsons, London, 1920; Simpkin Marshall, London, 1928.
One Day Awake (A Modern Morality), *Chapbook* No. 32, The Poetry Bookshop, London, Dec. 1922.
Real Property, The Poetry Bookshop, London, 1922.
Harold Monro, The Augustan Books of English Poetry, edited by Humbert Wolfe, Ernest Benn, London, 1927.
The Earth for Sale, Chatto and Windus, London, 1928.
The Collected Poems of Harold Monro, edited by Alida Monro, with a biographical sketch by F. S. Flint and a critical note by T. S. Eliot, Cobden-Sanderson, London, 1933.
The Silent Pool and Other Poems, chosen by Alida Monro, Faber and Faber, London, 1942.

ii *Books and periodicals edited by Monro.*

The Poetry Review. The Saint Catherine Press, 34 Norfolk Street, Strand, W.C. Monthly, Jan.–Dec. 1912.

Poetry and Drama, 35 Devonshire Street, Theobalds Road, London, W.C.1. Quarterly, March 1913–Dec. 1914.

The Chapbook (Nos. 1–6 issued as *The Monthly Chapbook*), The Poetry Bookshop, 35 Devonshire Street, Theobalds Road, London, W.C.1. Monthly from July 1919 to June 1921; February and May 1922; monthly from July 1922 to June 1923; annual volumes for 1924 and 1925.

Twentieth Century Poetry, An Anthology Chosen by Harold Monro, Chatto and Windus, London, 1929.

2 UNPUBLISHED MATERIALS

The main sources of unpublished material are given below. The remainder have been mentioned in footnotes.

The Harold Monro Collection
The Library, The University of California, Los Angeles.

The Collection comprises: (i) some 1500 letters (*circa* 1910–1935). The majority, from 239 correspondents, are addressed to Monro or his wife and have some bearing on their work. In some cases carbon copies of Monro's replies are preserved.

(ii) Monro's literary MSS. MS or typescript versions of most of Monro's published verse and prose are included. In addition there is a quantity of unpublished verse, much of it fragmentary. The most substantial item is 'Jehovah', which exists in up to a dozen versions, some very fragmentary. The unpublished prose includes short plays and essays which are classified as juvenilia, and lecture notes, articles and short stories of various dates.

(iii) nine literary MSS sent to Monro by his correspondents.

(iv) ephemera—press cuttings, brochures, leaflets regarding Monro's correspondents, etc.

The Maurice Browne Collection
The Library, The University of Michigan, Ann Arbor.

The Collection includes an extensive correspondence between Browne and Monro, dating from 1902 to 1928, and some letters from Dorothy Monro (*neé* Browne) to her brother. There is also a large collection of material relating to the Samurai Press.

The Sir Edward Marsh Collection
The Berg Collection, New York Public Library.

The Collection includes correspondence between Marsh and Monro, dating from 1912 to 1925, which deals with the publication of *Georgian Poetry* and with Monro's verse.

3 SELECTED CRITICISM AND REMINISCENCE

AIKEN, CONRAD, *Ushant, An Essay* (New York, 1952).

ALDINGTON, RICHARD, *Life for Life's Sake* (New York, 1941).

BAX, CLIFFORD, *Some I Knew Well* (London, 1951).

BOWEN, STELLA, *Drawn from Life* (London, 1941).

BROWNE, MAURICE, *Recollections of Rupert Brooke* (Chicago, 1927).

Too Late to Lament (London, 1955).

CHURCH, RICHARD, 'The Works of Harold Monro', *New Statesman and Nation* (3 June 1932).

COURNOS, JOHN, *Autobiography* (New York, 1935).

DEL RE, ARUNDEL, 'Georgian Reminiscences', *Studies in English Literature* (English Seminar, University of Tokyo, 1932, 1934).

DRINKWATER, JOHN, *Discovery, Being the Second Part of an Autobiography 1897–1913* (London, 1932).

ELIOT, T. S. 'Reflections on Contemporary Poetry', *Egoist* IV (Sept. 1917) [review of *Strange Meetings*].

'Prolegomena to Poetry', *Dial*, LXX (April 1921) [review of *Some Contemporary Poets (1920)*].

'Critical Note', *Collected Poems of Harold Monro* (London, 1933).

FARJEON, ELEANOR, *Edward Thomas, The Last Four Years* (Oxford, 1959).

FLETCHER, JOHN GOULD, *Life is my Song* (New York, 1937).

FLINT, F. S. 'Verse Chronicle', *Criterion* XI (July 1932).

'Biographical Sketch', *Collected Poems of Harold Monro* (London, 1933).

GOLDRING, DOUGLAS, *Odd Man Out* (London, 1935).

The Nineteen-Twenties (London, 1945).

GUTHRIE, ROBIN, 'James Guthrie: Biographical Notes', *The Amateur Book-Collector* IV (Oct. 1952).

GRIGSON, GEOFFREY, 'Coming to London', *London Magazine* III (June 1956).

HASSALL, CHRISTOPHER, *Edward Marsh, Patron of the Arts* (London, 1959).

Rupert Brooke, A Biography (London, 1964).

KREYMBORG, ALFRED, *Troubadour, An Autobiography* (New York, 1925).

LOWELL, AMY, 'A Letter from London', *Little Review* I (Sept. 1914).

'The Poetry Bookshop', *Little Review* II (May 1915).

MACAULAY, ROSE, 'Coming to London', *London Magazine* IV (March 1957).

MAGALANER, MARVIN, 'Harold Monro—Literary Midewife', *Arizona Quarterly* V (Winter 1949).

MARSH, SIR EDWARD, *A Number of People* (London, 1939).

MONROE, HARRIET, 'Nerve-Emotions', *Poetry* XXXVI (Aug. 1930) [review of *The Earth for Sale*].

'Harold Monro', *Poetry* XL (May 1932).

A Poet's Life (New York), 1938.

OULD, HERMAN, *Shuttle* (London, 1947).

PLOMER, WILLIAM, 'Coming to London', *London Magazine* II (June 1955).

EZRA LOOMIS, POUND, 'Harold Monro', *Criterion* XI (July 1932).

[review of *Collected Poems*] *Spectator* (23 June 1933).

Letters: 1907–1941, ed. D. D. Paige (London, 1951).

SAVAGE, D. S. 'Harold Monro: A Study in Integration', *Poetry* LX (Sept. 1942).

SERGEANT, E. S. *Robert Frost: The Trial by Existence* (New York, 1960).

SITWELL, SIR OSBERT, *Laughter in the Next Room* (London, 1949).

SKELTON, ROBIN, *The Poetic Pattern* (London, 1955).

SPENDER, STEPHEN, [review of *Collected Poems*]. *Criterion* XII (July 1933).

ANON, 'A Poet and his Ideal', *Times* (17 March 1932).

'Harold Monro's Poems', *Times Literary Supplement* (8 June 1933).

Index

INDEX

284